REGULATION A+

HOW THE JOBS ACT CREATES OPPORTUNITIES FOR ENTREPRENEURS AND INVESTORS

Paul M. Getty
Dinesh Gupta
Robert R. Kaplan, Jr.

Apress®

Regulation A+: How the JOBS Act Creates Opportunities for Entrepreneurs and Investors

ISBN-13 (pbk): 978-1-4302-5731-8

ISBN-13 (electronic): 978-1-4302-5732-5

Trademarked names, logos, and images may appear in this book. Rather than use a trademark symbol with every occurrence of a trademarked name, logo, or image we use the names, logos, and images only in an editorial fashion and to the benefit of the trademark owner, with no intention of infringement of the trademark.

The use in this publication of trade names, trademarks, service marks, and similar terms, even if they are not identified as such, is not to be taken as an expression of opinion as to whether or not they are subject to proprietary rights.

While the advice and information in this book are believed to be true and accurate at the date of publication, neither the authors nor the editors nor the publisher can accept any legal responsibility for any errors or omissions that may be made. The publisher makes no warranty, express or implied, with respect to the material contained herein.

Managing Director: Welmoed Spahr
Acquisitions Editor: Robert Hutchinson
Developmental Editor: Matthew Moodie
Editorial Board: Steve Anglin, Pramilla Balen, Louise Corrigan, James DeWolf, Jonathan Gennick, Robert Hutchinson, Celestin Suresh John, Michelle Lowman, James Markham, Susan McDermott, Matthew Moodie, Jeffrey Pepper, Douglas Pundick, Ben Renow-Clarke, Gwenan Spearing
Coordinating Editor: Rita Fernando
Copy Editor: Kezia Endsley
Compositor: SPi Global
Indexer: SPi Global
Cover Designer: Friedhelm Steinen-Broo

Distributed to the book trade worldwide by Springer Science+Business Media New York, 233 Spring Street, 6th Floor, New York, NY 10013. Phone 1-800-SPRINGER, fax (201) 348-4505, e-mail orders-ny@springer-sbm.com, or visit www.springer.com. Apress Media, LLC is a California LLC and the sole member (owner) is Springer Science + Business Media Finance Inc (SSBM Finance Inc). SSBM Finance Inc is a **Delaware** corporation.

For information on translations, please e-mail rights@apress.com, or visit www.apress.com.

Apress and friends of ED books may be purchased in bulk for academic, corporate, or promotional use. eBook versions and licenses are also available for most titles. For more information, reference our Special Bulk Sales–eBook Licensing web page at www.apress.com/bulk-sales.

Any source code or other supplementary materials referenced by the author in this text is available to readers at www.apress.com. For detailed information about how to locate your book's source code, go to www.apress.com/source-code/.

Apress Business: The Unbiased Source of Business Information

Apress business books provide essential information and practical advice, each written for practitioners by recognized experts. Busy managers and professionals in all areas of the business world—and at all levels of technical sophistication—look to our books for the actionable ideas and tools they need to solve problems, update and enhance their professional skills, make their work lives easier, and capitalize on opportunity.

Whatever the topic on the business spectrum—entrepreneurship, finance, sales, marketing, management, regulation, information technology, among others—Apress has been praised for providing the objective information and unbiased advice you need to excel in your daily work life. Our authors have no axes to grind; they understand they have one job only—to deliver up-to-date, accurate information simply, concisely, and with deep insight that addresses the real needs of our readers.

It is increasingly hard to find information—whether in the news media, on the Internet, and now all too often in books—that is even-handed and has your best interests at heart. We therefore hope that you enjoy this book, which has been carefully crafted to meet our standards of quality and unbiased coverage.

We are always interested in your feedback or ideas for new titles. Perhaps you'd even like to write a book yourself. Whatever the case, reach out to us at editorial@apress.com and an editor will respond swiftly. Incidentally, at the back of this book, you will find a list of useful related titles. Please visit us at www.apress.com to sign up for newsletters and discounts on future purchases.

The Apress Business Team

Contents

Foreword

This book is a must-read for all entrepreneurs who need to raise capital to grow their businesses.

The launch on June 19, 2015, of "Regulation A+"—the colloquial shorthand for the SEC rules that amend, expand, and replace Regulation A of the Securities Act of 1934 as mandated by Congress under Title IV of the JOBS Act of 2012—marks the most powerful positive change in the securities industry since 1934.

During more than 40 years in the venture capital industry, I have personally been close to the growth challenges faced by smaller firms, and I have assisted many companies to raise public and private capital. During the past 20 years I have witnessed a steady decline in the number of new companies that have been able to successfully access the public markets and seen the number of IPOs and publicly listed firms decline in the United States relative to other countries. In recent years I concluded that the increasing obstacles faced by small companies to raising growth capital had reached a crisis, and I felt it was time to change the regulations responsible for the slow-down.

I decided to get personally involved by helping to architect the required changes to allow small companies to regain the ability to raise capital not only from larger funds and wealthy investors but also from small investors. It was critically important that smaller companies be enabled to provide more liquidity and tradability in the shares they sell to their investors than they could by selling the currently popular Regulation D securities. Over the course of several years, I worked with numerous people, including U.S. senators and congressmen, to help craft Title IV of the JOBS Act as the platform for Regulation A+. I believe Regulation A+ as constructed by the SEC will play a crucial role in helping small companies raise the necessary capital to grow their businesses and in reinvigorating this stalled sector of the U.S. economy.

The authors have done an excellent job of compiling and interpreting all the relevant materials to produce a very useful guide to Regulation A+, explaining its beneficial features and the practical considerations and techniques for putting them to best use in a variety of businesses. This is a complete guide for entrepreneurs who need to evaluate their new range of options for raising capital to grow their businesses. Chapters 1 and 2 review and evaluate the various options for capital formation and what may or may not work for a particular situation. Chapter 3 details the various elements of Regulation A+ and compares them to the corresponding elements of the other options in terms of benefit, cost, and time for funding. Chapter 4 examines the applications and limitations of Regulation A+. Chapters 5 through 8 provide all the details small companies need to use Reg A+ to raise capital and manage stock listings if they choose to allow secondary stock transactions. The final chapter summarizes the appropriate uses and applications of Reg A+. The appendices contain reference material from the SEC and other relevant sources. The text is illustrated by numerous tables and charts.

I congratulate the authors of *Regulation A+: How the JOBS Act Creates Opportunities for Entrepreneurs and Investors* on their timely creation of this authoritative and accessible guide designed to assist the millions of U.S. entrepreneurs who are now eligible to capitalize on the rich opportunities for small company growth afforded by Reg A+.

—Bill Hambrecht

Founder and Chairman, WR Hambrecht + Co

About the Authors

Paul M. Getty has been an active venture capitalist with technology investment firms Venture Navigation and Satwik Ventures. He also is a co-founder of First Guardian Group, a national real estate investment and management firm that has completed over $800 million in transactions. His prior operating experience spans over 25 years as a serial entrepreneur and executive officer in firms that resulted in investor returns of over $700 million through multiple successful IPOs and M&As. Paul is a frequent speaker on investment topics at industry conferences. He is also the author of *The 12 Magic Slides* (Apress, 2013). Paul is a licensed real estate broker and holds Series 63 and Series 22 securities licenses. He has an MBA in finance from the University of Michigan, with honors, and a bachelor's degree in chemistry from Wayne State University.

Dinesh Gupta co-founded Satwik Ventures (www.satwikventures.com), a seed-stage technology venture fund in 2000. Satwik Fund has invested in over 25 early stage start-up technology companies. Dinesh has served on the boards of several of these companies. These companies received co-investments in excess of $1 billion from major Silicon Valley VC funds and many had successful exits via IPOs and mergers. Dinesh also co-founded First Guardian Group with Paul Getty. He is a licensed estate professional and holds Series 63 and Series 22 securities licenses. Dinesh has an MBA in marketing and finance from Santa Clara University, and a bachelor's degree in mechanical engineering from the University of Delhi, India.

Robert R. Kaplan, Jr. is currently managing partner of Kaplan Voekler Cunningham & Frank PLC, based in Richmond, VA. Rob has been referred to as the guru of Reg A+ due to his involvement and influence in bringing about new changes that will have a dramatic impact in rekindling investor interest in alternative investments. He is a leading speaker on Regulation A+ and has been featured in numerous financial publications and on syndicated TV/radio shows. He holds a J.D. from Marshall-Wythe School of Law, College of William and Mary, and an A.B. from College of William and Mary.

Acknowledgments

This book was conceived almost three years ago but stalled due to the SEC not finalizing the rules for implementation of Regulation A+ until June of 2015. During this journey so many people helped, inspired, and contributed to this book. We are grateful to all them.

To Dan Zinn and Cromwell Coulson, OTC Markets Group, David Dobkin, ASMZ Capital, and Steven Nelson, Continental Stock Transfer and Trust, for making valuable contributions to Chapter 8 on secondary trading of Reg A+ Securities.

To David Weild IV and Edward Kim of Weild & Co, for providing very insightful data and inputs on reasons for the decline of publicly financed firms in the U.S., plus adding valuable charts and content.

To Kate Mitchell for spearheading important efforts to raise awareness of capital formation issues to members of congress and also for allowing use of presentation materials.

To Rita Fernando and Robert Hutchinson of Apress, for their excellent work in editing the entire book in addition to patiently working with us on this project over three years.

To Erik Carlson, Jason Hogin, and Laura Ede, our colleagues at First Guardian Group, for reviewing and editing the final content.

To T. Rhys James of Kaplan Voekler Cunningham & Frank, for his valuable assistance in the preparation of portions of this book.

Lastly, thanks to our wives Jan Getty, Usha Gupta, and Kristen Kaplan, for inspiring us to share our life experiences with entrepreneurs and help them to achieve their dreams, thereby revitalizing the U.S. economy.

Introduction

Why Did We Write This Book?

"Connecting small entrepreneurs with small investors"

We Have Been On Both Sides of Funding

Over the last 20 years we have made dozens of investments in small growth companies as well as raised capital for scores of projects in the fields of high technology and commercial real estate or represented any number of individuals or entities doing just that. During this period we met hundreds of entrepreneurs who needed capital and scores of VCs, bankers, and both high net worth and small investors. In reflecting back on those experiences, certain messages became quite evident from these personal experiences in addition to a huge amount of data that validates the conclusions contained in this book.

Too Many Missed Opportunities

Over the years we have seen many worthwhile projects that either never get started or had a short life due to the limited amount of available capital that entrepreneurs could raise due to increasingly limited capital-raising options available to them. Eventually only a small number of projects actually received adequate capital and many good projects that could have been very successful died prematurely.

Small Investors Left Out

When raising investment funds on behalf of entrepreneurs, many small investors wanted to participate but had to be turned away as they did not meet the accredited high net worth criteria imposed by the SEC. Although the collective numbers and wealth of smaller investors is greater than the fewer high net worth investors, these investors were denied opportunity to participate in many attractive investment opportunities.

No Liquidity for Years for Investors

Most of the private investment opportunities obtain their funding in Regulation D private offerings, and, in most cases, investors had to wait 10–15 years to achieve returns, if any, due to the illiquid nature of Regulation D offerings. Many times, companies were unable to raise additional capital and had to close their doors. Investors lost all their money because they could not raise further capital in the public markets.

How Do You Make Sense of a Changing Landscape?

While Regulation A+ is a very powerful and positive development in addressing fundraising and liquidity issues faced by entrepreneurs as well as providing investment options to small investors, it is not going to be an easy path to success. There are hundreds of large funds, broker-dealers, and others who have a strong vested interest in maintaining the "status quo," or are timid when it comes to uncertainty concerning a new market. Therefore, we felt it was critical that larger groups of entrepreneurs and investors be introduced to the benefits they can draw from utilizing Reg A+ for their next capital raise, relative to all other options they may have. Demand builds markets!

Since the passage of JOBS Act in 2012, there is a huge overload of sometimes confusing and conflicting information on the Internet concerning the JOBS Act and Regulation A+. We felt it was important to take a top-down approach to develop an easy-to-understand and, hopefully, useful guide to facilitate making a proper evaluation of this exciting new option for capital raising and investing.

Introduction

With overwhelming bipartisan support, the *Jumpstart Our Business Startups Act* (the JOBS Act) was passed in April, 2012.[1] It ushered in a new era of capital formation and job creation that is already being predicted by many to have a profoundly positive, transformational impact on the U.S. economy. For reasons detailed in this book, we believe one of the most impactful areas of the JOBS Act is the creation of important updates to Regulation A. Regulation A is a Securities and Exchange Commission (SEC) regulation that permits firms to raise capital with less burdensome requirements. This paves the way for many companies to raise capital via "mini-IPOs" (Initial Public Offerings), which are far less costly than full IPOs but achieve many of the same objectives.

Prior to the JOBs Act, investments in non-publicly traded firms were effectively limited to wealthy individuals and institutions. Provisions of the JOBs Act, including Regulation A+, are a major game changer and now allow entrepreneurs to more easily access a much larger pool of potential investors who have previously not been permitted to invest in emerging businesses.

Federal law requires all offers to sell securities and all sales of securities to be registered unless an exemption to registration applies. A security is broadly defined as "an investment contract, transaction, or scheme whereby a person invests his money in a common enterprise and is led to expect profits solely from the efforts of others." Securities typically involve investments in intangible items such as a share of stock rather than tangible items such as a house or a car. If you are seeking to raise money for a business, you will be offering a security and must comply with existing laws. Since the registration of a security can be costly and time-consuming, many firms seeking to raise funds often seek to obtain one or more exemptions from registration.

---

[1] https://www.sec.gov/spotlight/jobs-act.shtml

Obtaining an exemption can pose additional challenges since exemptions usually have restrictions that limit the types of investors who can be attracted and also impose added administrative overhead. The most common used exemption from securities registration is Regulation D ("Reg D") promulgated under section 4(2) of the Securities Act of 1933 as amended. Firms electing this exemption are limited to obtaining funds from wealthy or "accredited" investors or institutions, which severely limits the potential pool of investors who are allowed to invest under this exemption. Also a commonly used Reg D exemption, called 506, prohibits public solicitation and general advertising to attract investors.

Under the new Regulation A ("Reg A+"), a company may raise up to $50 million in a 12-month period and it may offer its shares to both accredited and non-accredited investors, with some limited restrictions on the amount of a non-accredited investor's investment. In addition, Reg A+ has no restrictions on general solicitations or advertising.

Among the most compelling benefits to entrepreneurs of structuring an offering under Reg A+ is the ability to attract both accredited and non-accredited investors and take advantage of public advertising to expose their offerings. Since less than 1% of population qualifies as an accredited investor, Reg A+ provides a means for entrepreneurs to access the other 99% of potential investors and thereby greatly expand the potential pool of funds to draw from. Firms that are unable to attract a sufficient amount of funds from accredited investors can utilize Reg A+ to tap into their customer base or into regional investors who may be familiar with the firm or have an affinity to invest locally. To better understand the objectives of the JOBS Act, it is important to first understand several negative trends that have created the need for the new legislation.

Historically, capital raising in the United States has been a function of operating in one or two spaces—an IPO, with a complete registration of the offering of securities, or a "private" offering, usually under Regulation D. Prior to roughly 20 years ago, we saw a much more diverse number of IPOs based on size, maturity of the issuer, industry, and strategy of the business. IPOs were also conducted by a more diverse set of financial institutions, both in market focus and region. We have seen this window steadily narrowing since that time for reasons discussed in this chapter. The result has been that more companies seeking capital have to look to private transactions, either through private equity groups/venture capital firms or Regulation D offerings to individual or "retail" investors. As discussed in this chapter, this has resulted in a seriously more challenging market to raise capital privately. For reasons detailed throughout this book, we believe that Regulation A+ provides a viable alternative to Regulation D and private equity for growing businesses outside of more traditional registered public offerings.

IPOs and Job Creation: Coupled Trends

From 1996 through 2011, the number of companies entering the U.S. capital markets through IPOs dropped dramatically relative to historical norms. During this period, listings on U.S. national stock exchanges declined from 8,800 companies to less than 5,000. Over the years from 2001 to 2012, IPOs were down to about a hundred per year versus 300–400 a decade ago[2] (Figure 1-1). This downward trend has been more severe than the potentially offsetting economic cycles during that period and had a negative impact on U.S. job creation. In fact, by one estimate, the decline of the U.S. IPO market has cost America as many as 22 million jobs through 2009.[3] During this same period, competition from foreign capital markets intensified, and new listings on overseas exchanges doubled. Today, less than 10% of global firms choose to list on U.S. exchanges, compared to 48% in the 1990s.[4] This slowdown in U.S. IPOs and the diversion of global capital away from the U.S. markets has slowed American job growth and threatens to undermine U.S. economic superiority for decades to come.

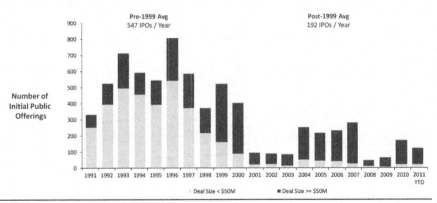

Figure 1-1. Number of IPOs per year, 1991–2014. The number dropped steeply in 1996 and remained low until 2013, when a rebound occurred owing in part to the impact of the JOBS Act. (Source: IPO Task Force, "Rebuilding the IPO On-Ramp," October 20, 2011)

---

[2]http://online.wsj.com/article/SB10001424052970203986604577253250236327264.html

[3]D. Weild and E. Kim, Grant Thornton, A Wake-up Call for America at page 2 (November 2009).

[4]http://www.pwc.com/en_US/us/transaction-services/publications/assets/capital-markets-2025.pdf

David Weild, former Vice Chairman of NASDAQ, published findings that it takes 360 new corporate listings a year to replace what is lost in an average year from mergers and acquisitions and regulatory delistings. We have averaged only about 150 IPOs a year since 2000. Weild further characterized the IPO spurt in 2013 and 2014 as "dead cat bounce" years coming off the highly depressed years of the credit crisis, which began in 2007–08. In spite of champagne corks popping on Wall Street, neither 2013 nor 2014 generated the 360 corporate IPOs needed to even tread water.

As troubling as these statistics are, the failure of the United States to keep pace with international markets further underscores its growing inability to maintain its lead in fostering entrepreneurial growth and capital formation (see Figure 1-2).

Percent Change in Number of Listed Companies for Selected Markets
Indexed to 1997 (1997=0)

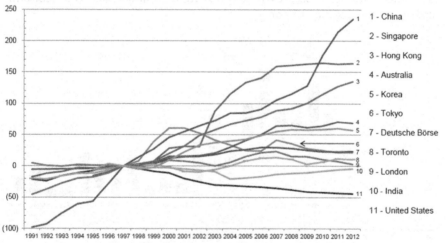

Sources: Weild & Co., World Federation of Exchanges and the global stock exchanges
China includes Shanghai S.E. + Shenzhen S.E. India includes National S.E. + Bombay S.E.
Based on the number of listed companies at year-end, excluding funds, as of Dec. 2012.

Figure 1-2. Percent change in number of listed companies for selected markets

During an interview with the authors, Mr. Weild recounted congressional reaction to this chart as a hearing of the House Financial Services Subcommittee on Capital Markets and Government Sponsored Enterprises.

Congressman: "Mr. Weild, who is on the top of this chart?"

Weild: "China is, sir."

Congressman: "Who is at the bottom of this chart, Mr. Weild?"

Weild: "The United States is, sir!"

Congressman: "Which one would you like to be Mr. Weild?... On second thought, don't answer that!"

Jobs and IPOs

The relationship between IPOs and job creation has been widely studied. One such study by the Ewing Marion Kaufman Foundation concluded the following:

> *While many young businesses fail, the young businesses that have survived have exhibited high average growth rates (with the latter dominated by the most rapidly growing young businesses). In addition, the evidence shows that the high-growth surviving young firms have contributed substantially to productivity growth.[5]*

A study[6] presented to the U.S. Treasury by the IPO Task Force, a cross-industry group, reported that 92% of a typical company's employment growth occurs after the IPO (Figure 1-3).[7]

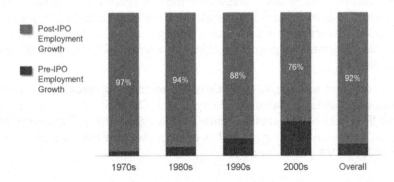

Figure 1-3. Significance of IPOs to job creation shown by the relative proportions of post-IPO employment growth and pre-IPO employment growth in companies that raised capital through IPOs per decade, 1970-2010. Source: IPO Task Force August 2011 CEO Survey

[5]http://www.kauffman.org/uploadedfiles/bds_2012.pdf
[6]http://www.google.com/url?sa=t&rct=j&q=&esrc=s&source=web&cd=2&ved=0CDMQFjAB&url=http%3A%2F%2Fwww.nvca.org%2Findex.php%3Foption%3Dcom_docman%26task%3Ddoc_download%26gid%3D805%26Itemid%3D93&ei=Zq67U0iJP0bc2Q XPoYGIAg&usg=AFQjCNEF440xGxfY1WaYrNrm9qD1EysZBw
[7]http://www.google.com/url?sa=t&rct=j&q=&esrc=s&source=web&cd=2&ved=0CDMQFjAB&url=http%3A%2F%2Fwww.nvca.org%2Findex.php%3Foption%3Dcom_docman%26task%3Ddoc_download%26gid%3D805%26Itemid%3D93&ei=Zq67U0iJP0bc2Q XPoYGIAg&usg=AFQjCNEF440xGxfY1WaYrNrm9qD1EysZBw

Another study, prepared by Grant Thornton LLP, cites that the United States has lost more than 22 million jobs because of lost IPOs since the 1990s.[8] While the drop in IPOs does not solely account for the weak job growth of the past decade, it is difficult to look at the data and not conclude that steps to reinvigorate IPOs would have a positive impact on job growth.

The decrease in IPOs raised a number of concerns that were directly related to the creation of the JOBS Act. Since the drop in IPO activity has been most severe among small firms,[9] reducing burdens for smaller companies became a central focus of the JOBS Act.

Why Have IPOs Declined?

A number of factors contributed to the decadal decline in IPOs (Table 1-1), including market changes and growing governmental regulations. Electronic trading, which started in the mid-1990s, put downward pressure on trading commissions and fees that in turn paid for ongoing market coverage—especially for smaller issues.[10] The elimination in 2001 of traditional spreads by the introduction of *decimalization*[11]—moving stock-tick intervals from a sixteenth of a dollar to a penny—hastened the departure of many analysts and market makers from traditional brokerages to hedge funds. There, they could make a better living working in the new world of high-frequency, zero-spread trading.

Added costs and administrative burdens due to creeping regulation—including Gramm-Leach-Bliley,[12] Sarbanes-Oxley,[13] and Dodd-Frank[14]—have further limited IPO options for smaller issuers. As a result, the average time from company inception to going public has been pushed out from 4.8 years in the early 1980s to 9.4 years since 2007.[15]

---

[8]https://www.grantthornton.com/staticfiles/GTCom/Public%20companies%20 and%20capital%20markets/gt_wakeup_call_.pdf at Page 2
[9]http://www.sec.gov/info/smallbus/acsec/acsec-090712-ritter-slides.pdf
[10]http://www.grantthorton.com/staticfiles/GTCom/files/GT%20Thinking/ IPO%20white%20paper/Why%20are%20IPOs%20in%20the%20ICU_11_19.pdf
[11]http://betanews.com/2012/09/05/stock-market-decimalization-kills-ipos-and-ruins-the-economy/
[12]http://business.ftc.gov/documents/bus53-brief-financial-privacy-requirements-gramm-leach-bliley-act
[13]http://smallbusiness.chron.com/sarbanes-oxley-act-2002-affect-small-business-owners-877.html
[14]http://www.washingtonpost.com/business/capitalbusiness/commentary-how-the-dodd-frank-act-hurts-small-businesses/2012/03/19/gIQAja7RaS_story. html
[15]Thomson Reuters and the National Venture Capital Association

In this environment, smaller firms are simply unable to afford the cost of raising capital, and market makers are unwilling to cover companies until they have become much larger than was the case earlier. The average cost of going public coupled with the costs of regulatory compliance have limited the IPO option to fewer and fewer companies (Figure 1-4).

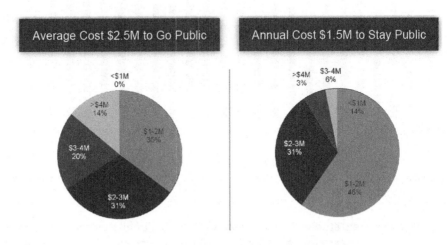

Costs Including SOX, Legal, Accounting

Source: IPO Task Force August 2011 CEO survey of incremental IPO costs from 35 CEOs of companies that went public since 2006; **Consistent With Independent Review of Public Filings for 47 2011 IPO's Raising Less Than $200M (Avg. Cost of $3M for IPO)**

Figure 1-4. Average costs to go public and annual costs to stay public. Source: IPO Task Force August 2011 CEO Survey

The reduction in IPOs has also led to a significant decrease in opportunities for the investors and employees of growth companies to gain liquidity for their shares. This has in part led to an increase in merger and acquisition (M&A) activity as companies seek exits for their investors (Figure 1-5). Ironically, the rapid increase in M&A has thwarted the growth of jobs since many firms lose employees after being acquired by larger firms.[16] Arguably, if many of these acquired companies had the option to go IPO instead to raise capital, the United States likely would have created more jobs.

---

[16]http://www.americasjobexchange.com/career-advice/impact-of-mergers-and-acquisitions

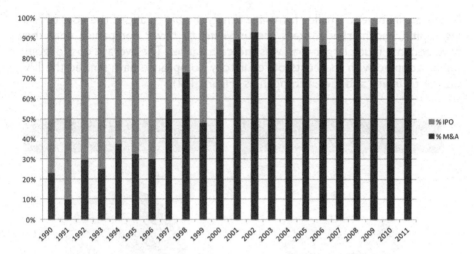

Figure 1-5. Relative proportions of mergers and acquisitions and IPOs as means of providing investor liquidity per year, 1990-2011. (Source: Thomson Reuters, National Venture Capital Association)

At the same time, studies indicate that 50% to 80% of all mergers fail, further dampening prospects for job creation and revenue growth.[17] The cumulative loss to the economy stemming from the inability of so many companies to raise growth capital at earlier stages in their maturity cycle is suggested by the positive impact that successful startups that are able to grow and remain independent have on U.S. GDP.

Challenges in Raising Growth Funds from Venture Capital Firms

Contrary to the belief of many aspiring entrepreneurs, only a miniscule number of firms succeed in obtaining funds from venture capital firms. Of the approximately 2 million businesses that are created each year, only 600–800 firms—far less than 1%—are funded via venture capital.[18] The majority of venture capital funds seek early-stage companies with strong business plans and management teams who have aspirations to grow to $100M+ in revenues and exit in less than 10 years. Due to the highly risky nature of early-stage investing, VC firms need to achieve very high returns on a portion of their portfolio

[17]http://www.caxtongrowth.com/images/resource/why_fail.pdf
[18]http://en.wikipedia.org/wiki/Venture_capital

to offset the losses on the remaining firms that do not achieve success. The typical investment criteria are set far above where most traditional business would qualify.

Furthermore, the types of investors who invest in typical venture capital deals are willing to lose substantial equity on many failed opportunities in order to realize a far greater return on the few companies who are able to realize extraordinary returns. The high-risk high-return nature of venture capital not only limits the types of firms that can succeed in attracting venture capital, but also highly limits the pool of potential investors who have the capacity to assume great risk.

While later-stage companies with established business lines and customers can pose less risk to VC investors, the required high hurdle rates of return still severely limit the number of later-stage firms that can obtain VC capital. Also, the capital needs of later-stage firms are typically greater and can often exceed the level of resources that can be provided from VC investors—even if their strict investment criteria can be met. Finally, since most VC firms have an investment horizon of no more than 10–12 years owing to caps on their ongoing management fees, there is a declining incentive to support mature companies that require added growth capital.

Challenges in Obtaining Other Sources of Capital

Once a new business has proven its business model, established a market presence, and developed product lines and distribution channels broad enough to meet the requirements of its largest customers, it may face its greatest capital demands. Cash flow from operations is often not sufficient to meet the needs of more mature companies, and the lure of obtaining funds from public markets can be compelling even in face of the growing number of obstacles.

It is common to find firms that have grown modestly for many years only to reach a plateau. New capital is then needed to restart their upward growth by providing the needed resources to take advantage of new opportunities. Funds raised by later-stage firms are often used to expand penetration into markets, acquire smaller firms, increase investment in R&D, and strengthen their balance sheets. All this improves their credit standing and attractiveness to investors and raises the value of their firms.

Whether a business owner is looking to modify his current capital structure or seeking new growth capital, money is hard to come by today. Excluding IPOs, the sources of external growth capital include bank loans, industry alliances, factoring of receivables, and investors. Not only are these types of sources more difficult to tap into, but they also can create additional liabilities and exposure for the firm's executives. Short-term debt can be very helpful to raising capital for tactical projects, but companies saddled with excessive long-term debt find that the value of their firm, relative to industry norms, is significantly impacted.

Regulation D

One of the most common and popular ways to raise growth capital outside of a public stock offering has been to privately offer ownership interests using a registration exemption under the Securities and Exchange Act of 1933 called *Regulation D* ("Reg D"). The amount of capital raised under Reg D offerings is well over $1 trillion annually. Regulation D has been used as a means of raising capital ranging from seed-stage "mom and pop" investments to hundreds of millions of dollars for later-stage firms owing largely to reduced SEC reporting requirements and the relative speed in which offering[19] materials can be produced. Although Regulation D offerings are the primary means today for raising growth capital for early-stage ventures or specific short-term (2–5 years) projects, they suffer from the following limitations and restrictions:

- Private fundraising under Regulation D is largely limited to *accredited investors* who have a net worth in excess of $1M, excluding their primary residence[20] or income of more than $200,000 per year (or $300,000 per married couple) during the past two years or to qualified institutions.

- Trading of Reg D shares is highly restricted and cannot be done in public markets. As a result, Reg D investments are considered "illiquid" and invested funds can be tied up indefinitely (anywhere from 5 to 20 years) unless there is a sale of the firm or an IPO.

---

[19]https://www.sec.gov/divisions/riskfin/whitepapers/dera-unregistered-offerings-reg-d.pdf at Page 2

[20]While the value of the primary residence is excluded, if the Fair Market Value (FMV) of the primary residence is below the loan value, the added debt beyond FMV must be further subtracted to determine if the net worth of an investor meets the accredited investor definition. For example, if an investor's personal residence is worth $500K and the mortgage owned is $600K, $100K needs to be subtracted when computing net worth.

- Due to poor performance of many investments that have been made under Reg D, many broker-dealers are unwilling to consider offering new Reg D investments to their clients. Although the Reg D investment structure was not primarily responsible for the failure of investments during the recent economic downturn, "Reg D" has been stigmatized and regulatory boards such as FINRA have placed added burdens on securities reps who offer such securities. Liability insurance premiums have also skyrocketed for those intermediaries that offer Reg D securities.

The lack of liquidity of Reg D also creates valuation problems. Since no public market exists, it's difficult to impossible to assess the value of Reg D investments.

Effective September 23, 2013, the SEC adopted amendments to Regulation D that removed the previous prohibition against general solicitation. "General solicitation" is broadly defined in the amendment to include virtually any print, electronic, and other public means of exposing securities offerings to investors. While the general public may now become aware of new offerings, the amendment also limited investors who may purchase an advertised offering to only those who are "accredited investors." The amendment also placed additional burdens on issuers and broker-dealer intermediaries to verify the accredited status of each investor.

Even with these latest modifications, the growing backlash against Regulation D by many securities broker-dealers has further dried up capital raising options for smaller firms. The net result of these growing constraints to obtaining growth capital is that far too many promising companies are unable to take full advantage of transformational opportunities and are limited to relatively tepid growth due to capital starvation.

Chapter 3 systematically compares Regulation D with Regulation A+.

Note **Pre-JOBS Act** regulations made it increasingly difficult for both early- and later-stage companies to obtain the capital they needed when they needed it, and for investors to cash out in a timely manner.

An Overview of the JOBS Act

The major goals of the JOBS Act are to reinvigorate job growth and create new capital formation opportunities, especially for smaller firms requiring more growth options. After a long period of increasing regulation and constraints in finance, the JOBS Act is having a dramatic effect in moving the regulatory pendulum back toward easing the process of capital formation and increasing economic growth.

The JOBS Act is comprised of the following six titles (sections), considered in turn.

Title I: Reopening American Capital Markets to Emerging Growth Companies

Most commonly referred to as the "IPO On-Ramp" legislation, Title I provides smaller companies new options and incentives for going public through a process whereby public company obligations are phased in over time. This title creates a new category of companies referred to as *emerging growth companies* (EGCs).[21] A firm may elect to become an EGC and realize related benefits under the title, provided its sales are less than $1 billion per year.

Under Title I of the JOBS Act, an EGC[22] is allowed numerous exemptions from and relaxations of costly reporting and disclosure requirements and rules, such as the following:

- A five-year grace period from certain reporting under current federal law and regulations.

- To use reduced financial disclosures, including only two years of audited financial statements and less-stringent executive compensation reporting standards.

- To confidentially pre-file its IPO registration statement with the SEC for its review.

- To "test the waters" for its prospectus with select qualified investors.

---

[21]http://www.sec.gov/divisions/corpfin/guidance/cfjjobsactfaq-title-i-general.htm
[22]An Emerging Growth Company is defined as a company which:
   (a) Has under $1 billion in revenue;
   (b) Completed its IPO less than five years ago;
   (c) Has less than $1 billion in non-convertible debt; and
   (d) Is not a "Large Accelerated Filer" under the Securities Exchange Act of 1934.

Title II: Broader Access to Capital for Job Creators

Title II removes the prohibition against general solicitation and general advertising in private offerings under Regulation D, provided that all of the purchasers of securities are accredited investors.[23] However, the securities remain restricted from resale. This title also addresses certain issues for intermediaries including broker–dealers, and includes provisions that ease fundraising under Rule 144a.

Title III: Crowdfunding

Title III provides an exemption for *crowdfunding*—raising funds broadly through Internet portals—by permitting offerings up to $1 million. Requirements targeted at investor protection are imposed on the issuer and on the intermediary involved in the crowdfunding effort. This title also addresses certain broker-dealer issues for intermediaries. The following constraints and limitations are included in Title III:

- Crowdfunding must take place with an approved offering document that will likely require an attorney and be placed through either registered or regulated funding portals or broker-dealers that meet certain requirements, thereby raising costs that will limit the amount of net capital that can be obtained.

---

[23]In the US, an *accredited investor* is defined by the following:

1. A bank, insurance company, registered investment company, business development company, or small business investment company;

2. An employee benefit plan, within the meaning of the Employee Retirement Income Security Act, if a bank, insurance company, or registered investment adviser makes the investment decisions, or if the plan has total assets in excess of $5 million;

3. A charitable organization, corporation, or partnership with assets exceeding $5 million;

4. A director, executive officer, or general partner of the company selling the securities;

5. A business in which all the equity owners are accredited investors;

6. A natural person who has individual net worth, or joint net worth with the person's spouse, that exceeds $2 million at the time of the purchase, or has assets under management of $1 million or above, excluding the value of their primary residence;[2][3]

7. A natural person with income exceeding $200,000 in each of the two most recent years or joint income with a spouse exceeding $300,000 for those years and a reasonable expectation of the same income level in the current year; or

8. A trust with assets in excess of $5 million, not formed to acquire the securities offered, whose purchases a sophisticated person makes.

- Issuers need to file financial statements annually and file reports of the operations with the SEC.

- Issued shares are restricted and cannot be traded for one year.

- Eligible firms are limited and cannot include foreign issuers and investment companies.

- Individual investors are limited to investing only up to

  - the greater of $2,000 or 5% of annual income or net worth (for small investors); or

  - 10% of the investors' annual income or net worth, up to $100,000, if such an annual income or net worth equals or exceeds $100,000.

Shortly after the JOBS Act legislation was announced, the crowdfunding provisions became an immediate lightning rod, attracting cash-hungry startup entrepreneurs, wannabe portal firms, and harsh critics fearful that scam artists would bilk hapless investors under the proposed new rules. Proponents were quick to point out that the investor safeguards in the JOBS Act are sufficient to balance crowdfunding risks and benefits, and that many other less-regulated investment options, such as investing in common stocks, are permitted today.

Also cited was the fact that government-encouraged sales of lottery tickets and other forms of gambling at about $140 billion per year dwarf the $40 billion or so of investment funds in startups/growth firms made each year. Yet crowdfunding continues to be portrayed by many of its critics as a vehicle for victimizing unsuitable investors.

Despite Title III constraints and media criticism, crowdfunding has begun to play a significant a role in providing new options for smaller firms to raise capital.

Title IV ("Regulation A+"): Small Company Formation

Title IV—commonly referred to as "Regulation A+" or "Reg A+"—amends the previous Regulation A legislation in the following areas:

- Title IV increases the amount permitted to be raised from $5 million to $50 million each year indefinitely.

- Shares are generally unrestricted and can immediately be traded, thereby providing liquidity to investors, management, and employees holding shares.

- Advertising and general solicitation are generally permitted.

- Non-accredited investors are allowed to invest.

- A broad number of firms can raise funds.

- Title IV requires slightly more detailed SEC-specified offering disclosures.

- Title IV requires annual audited financial statements to be filed with the SEC.

- Larger Reg A+ offerings—called "Tier 2" and discussed in Chapter 2—are exempt from state "blue sky" reporting requirements.

- Title IV requires ongoing reporting to the SEC but with fewer disclosure requirements than for traditional "public" companies.

On June 19, 2015, the SEC adopted the final rules for Regulation A+ in response to ongoing comments received since the initial framework was outlined in the JOBS Act. The final rules are largely consistent with the original intent of the JOBS Act with several important updates. Per the final rules, Regulation A+ includes two tiers: Tier 1 for offerings up to $20M and Tier 2 for offerings up to $50M—both within any twelve month period. The differences in the tiers are largely due to differing reporting and disclosure requirements. Most significantly, issuers who meet Tier 2 disclosure and reporting requirements are exempt from state blue sky pre-sale reviews, which have been cited as one of the major obstacles that previously limited the attractiveness of Regulation A as a means of fundraising. A more complete discussion of the final rules for Regulation A+ can be found in Chapter 5.

We believe Regulation A+ can provide a more attractive means of raising capital for many growing companies than either the Regulation D private placement or the traditional IPO. The benefits and trade-offs of Regulation A+ form the central theme of this book.

Note Regulation A+ is a huge new development for growth companies: it can indeed serve as a "mini-IPO" for many companies. It is the subject of this book.

Title V: Private Company Flexibility and Growth

Title V increases the 1934 Exchange Act registration shareholder-of-record threshold from 500 to 2,000 (only 500 of which can be non-accredited investors).

Title VI: Capital Expansion

Title VI increases the shareholder-of-record threshold from 500 to 2,000 for banks and bank holding companies, and it provides that a bank or bank holding company could terminate the 1934 Exchange Act registration if the number of holders of record drops to less than 1,200.

These changes are significant. The 1934 Exchange Act and its related rules currently require a company to register with the SEC and file periodic public reports if, on the last day of its fiscal year, the company had total assets exceeding $10,000,000 *and* a class of equity securities generally held of record by 500 or more persons (both conditions must be met).

Under Title V and Title VI of the JOBS Act, the number of shareholders of record that a company may have before it must register under the 1934 Exchange Act is increased from 500 to 2,000 or by 500 or more persons who are not accredited investors—thereby reducing regulatory burdens and related costs. The threshold for total assets remains unchanged at $10,000,000. Shareholders who received their securities through an employee compensation plan or an offering conducted under the "crowdfunding" exemption in Title III of the JOBS Act do not count toward the holders-of-record thresholds.

Implications and Overview of the Book

This book is primarily a how-to guide on utilizing the new Regulation A+ rules to raise capital from accredited investors and institutions in addition to more than 100 million non-accredited investors and to provide liquidity in the most effective manner for all stakeholders. That includes management, current and future investors, and service providers such as attorneys, auditors, i-Banks, financial advisors, research analysts, and so forth. "It takes a village to grow a child," and that tight and intimate coordination of all members of the fundraising team is required to achieve a successful outcome. We will therefore discuss the roles and responsibilities of the various team members throughout the book and suggest coordination processes that we believe will assist firms in obtaining their fundraising objectives.

This book has two critical objectives for the reader seeking to successfully utilize Regulation A+:

- Education about the processes involved

- First and foremost, how and where to seek advice and resources to accomplish fundraising and, if possible, liquidity goals

Do you have customers and growing revenues? Do you have a good-enough story to attract investors who are seeking not only a return on their capital, but also a return *of* their capital? Can your company stand up to close scrutiny by due-diligence analysts? If so, the good news is that your firm may be able to successfully raise growth capital under Regulation A+—even if you are not the next Google, Apple, or LinkedIn.

Regulation A+ opens up potential fundraising channels that may not require the high multiple returns that many venture capital firms require. Indeed, there are many qualified investors who seek opportunities to invest in solid, growing bread-and-butter businesses but who before Regulation A+ did not have a means of doing so. This book explores potential fundraising channels in more detail, including suggestions on finding appropriate investors for your firm.

Although it might seem that growing the use of Regulation A+ would tend to diminish the popularity of the current IPO or Regulation D private placement fundraising approaches, we believe Reg A+ simply expands the scope and opportunity for fundraising by allowing many non-accredited investors to profit from pre-IPO growth companies by diversifying and optimizing the selections of their investments. For example, it may be important for an early-stage startup to seek its initial capital and guidance from angel investors or a VC firm via a Regulation D private placement; whereas later-stage firms may seek much lower-cost capital through an mini-IPO based on Reg A+ and continue a growth trajectory that might otherwise stall in the absence of growth capital.

Tip   Reg A+ is in its infancy. The investment and entrepreneur communities must still work out optimal ways of working together to raise growth capital. A number of open issues still remain which are likely to be addressed by market reaction to Regulation A+ offerings in addition to further rulings that are likely to take place. The good news lays in the significant progress that has been made to date and the positive momentum that is moving to open up new funding options to benefit both entrepreneurs and investors.

Overcoming Challenges to Going Public

Regulation A+ creates options for firms to raise capital beyond a Reg D and without a public registration, but instead via a mini-IPO that can be accomplished with less cost, time commitment, and resources than a full-blown IPO. However, an IPO is an IPO and, whatever type you choose, the outcome and many of the related issues are similar. Let's start with a basic question.

Should My Firm Go Public?

Historically, many of America's young companies have pursued the acquisition of later-stage growth capital through initial public offerings (IPOs) in order to have access to the additional capital they needed to hire new employees, develop their products, and expand their businesses globally. Fundraising via IPOs has enabled many companies to generate new jobs and revenue for the U.S. economy, while investors of all types have been attracted to ensuing growth to build their portfolios, personal incomes, and retirement accounts.

The advantages of going public include:

- Funds are obtained from the offering, which can be used for added research and development, hiring additional personnel, expanding infrastructure, building international distribution channels, retiring existing debt, acquiring other companies, or diversifying product lines.

- Public offerings will often improve the balance sheet of the company, allowing the firm to obtain future capital or debt under more attractive terms. If a stock performs well in the aftermarket, additional capital can be raised from the public and from institutions. Once a public market has been created for a stock and, if it performs well in the continuing aftermarket, substantial additional equity capital can be raised on favorable terms. The added security that comes in having a tradable stock with a market value increases future financing options.

- The market value of a public company can be substantially higher than a private company with the same structure in the exact same industry. Statistics published by the U.S. Chamber of Commerce say that sellers of private companies receive an average of four to six times their net earnings. Whereas, public companies sell at an average of 20–25 times their net earnings. High-tech companies with good growth prospects can be valued even higher.

Investors in a private company will tend to discount the value of its stock due to its lack of liquidity. Furthermore, added disclosures and reports by third-party analysts who are often present for public companies tend to drive higher market values for their shares. Therefore, public companies are often valued much greater than comparable private companies in the same or similar industries. The availability of other alternatives to raising capital permits a public company greater leverage in its negotiations with investors. Most institutional and individual investors prefer investing in a public company since they have an *exit*—meaning they can sell their stock in the public market. Many companies that were private and about to be purchased went public to be purchased at a much higher price.

Here are additional benefits provided by going public:

- If a publicly traded firm chooses to grow via acquisition of other firms, it can use its own securities to acquire firms with minimal impact on its cash balances.

- Businesses with public stock are typically better equipped to attract and hire quality personnel if they can include stock or stock options that have market liquidity. Also, since compensation from stock options may be taxed at lower capital gains rates than ordinary income, a more attractive compensation package can be offered to attract employees.

- Public companies generally enjoy greater market visibility, benefit from stronger branding of their products and trademarks, and also can improve the attractiveness of their goods and services to more discriminating customers who prefer to trade with companies whose financials and market value are more visible. Owners and employees of publicly traded firms often realize a greater sense of fulfillment and well-being in knowing that their investments of time and money can have a high degree of liquidity.[1]

- The initial sale of stock can provide cash to management, employees, and existing investors. Underwriters will usually view any excessive *cash-out* with disfavor since it may be perceived as a *bail-out* to the investing public that reduces the amount of the funds raised which go into building the company. However, underwriters will place limitations on cash-out through lock-ups (that is, delaying the sale of shares of by insiders until some time has passed after outside investors have purchased the stock) and will also limit cash-outs by senior insiders to no more than 10% or 15% of the offering. Nevertheless, the liquidity that is ultimately achieved by going public is a powerful tool to motivate company performance.

---

[1] www.grantthornton.com/staticfiles/GTCom/files/services/PHB/Going%20Public_Web.pdf, page 3

- Public offerings create a source of liquidity for employees and investors who require an exit within a finite period to achieve expected returns on their investments. When a company remains private, its value cannot be easily calculated or realized without a marketplace for its stock. Furthermore, many investment funds are established with a finite holding period, typically 10 years, and they need to realize liquidity or face issues, including loss of management fees, potential penalties to the managing partners, and/or lack of resources to continue to manage funds beyond their stated expiration period.

The disadvantages to going public include:

- By definition, going public carries with it a responsibility for greater disclosure of the company's financials, business strategies, and data on key executives and board members, including compensation details. Once a company's publicly traded stock is being followed by analysts and market makers, comparisons of performance to competitors will be more frequent and comprehensive. By contrast, owners of privately held firms often have concerns that the exposure of information on sales, profits, competitive position, key customers, and material events may place their companies at a competitive disadvantage and/or provide unwelcomed exposure to their personal compensation plans.

- A public listing can be expected to reduce flexibility by management. Some actions that could be taken unilaterally by executives of a private firm may now need to be approved by shareholders and/or outside directors. Also certain business opportunities that may have been available personally to the firm's executives may now need to be turned over to the company.

- Once a company's stock is publicly listed, management decisions will tend to be biased based on the impact to near-term stock value. As a result, there may be tradeoffs that result in short-term gains at the expense of strategic investments and decisions.

- The added expenses and administrative overhead of maintaining a public listing can be significant. While the reduced reporting regime under Regulation A+ will significantly lower these expenses relative to a traditional IPO, firms should carefully consider the added legal, accounting, and administrative expenses before making a decision to raise capital through an IPO.

- Control by insiders is likely to diminish when greater portions of the stock ownership shift to external investors.

- Executive management and board directors are subject to greater liability when their stock is public, including class actions and derivative lawsuits regarding violations of securities or corporate laws. Exposure to nuisance and even frivolous lawsuits may increase and require significant expense and investment of time to defend.

- Tensions can develop due to conflicts between tax implications to executives versus those of investors on certain decisions, such as to whether to pay dividends. Also since public markets often place a higher value on publicly traded firms versus those that are privately held, estate taxes when leaving equity to heirs are likely to be higher.

Obviously, going public does not automatically turn a poorly-run unprofitable company into a more valuable one overnight. The public spotlight can magnify both positive and negative factors—with bad news often given more weight by public investors. Fortunately, companies that are contemplating public financing options can seek preliminary feedback on their likely success through interviews with investment bankers and broker-dealers. They can also potentially take advantage of the "testing of the waters" provisions of the JOBS Act to receive direct investor feedback.

THE ROLE OF THE UNDERWRITER

Underwriters are IPO specialists who typically work for investment banks. Their responsibilities include verifying the firm has complied with all regulations, filed all required fees, and completed required financial data that will be presented to investors. Underwriters also interact with larger potential buyers of the firm's securities, such as pension funds and insurance companies, to assess their interest in acquiring shares and also providing inputs for setting suitable IPO prices. The key objective in setting an IPO price is to strike a balance to insure that the full offering is sold out at a price that ensures anticipated proceeds to the issuer. Larger issuers are typically able to obtain guarantees from their underwriters of proceeds from securities sales. If the underwriters are unable to sell all the offered securities, they are required to purchase the excess. Underwriters for smaller issuers, including those using Regulation A+ for mini-IPOs, typically do not offer guarantees but instead work on a "best efforts" basis. An underwriter is not required for a Regulation A+ offering. The issuer may set its own price and sell its stock based on market receptivity. However, the use of third parties to assist in determining a realistic stock value so that fundraising goals are achieved is highly recommended.

What Are the Considerations in Seeking Public Financing?

Presuming that your firm has generally weighed the pros and cons of going public and still wishes to move forward with some form of IPO (whether a mini-IPO via Regulation A+ or a full-blown IPO), what are some of the considerations that underwriters will consider when deciding if they will assist you in raising capital?

Since we believe that Regulation A+ is best suited for established companies that have growing revenues and customer bases, and who are seeking expansion capital to further fuel growth of an already proven business model, we will focus our comments on established businesses.

Underwriters and analysts consider the following questions in determining the value of new public company:

- What is the prior earnings history of the company going back at least three years? To what degree have previous financials been audited?

- Do prior earnings generally meet prior projections and, if not, are there solid reasons for any missed projections?

- Do balance sheet and income and expense ratios fit industry norms and, if not, what is the explanation of these variances? What are the plans for correcting imbalances?

- Does the company have an experienced management team and board of directors that can adequately meet the added responsibilities of going public and achieving further growth objectives with the newly raised capital? Is there a plan in place for filling holes and a good succession plan for key contributors?

- How strong is the demand for the company's current and anticipated new products? How strong is the new-product pipeline?

- Who are the customers and how loyal are they? How certain are they to continue to buy the goods and services offered?

- What is the company's competitive position and how do its relative strengths and weaknesses measure up? Is the company a leader or at least a strong #2 in its region/market sector? Are the barriers to entry sufficient to maintain and grow market penetration in spite of competition?

- What are the planned uses of capital and impact on future growth?

- If the company is growing at more modest rates, will it be able to offer a dividend?

- Is the company in a "bread and butter" sector or in a hot growth area? If the latter, many hot growth areas receive excessive funding and there are shakeouts. Will this firm be a survivor?

- What is the impact of the financing on a possible exit via a merger or acquisition? Occasionally, a plan to take a company public can excite potential acquirers to make a move and purchase the company before its value is bid up in the public markets.

Interactions with investment bankers, analysts, and broker–dealers during their due diligence activities can be stressful and tend to reveal issues that must be first overcome before a public financing or that must at the least be taken into consideration in establishing the offering structure and pricing of the security.

How Competitive Factors Shape Determination of Market Value

Management should make a preliminary focus in identifying public companies that are in the same industry sector and in a similar stage of development to obtain an initial estimate of a likely pre-funding market valuation. This data should then be organized and shared with potential lead underwriters, who will apply their own methodology to determine what they believe will be a fair market valuation. Issuers should be prepared for a fair amount of "give and take" in this process and argue their case with as many facts as possible that can be justified by solid market data while setting aside wishful or unrealistic valuation targets.

It is useful to first define a continuum for comparable public companies in your business sector, ranging from "strong" to "weak" and identify factors that contribute to their relative positioning. In general, a "stronger" company will have established and proven products, a solid defensible technology with barriers to entry, and a proven management team that consistently sets and meets or exceeds investor expectations.

Start with these more obvious discriminators and then add others that fit the range of public companies that you believe investors will consider in setting the value of your firm. During this process, it is also useful to obtain and read copies of pre-registration and post-registration documents of similar firms in order to become familiar with the range of disclosures required by your market sector. This will give you a deeper sense of the potential market for the stock.

Once this general exercise is reasonably complete, give your executive team and trusted advisors an assignment to have them each place your firm in the overall continuum that you have created from your research. This should then be followed with group meetings where all participants can argue their various points of view in order to derive a defendable group consensus of where your firm fits against other public firms.

This exercise is a critical step in reshaping the perceptions of the management team toward thinking about their contributions as outside investors may see them. The shift of thinking from a private company to a public company mentality can be difficult for even some very capable executives to grasp and internalize—and this process may reveal issues that are best dealt with earlier than later.

It is also possible that an objective and honest appraisal of the likely market valuation may result in the conclusion that the valuation of the stock may be so low as to result in significant dilution of ownership interests to outside investors. Once again, such issues are better confronted early in the process.

The next area to better understand is how your company's future performance may differ from the overall sector's performance—both good and bad—and how those differences are likely to impact future value. While this analysis can have a bigger impact on market valuation, it is a more speculative area from which to reach objective conclusions.

At this point, external underwriters should begin to weigh in and provide their analysis and related conclusions. Keep in mind that different underwriters are likely to reach different conclusions and that the quality and depth of their feedback will be one of the determining factors for choosing one underwriter over another (see Chapter 6 for additional considerations).[2]

---

[2]One thing to be aware of when applying to a Regulation A+ offering is that a formal underwriting or investment bank is not necessarily the norm to establish the value of the company's stock. While Regulation A+ securities can be freely traded immediately, markets are not as established as with registered securities and the value is more likely to be set by the issuer who is selling the security. The process described above is even more important to be followed by executives because setting unrealistic stock values that are not supported by market data can lead to added company liability.

Ultimately establishing the market value of a company is a very complex process and will be influenced by many factors. The key is to identify all the variables as soon as possible that are likely to affect pricing based on analyzing industry comparables and also how investors will perceive future performance. What-if questions should also be posed once the valuation range has been set. For example, what happens if earnings are projected to increase X% during the registration process and they increase Y%?

After-Market Considerations

While a public market for Regulation A+ securities is yet to be established, we believe that many of the same considerations regarding after-market support that are required for full-blown IPOs will be in play.

Therefore, even with the Regulation A+ mini-IPO, it is critical to look beyond the IPO and consider new responsibilities that your firm will have in dealing with outside investors and meeting ongoing expectations. It is important to first understand that in today's volatile economic climate, firms need to do much more to attract the interest of often nervous and skeptical investors.

There are approximately 100,000 publicly listed firms worldwide, with about 5,000 companies on national exchanges in the U.S. (such as NASDAQ and NYSE) and an additional 10,000 firms listed on U.S. over-the-counter (OTC) markets in the United States. The majority of U.S. firms are microcap companies, having market values of $500 million or less. It is expected that the JOBS Act will create significant growth in the number of new public issues, thereby putting further pressure on young public companies to maintain ongoing efforts to attract interest in their stock.

While many investors gravitate toward better-known firms that are actively covered in the national financial press, there is still a large pool of investors out there who are willing to take a chance on investing in a small company at a low price (or price with a dividend), hoping to realize a larger return than might be possible with a better known firm. How to reach them and engage them is a problem most small companies face.

Today's investor is far more sophisticated than the investors of the 1990s and early- to mid-2000s. They are savvy and know how to use the Internet to do their due diligence on a company. They follow conversations on message boards, use social media, and do not invest for superficial reasons. As a CEO/CFO of a newly public small firm, you will need to become adept at setting and meeting realistic expectations. If you try to hide something from investors, they will inevitably find out what you are hiding and share their disappointments with other investors. This can have a destructive snowball effect, as everyone piles on by getting into the conversation and slamming your company.

■ **Note** Today's investors are sophisticated and they share information freely on the Internet. As an executive of a publicly traded company, you won't be able to hide bad news or bad numbers from them. So don't even try.

Investors don't expect miracles all the time, but they do want to know what is going on with the company. They would rather hear bad news or indifferent news from your company than find out that kind of news on a message board or on a social media platform. Investors who find out bad news from another source will absolutely skewer your company and your management team. Today's investor has a zero-tolerance policy for lack of communications from the companies they have put their hard-earned cash into. If you screw up and don't handle it properly, expect the repercussions to be swift and severe.

Unless your investors are kept informed on a regular basis, they will begin to speculate on what your company is doing. Believe us, you do not want them speculating. Their speculation is almost always going to be negative and will eventually begin to influence even your best supporters among shareholders. In short, in the absence of information, some of your investors will begin to fill in that void with information that is grossly inaccurate (or perhaps very accurate, depending on what your company is doing).

An ongoing program of communicating with your investors will make a big difference. Companies that do this right will be rewarded at a far greater level than the investment made. Carefully consider the added responsibilities and risks that will come when you begin public trading and disclosures. You and your company and its board of directors need to have a temperament that is suited to interfacing with the public. Today's investor also expects to be informed on a regular basis.

The motivation to go public is summarized in Figure 2-1. Raising capital to support future growth, differentiating your firm from competitors, and realizing higher value for your firm are all very compelling reasons to strongly consider the IPO option, especially in consideration of the reduced costs and reporting requirements introduced by the JOBS Act.

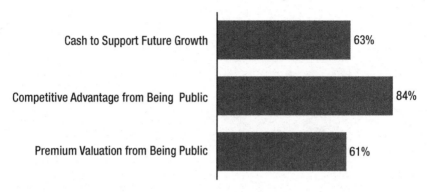

Figure 2-1. Why go public? (Source: IPO Task Force August 2011 CEO Survey)

Summary

Due to the avalanche of regulations and associated compliance costs that have occurred over the past 20 years, many firms simply no longer consider going public to raise growth capital. Even if you believe and, if trusted advisors tell you that your firm is not qualified to raise funds in public markets, it is now time for you to challenge this advice. In the chapters ahead, we present options that have been created by the JOBS Act that are already being utilized to varying degrees by a growing number of smaller companies. Against what has become conventional wisdom, these companies are succeeding in raising growth capital in ways very similar to how Apple, Cisco, Starbucks, and many other now large and famous firms first did many years ago. While the steps that we outline ahead are not suitable for all firms for a variety of reasons, there is no question that a new "old" has been created and is already having a very positive impact on capital formation.

Benefits of Regulation A+

Intel (INTC) went public in February 1971 with an IPO that raised $8M (million) supported by an underwriting group of 63 firms, of which fewer than 10 still exist. In March 1986, Microsoft (MSFT) went public with an offering of $58M with 116 underwriters, of which only about one quarter remain in operation in a similar line of business. Apple, Cisco, FedEx, Genentech, Starbucks, and many other firms are examples of small companies that raised growth capital outside of Regulation D via relatively small IPOs that helped them grow to become industry leaders.

By contrast, LinkedIn's IPO (LNKD) in May 2011 raised $358M with only six underwriters. For a myriad of reasons which were covered in more detail in Chapter 1, the increased burdens of regulation and compliance have not only resulted in fewer IPOs in recent years but have also resulted in significantly higher barriers to accessing public capital. IPO options have effectively dried up for smaller companies.

Growth capital is the most critical ingredient that fuels the growth of any business. As America grew to economic preeminence in the 20th Century, many growing young firms pursued IPOs to access the additional capital they needed to further develop their products, hire additional employees, and pursue international market opportunities. The ability to raise growth capital through IPOs allowed many promising companies to continue to produce new jobs and grow the U.S. economy, while all types of investors were able to enjoy the benefits of growing portfolios and retirement accounts.

The JOBS Act of 2012 has created a new kind of IPO that hearkens back to deals like Intel or Microsoft prior to when expense, regulation, and consolidation among players in the public securities markets pushed public offerings bigger and bigger, forcing smaller issuers deeper into the private markets to raise capital. This chapter will explain the benefits and applications of Regulation A+ as developed in the JOBS Act along with suggestions for entrepreneurs on how to take advantage of this new legislation to raise growth capital.

History of Regulation A

Regulation A ("Reg A") persisted in the same form continuously from 1934 to June 2015 to facilitate public financing by small companies through issuing public securities that were exempt from registration under the Securities Act.

The maximum amount of an offering pursuant to Reg A has been increasing over time, as follows:

- $100,000 – 1935
- $300,000 – 1945
- $500,000 – 1970
- $1,500,000 – May 1978
- $2,000,000 – October 1978
- $5,000,000 – 1980
- $50,000,000 – June 2015

To date, Reg A offerings have not been widely used, in part because the previous maximum permitted offering amount of $5M was considered excessively low in light of the costly regulatory requirements at state and federal levels.

Regulation A+ Overview

Prior to revisions made by the JOBS Act, Reg A's authority came from Section 3(b) of the Securities Act, which read:

> The Commission may from time to time by its rules and regulations, and subject to such terms and conditions as may be prescribed therein, add any class of securities to the securities exempted as provided in this section, if it finds that the enforcement of this title with respect to such securities is not necessary in the public interest and for the protection of investors by reason of the small amount involved or the limited character of the public offering; but no issue of securities shall be exempted under this subsection where the aggregate amount at which such issue is offered to the public exceeds $5,000,000.

Title IV of the JOBS Act revised Section 3(b) to now consist of a Section 3(b)(1) and a Section 3(b)(2), which reads as follows:

(b) Additional exemptions

(1) Small issues exemptive authority

The Commission may from time to time by its rules and regulations, and subject to such terms and conditions as may be prescribed therein, add any class of securities to the securities exempted as provided in this section, if it finds that the enforcement of this subchapter with respect to such securities is not necessary in the public interest and for the protection of investors by reason of the small amount involved or the limited character of the public offering; but no issue of securities shall be exempted under this subsection where the aggregate amount at which such issue is offered to the public exceeds $5,000,000.

(2) Additional issues

The Commission shall by rule or regulation add a class of securities to the securities exempted pursuant to this section in accordance with the following terms and conditions:

(A) The aggregate offering amount of all securities offered and sold within the prior 12-month period in reliance on the exemption added in accordance with this paragraph shall not exceed $50,000,000.

(B) The securities may be offered and sold publicly.

(C) The securities shall not be restricted securities within the meaning of the Federal securities laws and the regulations promulgated thereunder.

(D) The civil liability provision in section 77l(a)(2) of this title shall apply to any person offering or selling such securities.

(E) The issuer may solicit interest in the offering prior to filing any offering statement, on such terms and conditions as the Commission may prescribe in the public interest or for the protection of investors.

(F) The Commission shall require the issuer to file audited financial statements with the Commission annually.

(G) Such other terms, conditions, or requirements as the Commission may determine necessary in the public interest and for the protection of investors, which may include—

> *(i) a requirement that the issuer prepare and elec-*
> *tronically file with the Commission and distribute to*
> *prospective investors an offering statement, and any*
> *related documents, in such form and with such content*
> *as prescribed by the Commission, including audited*
> *financial statements, a description of the issuer's busi-*
> *ness operations, its financial condition, its corporate*
> *governance principles, its use of investor funds, and*
> *other appropriate matters; and*
>
> *(ii) disqualification provisions under which the exemp-*
> *tion shall not be available to the issuer or its prede-*
> *cessors, affiliates, officers, directors, underwriters, or*
> *other related persons, which shall be substantially simi-*
> *lar to the disqualification provisions contained in the*
> *regulations adopted in accordance with section 926*
> *of the Dodd-Frank Wall Street Reform and Consumer*
> *Protection Act.*

The JOBS Act hereby provides that the original exemption still exists but with a new variation allowing for a greater amount of capital to be raised with the same positive attributes of the original Regulation A (and with some more), albeit with additional requirements.

The SEC has followed this same scheme in its rulemaking around Reg A+, creating two tiers of offerings under Reg A+. Tier 1 is the original Reg A and, for the most part, keeps the original regulatory scheme in place while increasing the amount to be raised there under to $20M. Tier 2 offerings are offerings made pursuant to Section 3(b)(2) for up to $50M, and they are where we find the vast bulk of changes to Reg A.

■ **Tip** It's important to note that one does not need to offer more than $5M to take advantage of Tier 2, but you must follow the requirements of Tier 2 to use it.

The following sections discuss the major areas of consideration around Tier 1 and Tier 2 offerings: how each works generally and why one may opt to conduct one or the other.

Limits on the Amount of Capital

Reg A+ now allows legal issuers to raise up to $20M in Tier 1 and up to $50M in Tier 2 offerings in any 12-month period. It is conceivable for more than $50M to be raised in a given 12-month period by using different legal issuers and structuring the offerings in such a manner so that the SEC does not consider the offerings to be part of one common scheme of financing. For example, a real estate developer might need $50M each for multiple stand-alone development projects. The offering may be in the form of debt and or other flexible structures, e.g., it might provide dividends or other enhancements to attract various individual or institutional investors. Anyone considering such a course should seek the advice and assistance of experienced legal counsel.

In addition, $6M of the $20M under Tier 1 and up to $15M of the $50M under Tier 2 can be made up of securities of existing investors of an issuer. This provides an opportunity for owners of otherwise "restricted" securities not previously qualified under Reg A to be able to offer those securities for sale in the public market, thereby gaining the benefits of liquidity.

However, the SEC has further adopted a unique wrinkle to this rule. That being that secondary sales offered as part of an offering cannot exceed 30% of the aggregate offering price of the issuer's first offering or any subsequent Regulation A+ offering qualified within one year of the issuer's first offering. So, for example, if an issuer were to qualify $15,000,000 of new issuances in its first Regulation A+ offering, and then qualifies another $35,000,000 offering six months later, only $10,500,000 can be comprised of securities currently held by existing holders and offered for secondary sale through that offering. This does not apply to offerings 12 months after an issuer's first Reg A+ offering.

Who Can Qualify?

Tier 1 is available for any entity that (i) is formed in the United States or a province of Canada, (ii) has its principal place of business in the United States or Canada, and (iii) is not subject to reporting obligations under certain sections of the Exchange Act immediately before the offering.

At the same time, the following issuers are ineligible to offer or sell securities under Reg A+:

- Any issuer that is a development stage company that either has no specific business plan or purpose, or has indicated that its business plan is to merge with an unidentified company or companies (known as a *blank check company*).

- Any investment company registered or required to be registered under the Investment Company Act of 1940.

- Any entity issuing fractional undivided interests in oil or gas rights, or similar interests in other mineral rights.

- Issuers subject to disqualification under Rule 262 of Reg A+ for specific items of improper conduct. An issuer that is registered or must register under the Exchange Act of 1934 ("the '34 Act"), or one that is no longer a '34 Act-registered company by virtue of misconduct within the last five years.

Tier 2 follows this scheme, but also denies qualification for securities of issuers who failed to meet ongoing reporting requirements associated with securities previously qualified.

What Is Rule 262?

Pursuant to Rule 262 of Regulation A, an issuer will not be eligible to use the Regulation A+ exemption if it, or any of its "covered persons," are subject to one of several events of disqualification set forth in the rule at the time of initial filing. In addition to the issuer itself, an issuer's covered persons are:

- A predecessor of the issuer

- An affiliated issuer

- Any director, executive officer, other officer participating in the offering, general partner or managing member of the issuer

- Any beneficial owner of 20% or more of the issuer's voting securities

- Any promoter connected with the issuer at the time of the filing of the offering statement, any offer after qualification, or a sale

- Any person who has been or will be paid (directly or indirectly) remuneration for solicitation of purchasers in the offering (called a *compensated solicitor*)

- Any general partner or managing member of a compensated solicitor or any director, executive officer or other officer participating in the offering of a compensated solicitor or any general partner or managing member of such compensated solicitor

The following are events of disqualification:

- Criminal conviction within 10 years prior to the filing date of the offering statement (or five years, in the case of issuers, their predecessors and affiliated issuers) that are (i) in connection with the purchase or sale of a security;

(ii) involve the making of any false filing with the SEC; or (iii) arise out of the conduct of the business of an underwriter, broker, dealer, municipal securities dealer, investment adviser, or paid solicitor of purchasers of securities.

- Orders, judgments, or decrees of courts entered within five years before the filing of the offering statement that, at the time of the offering statement filing, restrain or enjoin the subject covered person from engaging or continuing to engage in any conduct or practice: (i) in connection with the purchase or sale of a security; (ii) involving the making of any false filing with the SEC; or (iii) arising out of the conduct of the business of an underwriter, broker, dealer, municipal securities dealer, investment adviser, or paid solicitor of purchasers of securities.

- Final orders of certain state regulators (such as state securities, banking, and insurance regulators) and certain federal regulators (such as federal banking agencies, the CFTC, or NCUA), if the order (A) at the time of filing bars the covered person from: (i) association with an entity regulated by the applicable state or federal regulator; (ii) engaging in the business of securities, insurance, or banking; or (iii) engaging in savings association or credit union activities; or (B) is a final order based on violation of law or regulation prohibiting fraudulent, manipulative, or deceptive conduct entered within 10 years prior to filing.

- Certain SEC disciplinary orders relating to brokers, dealers, municipal securities dealers, investment advisers, and investment companies and their associated persons to the extent such order is in effect at the time of filing.

- Cease and desist orders of the SEC to which the applicable covered person is subject as of the filing and which were entered within five years before the filing for scienter-based anti-fraud violations and Section 5 registration violations.

- Suspension or expulsion from, or suspension or barring from association with a member of a registered nation securities exchange or a registered national or affiliated securities association (such as FINRA), for any act or omission constituting conduct inconsistent with just and equitable principles of trade.

- Has filed, or was named as an underwriter in, any registration statement or Regulation A+ offering statement filed with the SEC that, within five years prior to filing of the offering statement, was subject to a stop order or order suspending the Reg A+ exemption, or at the time of the filing is subject of an investigation to determine whether to issue such an order.

- Is subject to a USPS false representation order entered within five years prior to the filing date of the offering statement.

An issuer will not be subject to disqualification for such events that occurred prior to the effective date of the revised Regulation A rules. However, an issuer will be required to disclose in its offering circular any matter that was an event of disqualification but for its occurrence prior to the effective date of the rules.

Offering Communications

Restrictions on Reg A+ offering communications involve advertising, solicitation, analyst–investor relations, and the use of broker–dealers, as treated successively in the sections below.

Advertising

Public advertising of securities qualified under Reg A+ may occur both during the filing process and after that process once the securities are qualified. Previously, the rules specified what written materials could be used once the initial filing with the SEC had been made. Under the new rules, that is not the case even permitting the use of "testing-the-waters" materials after the initial filing with the SEC.

"Testing the waters" is a concept that has been in Reg A for a long time. Essentially, the idea is that the issuer may feel out the market's interest in an offering prior to incurring the expense and scrutiny of filing with the SEC through diverse media; for example, by engaging in a broad-based marketing campaign, using written materials, online content, or radio/TV to solicit indications of interest in an offering an issuer was considering conducting.

The issuer can even have a means of identifying potential investors and obtaining their contact information so that they could be approached directly to invest once the offering was being conducted. Issuers had broad latitude as to what could be included in those materials, provided that they were not misrepresentative or untruthful, but they must stop using them once an initial filing for a Reg A+ offering has been made with the SEC. From there on, issuers are very limited in what written material (including recordings of seminars that could be easily accessed) could contain during the pendency of the filing.

Under the new rules, same materials can continue to be used, provided there is a preliminary offering circular or notice as to where to find the latest version of the offering circular on the SEC's EDGAR system.[1] Hence, there are more flexible marketing options before filing than before the JOBS Act. The investment limit will not apply to accredited investors. In addition, both accredited and non-accredited investors are exempt from the investment cap if the subject securities of the offering are listed on a "National Exchange" as defined in the Exchange Act of 1934 (see the section, "The Backdoor IPO").

■ **Note** While the SEC's new rules liberalize the use of advertising materials, Tier 1 securities are not exempted from state blue sky laws (discussed below). One should carefully consider the interplay of State and Federal law with experienced legal counsel.

Who Can an Issuer Solicit to Invest, and Who Can Invest?

Generally, Reg A+ does not impose investor qualification standards, as in Regulation D. An issuer can solicit anybody and can take anyone as an investor. However, in Tier 2 offerings, non-accredited natural persons are subject to the investment limit in an initial issuance of not more than 10% of the greater of the investor's annual income and net worth, determined as provided in Rule 501 of Regulation D. As an example, an individual with $100,000 in annual income cannot invest more than $10,000 in a single Reg A+ offering.

Isolation of Analysts from Investors

In the more traditional public securities offerings, there are strict limitations on the sharing of information between the advisory function of an investment firm and its brokering or selling arm—the so-called "Chinese Wall." This is to prevent the sharing of insider information that could influence improper trading of the issuer's shares.

This prohibition is not applicable to Reg A+ and information can be shared freely but must be factual and not resulting in fraudulent misrepresentation.

---

[1] That said, if you're using a broker-dealer (BD) to place your securities, they may be subject to certain FINRA rules that govern how they use certain materials or what can be in them. Always coordinate your marketing efforts with your BD!

Use of Broker–Dealers

Many registered broker–dealers are expressing strong interest in raising funds for Reg A+ offerings due to lower regulatory concerns by FINRA and the lower *errors and omissions* (E&O) liability insurance costs associated with Reg A+ offerings relative to the more traditional Regulation D offerings.

Liquidity

As discussed, Reg A+ may be used by an issuer to conduct a primary offering of its securities with the proceeds to be used by the issuer, as well as to conduct a secondary offering of securities on behalf of selling security holders. The Tier 1 offering limits the amount to $6M offered by all selling security holders. The SEC has increased this amount for Tier 2 offerings to $15M. In short, 30% of the maximum value an issuer can offer to the public in securities under Reg A+ in a 12-month period can be made up of the securities of existing securities holders, and they can be offered on a continuous basis. But this cannot exceed 30% of the aggregate offering price of the issuer's first offering or any subsequent Regulation A+ offering qualified within one year of the issuer's first offering. So, for example, if an issuer were to qualify $15,000,000 of new issuances in its first Regulation A+ offering, and then qualifies another $35,000,000 offering six months thereafter, only $10,500,000 can be comprised of securities currently held by existing holders and offered for secondary sale through that offering. This does not apply to offerings made 12 months after an issuer's first Reg A+ offering.

SEC has also made the review of an issuer's mandatory ongoing reporting be sufficient to satisfy a broker-dealer's obligations under Exchange Act Rule 15c2-11 to review information about an issuer in connection with publishing quotations on any facility other than a national securities exchange. Huh? In other words, if a BD has the up-to-date reporting of a Tier 2 issuer, it can provide a public price quote on the security. This is crucial for trading these securities until established exchanges or alternative trading systems develop for Reg A+ securities. How else would they trade without some way to establish a price in the market?

The SEC has also suggested that the reporting associated with Tier 2 Reg A+ securities could meet the requirements for public information under Rule 144. As such, if an issuer were to qualify a class of equity securities and comply with requisite reporting for the same (discussed below), then any restricted securities otherwise complying with Rule 144 may be traded in the secondary market.

However, while the SEC opted to pre-empt state securities registration requirements for the initial issuance of securities, the SEC did not pre-empt state regulation of secondary activity associated with Regulation A+ securities. This means that someone seeking to sell their securities might have to register the securities in that state prior to sale, unless an exemption applies. Most states carry a number of exemptions, including those for trades not for the benefit of the issuer or that do not comprise arbitrage activity. So, the secondary market likely will develop first as a means for retail investors to reliably move in and out of positions they have held truly for investment. If further pre-emption of state securities develops, which is activity being discussed presently, the more institutional style investment, taking advantage of market forces, could develop.

Circular

Reg A+ securities are offered to investors through the offering circular, and the template for offerings circulars is Form 1-A. The new rules retain Form 1-A's existing structure, but make various revisions to the form. For Tier 2 offerings, Form 1-A is enhanced and requires disclosures of basic information about the issuer; material risks; use of proceeds; an overview of the issuer's business; an MD&A-type discussion; disclosures about executive officers and directors and compensation; beneficial ownership information; related party transactions; a description of the offered securities; and two years of financial statements. The disclosure requirements continue to be scaled as compared to registration under the Securities Act.

For Tier 1 offerings, audited financial statements are required only to the extent they were prepared for other Federal law purposes, but are generally required for state law compliance. For Tier 2 offerings, audited financial statements are required. For Tier 1 and Tier 2 offerings, the auditors of financial statements must meet the independence standards but need not be PCAOB-registered. For Tier 2 offerings, financial statements must be audited in accordance with PCAOB standards.

The proposed rule requires offering statements to be submitted and available through the SEC's EDGAR system. An issuer or broker-dealer is required to deliver only a preliminary offering circular to prospective purchasers at least 48 hours in advance of sale when a preliminary offering circular is used to offer securities. A final offering circular is required to accompany or precede any written communications that constitute an offer in the post-qualification period. In instances where delivery of a final offering circular is required, in lieu of mailing a paper copy of the final offering circular to the investor, an issuer may instead provide the investor with a notice, including the URL where the final offering circular, or the offering statement of which it is a part, may be viewed.

The proposed rule permits confidential submission of offering statements for first-time offerings under Reg A+. The initial confidential submission and subsequent confidential amendments and SEC correspondence regarding the submissions are required to be publicly filed as exhibits to the offering statement not less than 21 calendar days before qualification of the offering statement.

Ongoing Reporting Requirements

Tier 1 issuers will be required to provide certain information about their Regulation A+ offering on a new form, Form 1-Z.

Issuers in Tier 2 offerings are subject to an ongoing reporting regime.

Tier 2 issuers will be subject to an ongoing reporting regime and require:

- Annual reports on Form 1-K
- Semi-annual reports on Form 1-SA
- Current reports on Form 1-U
- Special financial reports on Form 1-K and Form 1-SA
- Exit reports on Form 1-Z

Form 1-K is required to be filed within 120 calendar days of the issuer's fiscal year-end and requires these disclosures:

- The issuer's business and operations for the preceding three fiscal years (or since inception if it's been in existence for less than three years)
- Related party transactions
- Beneficial ownership
- Executive officers and directors
- Executive compensation
- MD&A
- Two years of audited financial statements

The semi-annual report is required to be filed within 90 days after the end of the first six months of the issuer's fiscal year and is similar to Form 10-Q, although it is subject to scaled disclosure requirements.

A current report on Form 1-U must be filed within four business days of the triggering event and is required to announce:

- Fundamental changes in the issuer's business

- Entry into bankruptcy or receivership proceedings

- Material modifications to the rights of security holders

- Changes in accountants

- Non-reliance on audited financial statements

- Changes in control and changes in key executive officers

- Sales of 10% or more of outstanding equity securities in exempt offerings

The structure of these reporting requirements is intended to be somewhat analogous to the reporting scheme under the Exchange Act, but less burdensome from a substantive perspective.

State Blue Sky Laws

Many people don't realize that, in addition to the securities laws at the Federal level, each state has its own set of securities laws, commonly referred to as *Blue Sky* laws. Unless Federal law or regulation establishes that a security or manner of offering is exempt from requirements under state laws—a concept known as *preemption*—then an issuer must also comply with the registration requirements of the states in which it intends to sell.

Prior to the JOBS Act, under Reg A an issuer was required to register, or find an exemption under that state's law, in each state in which it intended to sell its securities. This requirement was viewed by many as a serious flaw of Reg A and contributed to its lack of popularity.

Title IV of the JOBS Act provides that offerings conducted under Section 3(b)(2) be treated as "covered securities," and not subject to state Blue Sky registration or review, if the securities are sold to "qualified purchasers" or listed on a national securities exchange. In the guidelines, the SEC has defined "qualified purchaser" to include all offerees and purchasers in a Tier 2 offering. The final rules eliminate the offeree in Tier 1 offerings from the qualified purchaser definition. As such, the entirety of the Tier 1 offering process will remain subject to state securities law registration and merit review requirements.

Consistent with the proposed rules, however, Tier 2 offerings will not be subject to state registration requirements or merit review. States will, of course, continue to have authority to require notice filing of offering materials and enforce antifraud provisions in connection with a Tier 2 offering.

As discussed above, unless the firm chooses to not have its shares trade on a national exchange such as NASDAQ, NYSE, or AMEX and instead opts for trading on an OTC exchange, state law can still apply to secondary trading which may impact the volume of trade activity.

■ **Tip** The removal of the requirement to comply with state Blue Sky regulations for Tier 2 eliminates one the chief obstacles to utilizing Regulation A+.

A point of particular focus by both the private securities bar and regulators in developing the rules for Reg A+ was the application of Section 12(g) of the Act to Regulation A+ securities. Section 12(g) provides a "fail-safe" for when issuers must submit to registering and reporting under the 34 Act upon achieving a certain size. Reporting under the 34 Act is the typical on-going reporting that public companies do. It is expensive and laborious, and implicates further regulations under SOX and Dodd-Frank. Under Section 12(g) an issuer with (i) $10,000,000 in assets and (ii) 2,000 "shareholders of record," 500 of which may be non-accredited in a given class of equity securities, must register and report under the Exchange Act.

While the JOBS Act did not exempt Reg A+ from Section 12(g), the SEC has provided a further specific exemption for securities issued in Tier 2 offerings from the Section 12(g), if an issuer[2]:

- Retains the services of a transfer agent registered under Section 17 of the Exchange Act

- Has a public float of less than $75M or, in the absence of a float, revenues of less than $50M in the most recently completed fiscal year

- Is current in its periodic reporting obligations

At the same time, an issuer that exceeds the Section 12(g) threshold and this exemption standard will still have a two-year transition period in order to register under Section 12(g) of the Exchange Act, and can do so as an "emerging growth company" if they still meet the definition.

---

[2]We have discussed here only the exemption set forth in the rules for Reg A+. An issuer can structure its offering to be in a "streetname", which can also allow one to avoid Section 12(g).

The "Backdoor" IPO

The final rules facilitate the ability of a Tier 2 issuer to list a class of Regulation A+ securities on a national securities exchange. The final rule permits a Tier 2 issuer that has provided disclosure in Part II of Form 1-A that follows Part 1 of Form S-1 or Form S-11 to file a Form 8-A to list its securities on a national securities exchange. Thereafter, the issuer is subject to Exchange Act reporting requirements, but is considered an emerging growth company.

How Regulation A+ Compares to Other Fundraising Options

Since the passage of the JOBS Act, discussion of Reg A+ has been largely overshadowed by other provisions of the act that relate to new rules regarding crowdfunding, public solicitation of investors, and less burdensome ways to go public via election as an EGC. All of these new JOBS Act fundraising provisions are also less understood than fundraising via a Regulation D private placement or via a traditional IPO.

Since these topics overlap with each other and also with Reg A+, there is currently much confusion even among attorneys, financial advisors, accountants, and others as to how these various provisions compare and contrast with each other. We conclude this chapter with a summary of each of these provisions and how they compare to Reg A+.

How Does Regulation A+ Compare to Regulation D?

The traditional exemption for raising capital for growth companies has been and continues to be Regulation D ("Reg D"). This regulation follows the Securities Act of 1933 under Rules 504, 505, and 506. This is by far the most commonly used mechanism for raising capital by private companies from seed stage to late stage. Almost $800–900B (billion) is raised per year in 15,000–20,000 offerings for a wide variety of private businesses in the United States. This far exceeds the capital raised in the 200-400 public offerings that occur per year.

Reg D contains the rules providing exemptions from the registration requirements, allowing issuers to offer and sell securities without having to register with the SEC. A Reg D offering is intended to make access to the capital markets possible for small companies that could not otherwise bear the costs of a normal SEC registration. While this may be the lowest cost mechanism to raise capital and avoids delays caused by a formal registration process, Reg D has many very serious problems both for the issuers and the investors. Reg A+ solves all those problems very effectively. The following sections summarize the downsides of a Reg D offering.

Lack of Liquidity

In contrast to Reg A+, which allows an immediate option for liquidity for investors if desired, one of biggest weaknesses of Reg D offerings is their lack of liquidity. These securities are private and there are very limited means for owners or investors to sell or exchange their investment until the company exits in an IPO or is acquired by another company in exchange for liquid consideration such as cash or stock in a public company. If the Reg D offering is for an investment in a project having a finite life—such as a real estate development, a movie, or an oil well—investment funds are largely frozen until the project produces profit distributions or is sold.

This liquidity problem has been especially challenging for many private companies ranging from startups to late-stage firms because such companies may not realize an acceptable liquidity event, such as an IPO or M&A, for 5 to 10 years or even longer. Furthermore, the SEC has strict requirements that discourage private sales of Reg D ownership interests, resulting often in steep discounts to fair-market value by investors who need to exit from their investments. Last, this lack of liquidity impacts the ability of firms to attract top talent because they are often unable to offer competitive stock option incentives due to a perception that their private stock has little actual value.

Accredited Investors Only

Reg D offerings can only be made to high-net-worth accredited investors or to qualified institutions per SEC rules without triggering laborious requirements that limit its efficacy or the amount one can raise. Minimum qualifying criteria require investors to have $1M in assets excluding their home and $200,000 of annual income for the past two years plus the current year or $300,000 including spouse. This is justified by the SEC to mitigate risky investments to small investors. This is a hugely limiting factor both for investors who have to disclose their financial details to qualify and also for issuers to document and ensure that investors are actually qualified. Reg A+ allows non-accredited retail individual investors with the only limitation being that the size of investment they can make per project may be limited by their income or net worth, Reg A+ also allows non-accredited investors to self-verify their income and net worth.

There is no limit to the amount that can be invested in a Tier I offering, while Tier II has limits tied to income and net worth. Unlike Reg D, where the issuer has to make reasonably sure they have an accredited investor buying the security, investors are now in charge of confirming their ability to qualify to make investments.

In a Tier II offering that will not be listed on a national exchange, a non-accredited investor is limited to investing the greater of 10% of their annual income or 10% of their net worth, excluding their principal residence. That's a per-offering limit, not a per-investor limit. So a policeman making $65,000 per year with a net worth of $250,000 can invest $25,000 in a local real estate project and another $25,000 in a new technology company that makes surveillance products.

Small Pool of Investors

The total pool of U.S. investors who can potentially invest in Regulation D offerings is estimated to be only 4 to 6M accredited investors plus a limited number of qualified institutions and large funds. By contrast, Reg A+ offerings can be offered to a pool of non-accredited investors numbering as many as 100M or more.

Limited Disclosures and Reporting

Due to Regulation D exemption provisions, the SEC has no specific guidelines for issuers outlining required minimum disclosures in the Private Placement Memorandums (PPMs) that accompany Regulation D offerings. Most PPM disclosures are inconsistent and tend to list a lot of risk factors that limit investors' ability to sell or ensure adequate performance by the issuer. No reporting requirements are mandated (See "Various Reg D Offerings") typically by Federal and state securities laws, which often leads to investors being the last to know about impending problems in the company and not having the ability to impact any change. In contrast, Reg A+ requires quarterly reporting and annual audited results to be made public to help investors understand the status and ongoing performance of their investment.

Control Issues among Investors/Management

Absence of specific SEC requirements, Reg D-funded private companies and projects usually struggle in establishing an appropriate balance between the role of company managers and investors. Balancing these roles can become complicated, leading to the failure of many investments due to disputes between investors and insiders. For example, in the case of VC-funded technology firms, VCs typically have a mandate to control the board of the company and management is often constrained to operate the firm in an optimum manner.

The most common disputed issue usually is timing to sell or liquidate the investment to provide liquidity to investors. Company management and employees are usually minor investors and draw ongoing salaries and bonuses and control the company with little participation by investors. Therefore, they do not want to lose control in case of a sale and they aren't incentivized to expedite liquidity.

Cash Calls and Wash-Outs

Since Reg D-funded companies have private status and are not allowed to raise additional capital through public offerings until there's an IPO, they typically end up raising more capital from their existing accredited investors or through new investors. Most companies do not perform according to the projected business plan. They are either doing better or worse or have short-term capital needs due to market conditions that are never predictable.

As a result, if company needs additional capital in a distress situation, they require existing investors to invest more capital to maintain their ownership position regardless if they want to or not (often called "pay to play"). For those investors who decide not to invest sufficient additional funds based on their pro-rata ownership amount, they end up losing some or most of their original investment in what is commonly called a "wash-out." This is one of the major deterrents to investing in Reg D placements.

Fundraising

Although the SEC does not impose many restrictions on Reg D offerings in terms of disclosures or reporting, the fundraising process is highly regulated and restrictive, which makes it expensive and time-consuming. Furthermore, due to added regulations and oversight imposed after the 2008 crash, many broker-dealers who formerly raised capital for Reg D offerings can no longer afford the increased insurance premiums and larger personal liability risk of failed Reg D offerings and have been discouraged from raising capital by such offerings.

Bad Boy Disqualification

Regulation D has an almost identical disqualification rule to Rule 262 under Reg A+. However, while in Reg A+ where disqualification only occurs if a disqualifying event exists at the time of filing your Reg A+ with the SEC, a disqualifying event that occurs *any time* while a Reg D offering is being conducted can invalidate the offering. This can create a lot of regulatory uncertainty if you are conducting a Reg D to a broad audience or for an extended time.

Cost of Fundraising

Although the cost of Reg D offerings may sometimes appear to be lower than Reg A+, if all the factors are taken in account, they are usually much higher. The following are the major cost components:

Legal and organization costs. Depending on the size and complexity of the offering, these can range from $25,000 to $100,000.

Marketing costs. Depending on the fundraising channel, these can range from $25,000 to $100,000.

Due-diligence cost. Third-party experts can range from $10,000 to $25,000.

Placements fees. These fees charged by brokers range from 5% to 10% of the amount of capital raised.

Cost of equity lost. This is by far the largest hidden cost of Reg D offerings and is usually ignored by the issuers. Because Reg D investments are not liquid and can take many years to exit, investors require higher premiums in the form of offering much lower valuation for the companies or opportunities where they perceive that their capital may be tied up for extended periods. For example, the valuation of a liquid public company is typical two times higher than that of a similar private company.[3] This means the founders and managers of the Reg D companies can lose a lot more of their ownership interest compared to a Reg A+ placement. This has greater liquidity.

Table 3-1 tabulates an investor's expectations in a typical Reg D technology company offering.

Table 3-1. Typical Returns Expected by Investors in Reg D Offerings

Investment Amount	Required IRR Percent	Years to Exit	Multiple Required
$1M	35	3	2.5
$1M	50	3	3.4
$1M	80	3	5.8
$1M	35	5	4.9
$1M	50	5	7.6
$1M	80	5	18.9
$1M	35	10	20.1
$1M	50	10	57.7
$1M	80	10	357

[3]http://www.sec.gov/Archives/edgar/data/1444706/000115752313000292/ a50544928ex99_1.htm. Keating Capital Article dated January 28, 2013.

Note the very steep increase in required returns when time to exit is pushed out. By contrast, Reg A+ shares can be immediately tradable and liquid—subject to demand for the stock, access to an exchange, and other important factors.[4]

Miscellaneous Drawbacks

There are several important considerations that impact Reg D offerings negatively due to higher cost and restrictions that can delay the offering:

- The "prior relation test" requires that if outside broker help is sought for fundraising, the broker agent must have a prior relationship with the potential investors for minimum of 30 days or more and cannot solicit investment in a new offering.

- No public advertising is allowed to the general public on the Internet, radio, or print media. An option provided in the JOBS Act allows public solicitation if the issuer chooses to use this option, but this requires a lot more scrutiny and written verification of investor communications and their financial records, which many investors prefer not to share, thereby making this option not very practical.

- PPM distribution and investor records must be maintained by the issuer.

- Financial records of the investors must be kept and maintained by the brokers.

- A due diligence report from a third party is typically required by the brokers, which can take 4-6 weeks, plus significant cost. This also poses risks for brokers and issuers if not done properly, because it provides guidance to investors regarding valuation and risks in the offering.

Various Types of Reg D Offerings

There are three options within the Reg D offerings. These provide different offerings limits and restrictions rules issuers have to follow.

---

[4]This is not to say that Regulation A+ shares are inherently more liquid than Regulation D. In fact, if the Regulation A+ shares do not have a market or little-to-no demand by external investors, there may not be any liquidity advantage. The key point is that through electing to use Regulation A+, the issuer will at least have the option to create early liquidity for their shares, whereas with Regulation D such an option does not exist.

Rule 504

Rule 504 provides an exemption for the offer and sale of up to $1,000,000 of securities in a 12-month period. The company may use this exemption so long as it is not a blank-check company and is not subject to the Exchange Act of 1934 reporting requirements.

Rule 504 allows companies to generally solicit and sell securities that are not restricted if one of the following conditions is met:

- The offering is made exclusively in one or more states that provide for registration of the securities under state law and require a delivery of a substantive disclosure document to investors.

- The registration and sale takes place in a state that requires registration and disclosure delivery, and the buyer is in a state without those requirements, so long as the disclosure documents mandated by the state in which you registered to all purchasers are delivered.

- The securities are sold exclusively according to state law exemptions that permit general solicitation and advertising, and you are selling only to accredited investors. However, accredited investors are only needed when sold exclusively with state law exemptions on solicitation.

Rule 505

Rule 505 provides an exemption for offers and sales of securities totaling up to $5M in any 12-month period. Under this exemption, securities may be sold to an unlimited number of "accredited investors" and up to 35 "unaccredited investors" who do not need to satisfy the sophistication or wealth standards associated with other exemptions. Purchasers must buy for investment only, and not for resale. The issued securities are restricted. General solicitation or advertising to sell the securities is not allowed.

Rule 505 offerings have strict requirements as to the form of disclosure and how financial statements are presented. Financial statement requirements applicable to this type of offering:

- Financial statements need to be certified by an independent public accountant.

- If a company other than a limited partnership cannot obtain audited financial statements without unreasonable effort or expense, the company's balance sheet, to be dated within 120 days of the start of the offering, must be audited.

- Limited partnerships unable to obtain required financial statements without unreasonable effort or expense may furnish audited financial statements prepared under the federal income tax laws.

Rule 506

A company may qualify for an exemption under Rule 506 if it satisfies the following standards:

- It can raise an unlimited amount of capital.

- It does not use general solicitation or advertising to market the securities.

- It sells securities to an unlimited number of accredited investors and up to 35 non-accredited investors. However, if offered to non-accredited investors, certain rules under 505 shall apply.

- The seller is available to answer questions by prospective purchasers.

- The purchasers receive restricted securities, which may not be freely traded in the secondary market after the offering.

In August 2012, the SEC issued new proposed regulations as required by the 2012 JOBS Act. These regulations add Rule 506(c) to allow general advertising and solicitation, effectively relaxing the prohibition on advertising in private placement offerings, but only for qualifying 506 private offerings made exclusively to accredited investors. It also places heightened verification requirements on determining whether or not an investor is accredited. If those standards are not met, the issuer could be forced to return funds and/or register the securities under the Securities Act.

Crowdfunding versus Regulation A+

Almost all the initial discussions in the public press regarding the implications of the new JOBS Act legislation focused on crowdfunding. Since the passage of the JOBS Act in 2012, crowdfunding advocates continue to publish far more content on a daily basis on the Internet than other JOBS Act-related provisions. While the promise of crowdfunding is clearly very attractive to many entrepreneurs, we believe that the current form of crowdfunding contemplated by the JOBS Act, but not yet implemented by the SEC, will fall far short of realizing the hoped-for objectives. Furthermore, we think that Reg A+ provides a number of benefits that will be embraced by many of today's fans of crowdfunding.

Crowdfunding has become a popular term recently due to the perception that any entrepreneur can potentially raise capital from the public at very low cost for any project over the Internet. One of the major reasons this is becoming very popular—and rightly so—is the fact that a large number of potential investors can be approached in a very short period and cost effectively, and they can invest small amounts of money individually to pool a significantly larger overall amount.

Although the term *crowdfunding* has come to be associated with any fundraising over the Internet, it has only been defined specifically for the first time in Title III of the JOBS Act.

■ **Caution**   Crowdfunding permitted by the JOBS Act has many more limitations than commonly perceived. Although the JOBS Act provides guidelines for public solicitation of investors, the rules and limitations for the various fundraising methods are quite different. The next section surveys and tabulates the strengths and limitations of each application in comparison to Reg A+.

The current and potential uses of all crowdfunding/Internet funding can be broadly broken into the following four categories.

Crowdfunding to Raise Capital as Donations

The most successful model in the category of crowdfunding to raise capital as donations has been Kickstarter—which was formed in 2009, long before the JOBS Act. Kickstarter is arguably the most successful means of Internet fundraising to date, helping thousands of entrepreneurs raise small amounts of capital to pursue their small projects and hobbies.

Kickstarter's platform allows individuals to contribute funds for a particular project related to something they like in return for a gift or a reward, or for prepayment of a product to be delivered at a future date in exchange for their contribution. Contributors cannot accept equity in the company or share profits from their investment.

The contributions may be typically as little as $5 to $5,000 per person and the total amounts raised typically range from $1,000 to $1,000,000. These funds are typically used to either pursue a personal hobby or create a proof of concept that is generally exciting to the general public at large.

In some cases, some entrepreneurs planning to launch legitimate companies have been able to successfully raise seed funding through Kickstarter to develop an initial proof of concept of their product.

Aside from limited use to raise seed funding, this donation model has not allowed serious entrepreneurs to raise significant equity or improve their ability to pursue scalable projects or raise adequate amounts of capital to attract serious investors who invest with profit sharing motives.

Use of Crowdfunding up to $1M for Small Companies under Title III of the JOBS Act

The purpose of Title III of the JOBS Act is to encourage small businesses to raise small amounts of seed funding for new product ideas. Its provisions include the following:

- A company can raise up to a maximum of $1M/year.
- This offering is exempt from both the SEC and state approval process.
- Both accredited and non-accredited investors may invest.
- Investors with less than $100,000 income per year shall be allowed to invest a maximum $5,000 but not greater than 5% of their annual income in each investment.
- Investors with income higher than $100,000 per year may invest a maximum of $10,000 or 10% of their annual income.
- Funds may be raised only through a FINRA-approved licensed BD-managed platform. Any other efforts shall be scrutinized very closely and may to lead to fines and penalties for platform principals.
- Offerings over $100,000 require a third-party audit.

- Shares sold are restricted for 12 months and thereafter will still remain illiquid absent a sale of the company or an SEC registration.

- There will be significant ongoing reporting requirements to the SEC regarding the offering and specifically regarding the investors in it.

Crowdfunding under Title III may seem like a good way to raise capital for seed funding but is riddled with many problems. Some of the problematic issues include the high cost and time it takes for evaluation and due diligence required by licensed BDs to underwrite any deal. Secondly, use of the Internet to solicit investors can be illegal and subject to harsh penalties. The web portals are allowed for investor information only and a full PPM is required to be reviewed by each investor to be able to invest. Licensed BDs also must qualify each investor and verify their financials. Finally, due to limitations on the amounts each investor may invest, each deal will require too many investors to raise any critical amount of funds above $600,000 to $800,000.

Use of Crowdfunding for Regulation D under Title II of the JOBS Act

Under Title II, Regulation D has been modified by including Rule 506(c), which allows:

- A company to solicit accredited investors using social media, radio, Internet, and traditional advertising.

- No limit on the amount of investment by each investor.

- No limit on the amount of total funds raised per project.

- Exemption from pre-approval or registration with the SEC or states, although limited reporting is required.

- No requirement to involve FINRA-approved BDs.

- If funds are raised without involvement of a BD, investors' accreditation details must be maintained.

While many features of Rule 506(c) seem attractive compared to Title III, the Title II provisions also have issues with the high minimum costs of raising smaller amounts of funds and the responsibility to verify and maintain investor financial records, which are not required for the normal Regulation D process without application of Rule 506(c). For example, if general solicitation is not used, investors simply need to certify their income without providing actual tax returns or proof of income, including bank statements in some cases. However, the Rule 506(c) option may be suitable and better for raising seed capital than crowdfunding under Title III.

Potential Use of Crowdfunding for Regulation A+ Under Title IV of the JOBS Act

The key features of Reg A+ pertinent to public solicitation/crowdfunding are the following:

- A company may solicit accredited or non-accredited investors using social media, radio, Internet, and traditional advertising (i.e., no investor financials required).

- Smaller amounts can be taken from a larger number of investors without fear of trigging 34 Act reporting.

- Allows up to $50M total funds raised per project per year.

- Pre-approval required from SEC (unlike Regulation D), but with available exemptions from states Blue Sky laws. Testing of waters is allowed before registration as long as no funds are accepted.

- Requires annual audited financials to be submitted to the SEC. However, limited reporting is required compared to any other public company.

- It has no requirement to involve FINRA-approved BDs (optional).

- Securities are tradable immediately, providing liquidity to investors and owners (subject to the existence and support of a secondary market in the stock).

- Securities may be offered as private or publicly tradable on alternative trading systems (ATSs) managed by BDs, OTC markets, and so on.

In comparison, Reg A+ solves many of the issues related to other alternatives for the use of crowdfunding. Companies can raise capital from the general public by any means of public solicitation—Internet, social media, radio, TV, or other means of advertising. Limits on the amount of capital and contribution by each investor are a lot more reasonable and meaningful. When you take full advantage of expenses relative to the amount of capital raised or benefits of liquidity, Reg A+ is clearly a much more powerful option for raising capital by use of crowdfunding.

Tip Crowdfunding via Regulation A+ overcomes many of the existing crowdfunding limitations. Under Reg A+, a crowdfunding campaign can target non-accredited investors, use public advertising, and may not require involvement of broker-dealers.

How Regulation A+ Compares to Going Public as an Emerging Growth Company

As noted in the "State Blue Sky Laws" section, Title I of the JOBS Act introduced a new category of small companies called *EGCs* and granted firms that elected this classification several important exemptions from regulations that govern public companies.[5] To take advantage of these exemptions, a firm must have total annual gross revenues under $1B for the most recently ended fiscal year per standard accounting principles. Furthermore, the firm's initial sale of common equity securities must have occurred after December 8, 2011.

In general, the goal of this provision is to provide incentives in the form of reduced reporting requirements to encourage more qualifying firms to launch a traditional IPO and be listed on a national stock exchange such as NASDAQ or NYSE.

Table 3-2 is a quick comparison of the requirements for an EGC vs. an IPO.

Table 3-2. Primary Exemptions for EGCs

Exemptions for EGCs	Traditional IPO Requirements
No compensation disclosures required	Compensation disclosure for executive officers named in IPO documents and subsequent annual reports
Two years of audited financial statements	Three years of audited financial statements
Two years of financial data in IPO documents and subsequent reports	Five years of financial data in IPO documents and in subsequent reports
Only management assessment of internal controls in reports subsequent to IPO (no auditor attestation required)	Management assessment and auditor attestation of internal controls in reports subsequent to IPO
Adhere to private company policies for new accounting standards	Adhere to public company policies for new accounting standards

---

[5]http://www.sec.gov/divisions/corpfin/guidance/cfjjobsactfaq-title-i-general.htm.

Additional provisions that pertain to EGC exemptions include the following:

- *Draft IPO registration submissions.* An EGC may confidentially submit a draft of its registration statement to the SEC for review prior to officially filing with the SEC (provided that the confidential submission and amendments thereto must be publicly filed with the SEC no later than 21 days prior to commencement of the EGC's road show). Reg A+ now has a similar provision.

- *Testing the waters.* In connection with a securities offering, an EGC may, either before or after filing a registration statement with respect to the offering, engage in oral or written communications with potential investors, but only those that are *qualified institutional buyers* (QIBs) or accredited investors.

- *Analyst reports.* BDs are allowed to publish or distribute a research report regarding the securities of an EGC.

- *Auditor rotation.* Any existing or future rules of the Public Company Accounting Oversight Board requiring mandatory audit firm rotation or auditor discussion and analysis will not apply to an audit of an EGC.

- *Say on pay.* An EGC will not be required to conduct the shareholder vote on executive compensation mandated under the Dodd-Frank Act until, at a minimum, three years after the first sale of the EGC's common equity in a registered offering.

In addition, neither the SEC nor any national securities association may enact rules or regulations that restrict the following roles:

- A broker-dealer or member of a national securities association from publishing or distributing any research report or making a public appearance with respect to the securities of an EGC during the post-IPO or other agreed upon lock-up period.

- Which associates of a broker-dealer or national securities association may arrange for communications between a securities analyst and a potential investor.

- A securities analyst from participating in communications with an EGC's management team if such communication is also attended by associates of a broker-dealer or national securities association member in a role other than securities analyst.

Use of EGC Provisions by Issuers

Since the passage of the JOBS Act in April 2012, there has been a significant increase in IPOs. More IPOs were done in 2013 than in any year since 2000 and it has been reported that 81% of the 222 companies that went public utilized at least some of the EGC provisions of the JOBS Act.[6]

Cost Comparisons of Various Options

An IPO has the following cost components:

- Accounting fees
- Legal fees
- Professional advisor fees
- Filing fees
- Financing or placement fees
- Exchange fees
- Management meetings, conference calls, roadshows, and related marketing expenses

Accounting fees, legal fees, professional adviser, and filing fees are largely dependent on the size and complexity of each transaction. Generally, IPO fees will range from several hundred thousand dollars to much more than a million dollars. *Financing* or *placement fees*, as these are called, are charged based on the amount of funding raised by the investment banking firm.

Table 3-3 compares a comprehensive list of costs of going public via the three available options—traditional IPO, qualified EGC, and Reg A+—as discussed in this chapter. The numbers assume a typical $50 M raise.

[6]http://www.reedsmith.com/files/Publication/127bcd23-1f75-494d-a702-f8627323025b/Presentation/PublicationAttachment/603c6c97-3d24-460a-bcf7-03f412c006b7/alert14054.pdf.

Table 3-3. Costs of Going Public via Traditional IPO, Qualified EGC, and Reg A+

	Traditional IPO	EGC IPO	Revised Reg A+
Total gross proceeds	$50,000,000	$50,000,000	$50,000,000
Underwriter spread	$3,500,000	$2,500,000	$2,500,000
Gross proceeds	$46,500,000	$47,500,000	$47,500,000
Advisory fees	$150,000	$100,000	$75,000
SEC registration fee	$5,805	$5,805	$00.00
FINRA filing fee	$5,167	$5,167	$5,167
Listing fee	$50,000	$50,000	$50,000
Printing expenses	$166,667	$41,667	$41,667
Legal fees and expenses	$500,000	$250,000	$150,000
Accounting fees and expenses	$400,000	$225,000	$100,000
Transfer agent and registrar fees	$8,333	$8,333	$8,333
Roadshow and miscellaneous	$83,333	$40,000	$20,000
Total Approximate Expenses	$1,369,305	$725,972	$455,972
Net Proceeds to Company	$45,130,695	$46,774,028	$47,044,028

These costs can vary significantly based on the selection of legal and accounting firms and invest-ment banks. Some costs may not apply to Regulation A+, such as the listing fee or transfer agent upon issuer's election.

Remember, going public is just the start of the process, not the end. Once a firm is a public company, there are significant ongoing incremental costs that must be considered, including the following:

- Director and officer insurance
- Accounting
- Legal
- Board compensation
- SEC filing costs for 10-Ks, 10-Qs, 8-Ks, and so on
- Financial marketing costs (analysts, market makers, and PR)
- Corporate governance setup and maintenance costs
- Lost productivity

The ongoing costs of remaining a public company on a national exchange such as NASDAQ, NYSE, or AMEX can range from hundreds of thousand dollars per year to well over one million dollars. The costs to remain public on non-national exchanges such as OTC markets may be much less but are nevertheless significant.

As small-cap IPO opportunities increase in volume, many smaller brokers and investment banks are expected to participate and become much more competitive, resulting in lower costs. In particular, Reg A+ public offerings are expected to save 30-60% for the IPO due to the simplification and reduced documentation and reporting requirements explained in this chapter, along with reductions in related legal and accounting costs.

We believe that the cost of Reg A+ offerings will go down significantly as the volume of mini-IPOs increases, issuers, investment banks, and new channels such as solicitation through the Internet evolve, making the process more efficient and more cost-competitive.

Table 3-4 summarizes the key similarities and differences between Reg A+ and other areas discussed in the preceding section and compares fundraising to a traditional IPO.

Table 3-4. Comparison of Fundraising Methods

	Regular IPO	Qualified EGCs	Regulation D Offerings	Reg A+ Issuers
Trading/Listing	Public/national exchanges	Public/national exchanges	Private/none	Public/alternative exchanges
Issuer Location	U.S. +Foreign	U.S. only but includes foreign subsidiary	Private/foreign	U.S. or Canadian only
Type of Business	Any	Any	Any	Very few limitations
Stage of Business	Very late stage, usually profitable or very high growth	Any but intended for small late stage	Any	Any, but intended for early stage
Amounts of Capital	Any	Any	Any; subject to some limitations	Up to $50M/ 12 months of shares
Investment Liquidity	Depends on support unless it is big, popular stock	Good with adequate info for investors and promotion	Very poor	Good with adequate info for investors and promotion
Company Revenue Limits	None, except exchange required	<$1B/year	None	Small, but no specific limit
Number of Investors	No limits	2,000 including <500 non-accredited	2,000 including <500 non-accredited	2,000 including <500 non-accredited if Tier II exemption does not apply
Type of Investors	Any	Any	Any	Any
Testing of Waters	Very limited	Yes	None	Yes
Amount of Investment Per Investor	No limit	No limit	No limit	No limit if accredited; 105 of greater of net worth or annual income in initial issuance

(continued)

Table 3-4. (*continued*)

	Regular IPO	Qualified EGCs	Regulation D Offerings	Reg A+ Issuers
Typical Cost (Based on use of Channel to Raise Capital)	$750K-$1.0M + 10% of capital raised plus discounts	$500-700K + 7% of amounts raised plus discounts	$50-100K + 7-10% of capital	$150-250K+ 5-7% of capital raised
Cost of Reporting and Compliance	High	Medium	Very low	Medium/Low
Complexity	High	Medium	Very low	Low
Securities Law 1933 Act	Yes	Yes with some exemptions for five years	N/A	Yes with lot of exemptions
Securities Exchange Law 1934	Yes	Yes with some exemptions for five years	N/A	No, unless Tier II exemption does not apply and have more than 2,000 investors (or 500 non-accredited)
Blue Sky State Laws	No	No if listed on national exchanges	Yes	No for initial issuance
General Solicitation Allowed	No	Yes	Yes	Yes
Applicable Federal Regulations	Securities Act of 1933/1934	Section 3(b) Securities Act of 1933 and 1934	Reg D, 502, 504, 506	Section 3(b) Securities Act of 1933
Main Offering Documents	S-1 + PSA	TBD	Private Placement Memorandum	Form 1-A or TBD
Audited Financials	3 years	2 years	No	Yes, but no limits
Executive Compensation Disclosure	Yes	Not for 5 years	No	No
Exemption from Dodd-Frank	No	For 5 years	Yes	Yes

(*continued*)

Table 3-4. (*continued*)

	Regular IPO	Qualified EGCs	Regulation D Offerings	Reg A+ Issuers
New Revised Accounting Standards	Yes	None for 5 years	No	No
Mandatory Audit Firm Rotation	Yes	Not for 5 years	No	No
Limitations Periods for Exemptions	No limit	5 years	No limit	No limit
Analyst Support required	Medium unless small cap	High	No	High unless low liquidity okay

Reg A+ Provides New Opportunities for Investment Banks and Intermediaries

JOBS Act legislation is already creating new business opportunities for many firms that support small issuers. At the beginning of this chapter, we discussed how firms such as Apple, FedEx, Cisco, and others were able to have successful smaller IPOs. During that era, there were many more investment banks, analysts, and intermediaries that focused on smaller issuers. Due largely to increased regulation over the past 25 years, the growing costs of going and staying public resulted in fewer small companies going public, and those firms that supported smaller companies gradually were gobbled up by larger firms that focused on larger offerings.

Because Reg A+ allows smaller companies to raise capital with mini-IPOs, it can be expected that there will be a resurgence of interest from investment banks and intermediaries to offer support services, plus an increase in law firms and accounting firms to service this new sector. In addition, the relaxed restrictions on solicitation and advertising may also allow banks and other participants to add value in other ways previously not permitted under the securities laws.

Potential issuers under Reg A+ are likely to view the new alternatives as more attractive compared to prior options. Regional investment banks may be especially well-positioned to capitalize on these new opportunities, given their existing relationships with smaller regional issuers and growth companies. It can also be expected that new trading sites and exchanges will emerge that will allow new investors to take advantage of the liquidity options that Reg A+ provides.

Reg A+ is likely to create incentives for smaller investment banks that currently feel left out by larger banks taking over the IPO placements and syndications. They will likely use newer models and utilize flexibility of soliciting retail and small institutional investors at lower costs through online marketing, portals, and lower commission and legal fees.

Summary

Regulation A+ has a huge potential to replace many private placements under Regulation D and provide a lower-cost alternative to conventional IPOs for many qualified small domestic and foreign companies that have encountered challenges in raising growth capital.

Reg A+ presents the best balance between regulatory oversight and flexibility of all the offering options for smaller or younger businesses. It provides the most flexibility for smaller issuers to go public and raise significant amounts of debt or equity over private placements at the lowest cost of any public offering option.

Reg A+ will attract many investors who have shied away from private placements due to lack of liquidity.

Although Reg A+ does provide a lot of flexibility for issuers by not requiring compliance with the more onerous registration provisions of the Securities Act or reporting as required by the Exchange Act of 1934, disclosure and transparency remain a primary requirement of investors in the marketplace. Beyond the reporting required under Reg A+, the issuer can and should voluntarily provide additional information for investors' knowledge to allow proper evaluation of the issuer's value proposition.

Reg A+ securities will have a number of trading platform options available as the volume of deals grow. Alternative trading systems such as OTC markets currently listed or Reg A+-dedicated exchanges will develop over time to expedite and make more efficient the current practice of or trades through inter-dealer bidding. National exchanges such as NASDAQ and NYSE will very likely provide comparable platforms in the future.

Issuers must recognize that post-IPO support is just as important as—or even more important than—the initial listing. It is ironic that many issuers spend millions of dollars in marketing to fight competition but do not see the marketing of their stock as their responsibility. Investors are one of the most important and critical members of the company's team.

Maintaining good investor relations cannot be overemphasized. Providing ongoing information to investors is what maintains stock liquidity and is highly correlated to price appreciation. It is highly recommended that issuers commit to adequate human and financial support critical to the long-term success of their stock. This could be the key difference between appreciating stock with lots of liquidity for investors or an "orphan" stock.

Because Reg A+ is new to most investors and issuers, it should be expected that its use will grow and expand over time, and there may be speed bumps along the way. Those issuers who are bold and not afraid to dive in to new pioneering opportunities such as Reg A+ will reap the very significant benefits and business growth intended by the JOBS Act.

Limitations and Business Line Considerations

Regulation A+ is designed to facilitate the capital-raising needs of a broad variety of businesses and industry types, but it's not for all issuers or necessarily the best way to achieve all business objectives. You need to weigh a number of important considerations to determine if it is the optimum means of accomplishing your fundraising goals. Some of these include, but are not necessarily limited to, the legal limitations on Regulation A+, investor priorities, and the post-capital raise obligations to maintain and grow the value of your investors' investments.

The easiest place to start is with the legal requirements to qualify to use Regulation A+.

Qualification Criteria for Regulation A+

Regulation A+ can be used to issue any equity, debt, or debt convertible into equity securities, except for fractional undivided interests in oil or gas rights, or similar interests in mineral rights and asset-backed securities.

As discussed in Chapter 2, for Tier 1 and 2 offerings, the following categories of potential issuers are precluded from the use of Regulation A:

- Any issuer not organized under the laws of the United States or Canada, or any State, Province, Territory or possession thereof, or the District of Columbia, with its principal place of business in the United States or Canada

- Any issuer subject to Section 13 or 15(d) of the Exchange Act (a company required to report publicly) prior to filing

- Any issuer registered or required to register as an investment company under the Investment Company Act of 1940

- Any issuer that had their registration revoked pursuant to a Section 12(j) of the Exchange Act within five years prior to filing an offering statement

- A development stage company that either has no specific business plan or purpose, or has indicated that its business plan is to merge with an unidentified company or companies (commonly referred to as a "blank check" company or a "public shell")

- An issuer issuing fractional undivided interests in oil or gas rights, or similar interests in mineral rights or asset-backed securities

- Any issuer that is subject to "Bad Acts Disqualification" under Rule 262.[1]

So, outside of these limitations, from a legal perspective the types of companies that can use Regulation A+ is pretty expansive. The real question for whom Regulation A+ would be right comes down to business factors—such as the maturity and character of the business that might attract investors—and the market realities of where demand might lie at a given time.

---

[1]Tier 2 issuers are also subject to the disqualification rules established under Rule 506(d) of Regulation D. These are broader rules than found under Rule 262 of Regulation A+ and should be carefully reviewed with counsel. Existing Tier 2 issuers may not use Reg A+ while they are not in compliance with their ongoing reporting requirements.

Investor Considerations

As discussed in Chapter 3, Regulation A+ provides a broad public capital-raising channel that does not have the excessive regulatory expense and burdens normally associated with traditional public offerings, and that also greatly increases the pool of potential investors as well as access to them through public advertising. Also, because of the liquidity that is permitted with Regulation A+ securities, market opportunities are likely to develop over time.

Regulation A+ presents an enormous opportunity for mid-market and smaller businesses that have otherwise been precluded from the public markets, as well as for smaller, industry-focused, regional investment banks, and intermediaries who have been edged out of participation in IPO opportunities by larger investment banks and support firms that focus on larger IPOs.

As discussed in Chapters 1 and 3, traditional fundraising via Regulation D is practically limited to accredited investors and select institutions. While it has been reported that there may be as many as 8.5 million accredited investors in the United States,[2] the number of active angel investors is far smaller—fewer than 400,000—but they accounted for funding about 73,000 ventures in 2014.[3]

Because Regulation A+ is not restricted to accredited investors, the pool of potential investors enlarged by non-accredited investors could be many times greater than the pool for Regulation D investors. So, for example, while the challenges of accessing and convincing investors to invest in generally risky investments, like startups, can be expected to be greater, firms who elect to use Regulation A+ will have many more potential investors that they can attract to such deals. In addition, Regulation A+ transactions will likely require significantly less documentation from investors than either Regulation D 506(b) or 506(c). As a consequence, crowdfunding portals, brokerage firms, and managements will likely find it easier to market Reg A+ securities, at least on the offering.

---

[2]"SEC Mulls Changes to Accredited Investor Standards," Devin Thorpe, Contributor July 15, 2014, URL: http://www.forbes.com/sites/devinthorpe/2014/07/15/sec-mulls-changes-to-accredited-investor-standards-18-crowdfunders-react/. This article also discusses a possible change in the definition of an accredited investor being contemplated by the SEC, which could reduce the total from 8.5 million to just 3.75 million, thereby significantly reducing the pool of potential investors for Regulation D offerings. This possible change will likely further accelerate the number of Regulation A+ offerings since they can be offered to all types of investors—both accredited and non-accredited.
[3]Center for Venture Research, Jeffrey Sohl, Director May 2014. URL: https://paulcollege.unh.edu/sites/paulcollege.unh.edu/files/webform/2014%20Analysis%20Report.pdf.

Since the passage of the JOBS Act, there are a growing number of platforms that make it easier to access smaller investors. Numerous sites such as the following offer access to large numbers of investors:

- www.gust.com
- www.equitynet.com
- www.angel.co
- www.startups.co

While these and similar sites have been largely limited to accredited investors and Regulation D offerings until now, the ranks of these and similar portals should swell in number and volume as non-accredited investors get more active in the Regulation A+ offerings that will be offered on their portals.

Securities Broker-Dealers

Due to greater access and availability of online information on investments in general, there has been a growing number of investors in recent years that prefer to invest directly and avoid the added fees associated with accessing investments through intermediaries such as securities brokers. However, many investors still seek out and rely on the inputs of qualified financial advisors before committing funds to new investments.

As of May 2015, there were roughly 4,000 licensed independent securities firms who employed over 600,000 financial advisors and support personnel in the United States.[4] Since each financial advisor typically has dozens or more clients, their ability to attract investor interest is enormous. Financial advisors often have significant influence over the investments that are made by their clients. As a result, they can often quickly raise significant funds provided they are convinced that a new investment opportunity is suitable for their clients.

Many traditional financial advisors and broker-dealer firms are generally skeptical of new investment ideas and will require much more due-diligence information in order to be convinced that an investment is suitable for their clients. This is in comparison to angel investors, who are investing from their own checkbook and are generally willing to take greater risks.

The majority of registered securities firms focus on providing services to *retail clients,* that is, persons investing for their own account, as opposed to institutional investors, venture capital groups, or other dealers in securities. As a

---

[4]http://www.finra.org/about

result of the enormous opportunity that Reg A+ can have for many securities firms, the growing retail sector (accredited and non-accredited) will generate more opportunities for securities dealers to assist entrepreneurs in raising capital for quality investment opportunities that can withstand the more extensive due-diligence criteria required by this fundraising channel.

What Is the Retail Investor Looking for in Any Investment?

It may be surprising, but we have found that most of today's retail investors are not looking to make a killing on their investments. They are generally more interested in not getting killed—that is, losing their money. The typical angel investor who is seeking a 10X or higher return in a technology startup is not representative of the typical retail investor. They are a very important segment within the retail channel, but care must be taken not to build a fundraising strategy exclusively targeting high-risk–high-reward type investors. Otherwise, entrepreneurs may miss attracting the larger pool of potential investors available to them.

Most retail investors seek predictable yield (stable regular cash flow) with limited downside potential (low risk of loss of their investment capital). They also like to obtain some guarantee of repayment, if possible, such as a personal guarantee or a pledge of some securities in debt offerings, to protect their investment. While investors generally accept more risk as their anticipated yield increases, a strategy that emphasizes capital preservation with some ongoing distributions along with some added security attracts the greatest number of retail investors for any given deal. Most retail investors do not have the ability to risk large amounts on the potential of high-growth investments or to conduct arbitrage plays in the secondary markets that have the potential to develop around Regulation A+.

"But wait!" you say. "My opportunity will not provide any income, and I need to find investors that are okay giving me money with the hope that I can eventually return them a big multiple on their investment."

There's nothing wrong with that—just realize that such a story will reduce the number of potential investors that you can target, and will therefore require a bit more planning in reaching the right investors, which may increase the time required to raise the total capital required. However, entrepreneurs can take some steps, even on riskier deals, to broaden their target investor pool.

- Look for ways in which investors can be offered some yield. Cash distributions are best, but preferred stock with some added upside over time attracts more investors than "common" stock.

- Raising capital through a debt offering, especially if there is some limited guarantee or pledge of collateral, attracts more investors than a pure equity raise.

- Since many investors rely on inputs from investment professionals, look to build your investment pitch in way that such advisors find your story to be attractive to their clients.

- Look for opportunities to take advantage of the greater liquidity options inherent in Regulation A+. While Reg A+ stock can in theory be traded immediately with few restrictions, it will require successful efforts to build interest in trading your stock post investment (see "After Market Considerations" in Chapter 5).

COMMON VERSUS PREFERRED STOCK

Common Stock

- Investors who hold common stock benefit from capital appreciation when/if the stock rises in value and through dividends.

- This means ongoing payment of dividends cannot be guaranteed.

- Holders of common stock also have the right to vote on company issues.

Preferred Stock

- Unlike common stock, preferred stock often guarantees dividends. The value of preferred stock is more stable since it is tied to interest rates and not as subject to market volatility as with common stock.

- Preferred stockholders receive a higher priority for dividend payments and also get paid ahead of common stock holders if the company is liquidated.

- Holders of preferred stock do not get voting rights in the business.

In our experience, preferred equity deals and debt-oriented products—that is, deals that are structured to require current dividends to be paid to the investor (currently 5-8%)—predominate right now. But as a larger volume of deals develops and analytic coverage for issuers becomes more sophisticated, it's likely a much larger variety of deals will develop, with the investor being able to ascertain the likelihood of dividends from solid fundamentals rather than the covenants associated with the security.

With more diversity in the opportunities for retail investors, there will be more opportunities for retail investors (as well as for securities firms who might assist to get an offering sold on a retail basis) to find good deals in their geographic backyard. Industries and companies they know likely hold more attraction for the retail investor who does not have the analytical resources of the institutional investor. So a retail-oriented approach to a capital raise is very likely to have a greater geographic focus proximate to the issuer.

For institutional investors, their desired investment profile can be much more value-add oriented than current yield-oriented, and they are willing to take more risk and consider many more situations for a chance at prodigious growth. The more sophisticated approaches and methodologies employed by successful institutional investors are supposed to reduce the risk related to this sort of investing. Those who invest with such institutional investors do so relying on the institutional investor's methodologies and diversification to mitigate risk, especially when they are investing with principals who have a proven track record.

Venture capitalists and other institutional investors might have the same priorities they have always had, yet can be expected to enter the Reg A+ market with a view to the liquidity offered by these securities as a risk-mitigation tool. They may also view the public disciplines that will be brought to their less mature firms as a training ground before they go to the "big show" of a full Wall Street offering. As a generality, however, institutional investors will be more motivated by growth and after-market value appreciation than retail investors.

After-Market Considerations

Regardless of whether the money is raised from retail or institutional investors, as sophisticated secondary markets develop for these securities, after-market considerations hold a big place in whether a given investment attracts capital. For the institutional investor, the ability to identify opportunities for growth in the market value of the securities will be a major motivator. For the retail investor, the added transparency and frequency of reporting associated with public securities allows the retail investor to identify companies with fundamentals (like strong management market positions or solid financials, for example) that allow for reliable yields and the ability to preserve value.

Those same fundamentals usually, in fact, lead to growth in market value and stock appreciation, but that is less of a focus of typical retail investors than wealth preservation. So the ability to create value in the public market will be key to successful Reg A+ offerings.

The retail investors are more focused, consciously or not, on organic growth to develop value. They are longer-term investors who are not looking to achieve big returns from market moves. These folks, for whom more limited volumes of trading due to awareness of Reg A+ or regulatory issues at state levels, are less of an issue if the market can price shares reliably and there is a pool of demand. The Reg A+ after-market will likely be dominated by retail investors for some time. Creating market value is primarily a function, as with any other securities, of the issuer being able to operate profitably and support growth. Having a management team with a strong record of producing prior investor returns is key, as in most capital-raising pursuits, to a successful Reg A+ program.

Value creation is also supported by the transparency of the issuer. Reg A+ issuers deal in essentially a public market. The law requires certain aspects of reporting, but the markets, more than anything else, demand that issuers provide meaningful and regular reporting as to operations, progress, triumphs, and setbacks of the company, so that the securities can receive market attention and be properly priced.

The markets, as with other public securities, also want to see corporate disciplines—regular board meetings, proper consents, annual meetings, shareholders votes, and so on—followed rigorously. This is intended to give the markets confidence in the information they are receiving about a company. It also communicates a focused management team. A focused, disciplined management team will be more likely to be trusted to make the company profitable and get the company back on course when setbacks do occur, which should help the company retain share value on a more consistent basis.

While the potential of trading Reg A+ securities now exists, there are many challenges that remain unless Congress steps in to remove several remaining hurdles that will inhibit a broad public market in these offerings. We will further explore these challenges and present possible solutions in Chapter 8.

Let's look at how Reg A+ applies to some specific industry sectors.

High Tech

Advanced technology can be a double-edged sword. On the one hand, technology can be a source of massive growth in the value of one's investment. On the other hand, the same cutting-edge nature of many of these investments also means they can be a source of significant risk for investors, especially if the technologies do not have analogies to present applications in the marketplace.

Depending on what types of investors a high-tech company is seeking to attract, the company will need to achieve certain development milestones to achieve its goals. Institutional players may be more willing to invest in a technology at an earlier stage of development in order to maximize the potential for growth in the market value of their investment. On the other hand, retail investors are likely to be less tolerant of development risk so a proven track record of revenue and profits will be more attractive to the typical retail investor (versus an angel investor).

Currently, the pathway to funding in the high-tech sector saturated by large VCs, whose models are to invest extremely large amounts of money for a commanding stake in technology companies, they believe, can conduct a billion-dollar IPO on Wall Street in a roughly five-seven year timeframe. The VCs bet big, so they expect to win big.

At the same time, there are any number of companies in the technology space that have achieved a certain level of proven growth in the development of their technologies and have even, in many cases, reached a meaningful level of real revenues. They are now too big to find the money they need from angel investors or friends and family. At the same time, however, they are also far too small or may lack the very high return potential to meet the criteria of the large VCs.[5]

Based on what we have discussed regarding investor priorities in this space, Reg A+ can provide a viable alternative to the large VCs, for many of these companies, by allowing them to access a retail base that focuses more on current revenue and opportunities for reliable, if more modest, growth.

For the institutional investor, Regulation A+ provides the opportunity to realize significant growth appreciation earlier in a company's growth cycle as compared to the often longer road leading to a traditional IPO.

Online Fundraising for Technology Opportunities

Online fundraising for Reg A+ offerings will continue to evolve but can be expected to focus more on offering overall lower cost fundraising options as compared to Reg D offerings and access to a growing pool of non-accredited investors. This will lead to a rebirth or conversion of many of the current online platforms.

---

[5]As pointed out in the article from *Forbes* in 2013 entitled "Why 99.95% Of Entrepreneurs Should Stop Wasting Their Time Seeking Venture Capital," very few technology companies are able to achieve hurdles that attract VC capital. Most entrepreneurs would be well advised to seek capital from non-VC sources. See http://www.forbes.com/sites/dileeprao/2013/07/22/why-99-95-of-entrepreneurs-should-stop-wasting-time-seeking-venture-capital/.

Since the passage of the JOBS Act in 2012, many online platforms have emerged for technology companies. Until now these platforms are all raising capital for Reg D offerings for accredited investors, but can be expected to expand to include Reg A+ offerings and broaden their reach to include non-accredited investors going forward.

Some of these funding companies are organized as registered securities brokers and accept fees as a percentage of capital raised, while others list offerings for a fixed marketing or consulting fee on their site, do not have any license, and work on a consultant basis. Here are just a few examples of popular portals that assist entrepreneurs in raising capital for technology firms.

- www.MicroVentures.com
- www.CircleUp.com
- www.Fundable.com

Low- or Medium-Tech Companies

Medium-tech businesses are those that have created new applications or derivations of existing and proven technologies, or provide adjunct products, or services necessary to the operation of higher technologies—such as a service firm that deploys a customized GPS system for tracking distribution/fulfillment, or a company that produces circuit switches necessary for fiber-optic networks.

Low-tech covers everything from brick-and-mortar manufacturing to service businesses without any particular emphasis on technology. For example, a regional restaurant chain.

In Chapter 1, we discussed the fact that many smaller and regional investment banks and brokerages that were previously cut out of the public markets now have the opportunity to re-enter the public markets with Reg A+. Nowhere is their presence felt more than in this category, as low- and medium-tech companies exist all around the country and not just in high-tech centers like Silicon Valley.

The population of these types of businesses permits a lot more flexibility in the use of Reg A+ to meet funding needs. Many investors are attracted to the local nature of the investments that can be had under Reg A+ and many low- and medium-tech firms with a regional business focus could benefit by attracting local investors with a Reg A+ offering.

The companies who are in the best position to exploit Reg A+ share the same characteristics that attract the attention and capital of investment banks and brokerages—revenues, a disciplined approach to corporate governance and reporting, and an experienced management team.

Real Estate

Investments in real estate are one of the major opportunity areas that can benefit from Reg A+. Many investors prefer real estate over other investments since it is often easier to understand, has tangible value that can be verified with readily available market data, often has an associated income stream, and can be visited. Investment timeframes are often more predictable due to the short-term nature of many of the projects; for example, developing a new shopping center, rehabbing an older apartment building, and so on. Real estate is also viewed to be a scarce resource ("they aren't making it anymore") that is more immune to the degree of volatility that is frequently experienced in other types of investments, such as in technology firms.

Overview of Real Estate Investments

While real estate is often owned free and clear of any debt, the typical real estate investment sought by investors includes both an equity component and a debt component. There is typically a cash-down payment and a bank loan or mortgage for the remainder required to purchase the property. Indeed one of the uniquely attractive aspects of real estate is the ability to acquire larger and more attractive properties through leveraging available cash (equity) with added debt.

Equity investments in real estate can be broadly categorized as either income or non-income producing properties.

Income properties are primarily acquired by investors seeking near-term investment returns resulting from rental income in combination with longer-term asset appreciation. Examples include residential properties, retail, commercial office, industrial and warehouse, student housing, gas stations, storage facilities, mobile home parks, and so on. Non-income properties can also be desirable investments if they appreciate substantially over the investment period. Examples include raw land and development projects that can be sold for a profit at a later date.

Many smaller real estate investments are completed by individual investors who invest their own funds and do not seek participation from outside investors—and are not candidates for Reg A+. Larger projects, however, commonly require participation from multiple investors under the supervision of a management entity. Larger projects having multiple investors are potentially suitable for Reg A+.

There are also many opportunities to invest in debt securities related to real estate. Many smaller investors lend funds to those seeking to acquire real properties and secure their loans against the value of the underlying property. If the loan is not repaid, the investor has recourse to gain possession of the real property and sell it to realize unpaid loan balances that may be due. The following investment structures are commonly used when multiple investors are sought to invest real estate assets whether they are income or non-income producing.

Deal-by-Deal Syndications

Larger real estate investments are organized by individuals or groups commonly known as syndicators. Their efforts focus chiefly on finding an attractive opportunity and then developing sufficient related information to attract multiple investors to participate in the investment, as well as preparing required documentation to meet ongoing reporting and regulatory require-ments. The syndicator may also remain involved as a manager of the project through the time of an eventual sale or exit. Examples include:

- An existing older apartment building that can be rehabilitated for profit and is offered to multiple investors

- A new development project for a retail, commercial, or multi-resident that will be sold upon completion to other investors who plan to hold the property for a long period

- Investment in larger parcels of raw land that are in a growth corridor and have long-term appreciation potential

Public and Private Equity Firms Investing in Multiple Projects

At the next tier, above deal-by-deal syndications, are private equity funds that offer investors the opportunity to invest in multiple projects in a common investment entity having similar characteristics. These types of investments are attractive to many investors since they can mitigate risk through diversifi-cation. Fund-oriented investments often have more experienced management teams in place and offer economies of scale that are not always available for individual projects. The investment portfolios of these larger firms are typically focused on similar asset classes—for example, retail, commercial office, multi-resident, and so on,—and specific risk categories with those asset classes.

Investment strategies typically focus on the following risk/reward categories:

- *Core*: These investments are focused on asset preserva-tion, have low or no debt, and provide low risk with pred-icable income. Stable fully leased multifamily properties in strong areas are most often found in these funds.

- *Value added*: These funds are structured to provide moderately higher returns with commensurately higher risk. Greater returns are achieved through investing in properties that can benefit from additional value-added investments that can result in a higher property value that exceeds the amount invested. The types of properties span all asset classes and typically have management or operational problems, require building improvements, and/or need additional capital to fund improved operations.

- *Opportunistic*: These funds are organized to provide the highest returns but also have high risk. Examples include investments in development projects, debt instruments, raw land, and specialty asset classes such as storage and billboards. The investments are typically of shorter-term duration and more oriented toward capital appreciation than income objectives.

The fund structures range from private equity funds organized as partnerships (LLC/LLP) to public and private Real Estate Investment Trusts (REITs).[6] Many larger firms trade on public markets and their shares can be easily traded.

Why Reg A+ Works Well for Real Estate

With the exception of a few large REITs that raise capital through IPOs, most real estate capital is raised via private placements utilizing the Reg D exemption discussed in Chapter 3. Approximately $100B dollars is raised annually for real estate using Reg D.[7]

Suffice it to say that the opportunity and benefits of utilizing Reg A+ for real estate offerings can be substantial.

As discussed in Chapter 3, the major benefits of utilizing Reg A+ instead of Reg D include the ability to advertise freely on any media channel, testing of waters prior to approval by the SEC, allowing participation by a large population of non-accredited investors, and options for immediate liquidity if

---

[6]https://en.wikipedia.org/wiki/Real_estate_investment_trust.
[7]http://www.forbes.com/sites/cherylsnappconner/2013/07/13/a-trillion-dollar-source-of-new-funding-the-secs-new-reg-d/ and http://www.sec.gov/info/smallbus/acsec/acsec103111_analysis-reg-d-offering.pdf.

required. As a result, Reg A+ can be an excellent source of funds and can significantly lower the overall cost of capital for many real estate opportunities requiring up to $50M in equity per year.[8]

In order to evaluate whether a specific real estate investment or fund should use Reg D or Reg A+, it is important to review the impact of the JOBS Act on both regulations and compare the overall pros and cons. One of the major benefits added by the JOBS Act is to allow use of the Internet and other media channels to reach a much larger investor base. This applies to both Reg D and Reg A+ offerings. However, as you learned in Chapter 3, while both Reg D and Reg A+ offerings can now be publicly advertised,[9] only issuers of Reg A+ offerings are allowed to accept non-accredited investors. This greatly increases the pool of potential investors.

Since the passage of the JOBS Act in 2012, use of online web sites to advertise offerings has been significantly expanding along with a growing number of funding platforms focusing on real estate offerings (see below). In June 2014, *The Wall Street Journal* estimated that $135M in real estate related debt and equity had been raised via online portals. While this is not insignificant, it is important to understand that while these sites could advertise to both accredited and non-accredited investors, only accredited investors could actually invest per the laws existing at that time. Since use of Reg A+ significantly broadens the number of potential investors, it is reasonable to assume that over a billion dollars of real estate investments annually could be funded via online platforms offering Reg A+ real estate investments.[10]

Raising Capital for Real Estate Projects

The process for raising capital for real estate projects can vary widely but mostly depends on the amount of capital required, type of project, holding period, type of investors, and their liquidity needs. While there are many aspects of Regulation A+ that make it the preferred choice relative to Reg D, here we evaluate and compare the three most critical aspects—process and time to raise capital, cost of capital, and liquidity options.

---

[8]Since most real estate investments are leveraged through the use of debt (i.e., the buyer obtains a loan for a portion of the property value), the actual amount of property that can be purchased can be significantly greater than the amount of invested capital. For example, an investor with $100,000 to invest can purchase a property valued at $200,000 if they are willing to obtain a $100,000 loan to add to their investment equity.

[9]https://www.sec.gov/info/smallbus/secg/general-solicitation-small-entity-compliance-guide.htm.

[10]William Skelley, CEO of iFunding, a real estate crowdfunding web site, has provided analysis on his company blog indicating that the worldwide market for real estate investments is in the range of $11 trillion. See http://blog.ifunding.co/.

Process and Time to Raise Capital

In the process of real estate fundraising for a Reg D offering, the first step is to prepare a detailed business plan. Then a derivative of this plan becomes part of a Private Placement Memorandum (PPM). This document is typically prepared by a qualified attorney and not only includes the business plan but also numerous disclosures for risk factors that investors need to be aware of and accept. The time needed to prepare a Reg D offering can range from two-eight weeks depending on the scope and complexity of the project.

The next step is to decide the channel for fundraising. The choice is largely between using an indirect sales approach consisting of registered securities broker-dealers and their agents (BDs) or direct selling by the issuer to qualified investors that they may directly know, such as friends, family members, and/or previous investors known to the issuer. The larger the capital raise, the more likely that the services of a securities broker-dealer will be required.

If BDs are engaged to assist with the fundraising, the lead BD will conduct extensive due diligence (DD), which typically takes several weeks to approve the offering for broader distribution for sale by their agents. Several additional BDs may be engaged as part of the selling group and the fundraising process begins.

Typically, only accredited investors are allowed to participate in Reg D offerings. Each investor must be carefully screened and his income and net worth properly documented before acceptance of funds. To complete the actual funding, Reg D real estate offerings can typically take three-six months depending on the amount of funds being raised and the success of the distribution channel.

Raising capital through use of the BD channel can not only be a long process, but it can be relatively expensive as compared to direct fundraising. In addition to the cost of preparing the offering, BDs will often charge as much as 10% of the amount being raised for due diligence, marketing, and brokerage commissions. BDs will often require that more comprehensive offering documents be prepared by the issuer that can result in added legal fees.

As discussed in more detail in Chapter 5, in order to raise capital for a Reg A+ offering, a business plan similar to Reg D has to be submitted to the SEC along with two years of audited financial statements and other disclosures as applicable. Approval of the SEC may take three to six months based on completeness of the submitted information. The next step is to decide the channel for actual fundraising and the targeted investor pools. Since both accredited and non-accredited investors are allowed to participate, almost anyone may invest in a Reg A+ offering, thereby raising the likelihood that an issuer could directly raise required capital without the involvement and added expense of a BD sales channel.

Another key feature of Reg A+ rules allows "testing of waters". This feature is very important, as it allows issuers to approach investors before formal fundraising begins to determine the level of potential interest in their offering, and the amount of investment they may likely receive prior to approval from the SEC. Once SEC approval is received, investors who were approached during the testing of the waters can send their funds to the issuer immediately. By using testing of waters, an issuer can work in parallel with investors to gauge investors' interest in the offering while the SEC is reviewing the Reg A+ filing instead of waiting for SEC approval before starting the fundraising process.

Overcoming SEC Approval Delays

Unlike Reg D offerings, which can begin fundraising without SEC approval, Reg A+ offerings must first be approved by the SEC. This can take three to six months. This can be negative in considering the use of Reg A+. For real estate projects that cannot tolerate the added approval cycle; for example, a redevelopment opportunity that was just acquired in a competitive bidding situation and needs to be quickly started, there are options that can be considered.

- Urgent projects can be acquired using short-term debt ("mezzanine debt") and then refinanced by funds that are raised after the SEC approval process has been completed.

- Documents submitted for approval to the SEC can list a specific acquisition project (e.g., a 200-300 unit apartment rehab project) while parallel efforts are underway to identify a substitute property. An amendment can then be made to the previously submitted documents prior to the final approval of the SEC, thereby reducing the overall timeline.

With some creativity, the Reg A+ process may not be as complex or time consuming as it appears due to the added SEC approval requirements. The overall time to raise capital can be similar to the Reg D process, with the added huge benefit of having a large population of non-accredited investors to participate as compared to a much smaller number of accredited investors, who can invest in Reg D offerings.

Using Online Portals to Reduce Costs and Access More Investors

As with technology and other investments, the overall cost of raising capital for real estate investments can be significantly lower for Reg A+ offerings if online portals are used to attract investors. Furthermore, many real estate projects that may not be suitable for BDs and their clients (such as higher risk value-added and opportunistic projects) may still be attractive to smaller non-accredited investors who are willing to make direct investments online.

Since the JOBS Act of 2012, there have been dozens of firms that have launched online funding platforms. While many more firms will emerge in the years ahead, we would like to briefly profile several of the more successful and better known firms that focus on real estate to provide the reader with a better understanding of business models that currently exist.[11] As of the print date of this book, these firms predominantly offer Reg D investment opportunities; however, most of these portals have indicated that they plan to add Reg A+ offerings as the new regulations take hold.

Online real estate funding portals have evolved into the following categories.

Commission-Fee–Based Fundraising

Traditionally, the most common form of compensation for intermediaries who raise capital for real estate offerings is to be paid a commission based on a percentage of the funds raised. However, this form of compensation can result in a requirement that the entity raising the funds may need to register as a securities broker-dealer, thereby adding more cost and overhead to the fundraising process.[12]

Fixed Fee for Advertising

Rather than charging commissions, these portals generate their primary income by charging the fundraising group a flat fee to list their property on their site in order to gain exposure to potential investors. Since the fees are not related to the actual monies that are raised, these portals operate more as advertising sites and are therefore not subject to securities laws.

---

[11]There is a significant discussion within the legal community as to whether online portals under each of the models need to register as securities broker-dealers. This should be evaluated with your legal counsel as you consider these options.
[12]An example of a portal in this category is http://www.circleup.com.

Groups raising funds will of course need to comply with applicable regulations when they engage with investors sourced by these sites and obtain funds. This type of public advertising via the Internet was formerly not allowed per the securities law, but the practice has since been allowed per the JOBS Act of 2012 under the new general solicitation regulations.[13]

To assist investors to determine which offerings are right for them, most of the real estate portals profile their advertised offerings using standard templates so that all offerings on the site can be easily compared to each other. Some sites require that all capital that is sought be raised before any capital is turned over to the company group seeking the funds. Other sites allow any monies raised to go to the fundraising group.[14]

Examples of portals in this category include:

Sidecar Fundraising

Portals engaged in this form of fundraising establish a new investment company—typically structured as a Limited Liability Company (LLC)—that mirrors a specific real estate investment for which they wish to raise capital. Acting as principals of this *sidecar* investment vehicle, they then can directly raise capital without registering as a securities broker-dealer. This capital is then deployed in the primary project.[15]

While traditional broker-dealers have been slow to embrace online portals, there is a growing trend among smaller regional broker-dealers to establish online to allow their established clients to obtain information on new offerings.

Summary

The selection of the fundraising channel is a critical decision and issuers need to carefully weigh the trade-offs among costs, time to raise funds, and capacity of the selected channel to produce desired funds. The lowest cost option is to directly access investors known to the fundraiser. Next is use of fixed fee online advertising channels. Next is the use of online broker-dealers. Finally, the most expensive is when traditional broker-dealers utilize financial advisers to raise capital from their clients. The range of cost is expected to be between 3–10% of the amount of capital raised, depending on the choice of channel.

---

[13]http://www.forbes.com/sites/tanyaprive/2013/09/23/general-solicitation-ban-lifted-today-three-things-you-must-about-it/.

[14]An example of a portal in this category is http://www.equitynet.com.

[15]Examples of portals in this category are www.realtymogul.com and www.cityfunders.com. Currently, such portals offer predominantly Reg D rather than Reg A+ opportunities. However it can be expected that there will be a shift into Reg A+ as more portal operators begin to take advantage of the added benefits.

The Key Elements of a Reg A+ Offering

Once a company has determined that a Regulation A+ offering is the correct path, the company, which is now a potential Regulation A+ issuer, has several initial decisions to make. If the issuer has engaged a principal underwriter or placement agent, the underwriter or agent may have significant input on these initial decisions. Many of these decisions will occur simultaneously with each other, or at different points in the process for different issuers. Here is a non-exhaustive list of these typical decisions, in no particular order:

- *Determination of offering size*: If the intended offering size is greater than $20M, an issuer will be required to engage in a Tier 2 offering, with the attendant audited financials and reporting requirements, and the benefit of state preemption.

- *Tier 1 vs. Tier 2:* If the issuer's intended offering size is $20M or less, the issuer may use either Tier 1 or Tier 2 of Regulation A+. The primary factors weighing in this decision are the advantage of state preemption relative to the initial offering versus the increased burden of filing audited financial statements with its offering statement and required periodic reporting in Tier 2 offerings.

If an issuer is considering utilizing Tier 1, it should carefully review the qualification regulations in the states it is targeting for sales, because many states have their own laws and regulations that require audited financials, which means that all but the most targeted Tier 1 offering is likely to include some audit requirements.

- *Plan of distribution:* The earlier an issuer can determine its plan for distributing its Regulation A+ securities, particularly whether it intends to engage underwriter(s) or placement agent(s) to sell its securities, the better. The method of distribution will likely have significant influence over the type and structure of the offered securities, and the underwriters and placement agents will likely have significant input.

- *Selection of third-party providers:* The vast majority of issuers will not have the in-house financial or legal personnel (and, of course, cannot have in-house auditors relative to a Tier 2 offering) to complete the regulatory requirements of a Regulation A+ offering. Early identification of skilled legal counsel and accountants will help an issuer avoid any early missteps that can poison the Regulation A+ journey.

  In order to file its offering statement electronically on the SEC's EDGAR system, the issuer will need to select a financial printer to "EDGARize" and file the offering statement. In addition to legal counsel, accountants, and a financial printer, the issuer may need additional third-party providers, such as transfer agents, escrow agents, trustees, and administrators, dependent upon the structure of its offering.

- *Selection of type and structure of security to be offered:* Regulation A+ offers broad flexibility in the type of security that may be offered, permitting equity securities, debt securities, and securities convertible or exchangeable into equity (but not asset-backed securities). This determination will depend on a balance between the capital requirements of the issuer and the features necessary to make the security appealing to investors. If the plan of distribution includes underwriters and/or placement agents, they will likely provide substantial assistance in structuring the offered securities.

- *Bad actor review:* Prior to embarking on a Regulation A+ journey, issuers must take care (and must continue to do so during the qualification process) that no members of their management team or any person who will be compensated for soliciting the securities to be offered—including under-writers, placement agents, and their management teams and registered representative—are subject to the disquali-fication events set forth in Rule 262 of Regulation A+. If a "bad actor" is discovered, the issuer must terminate that person, or it will not be eligible to use Regulation A+.

The previous list, as well as other initial determinations, provides the founda-tion for the preparation and filing of the offering documents, and many can be made during and in conjunction with the drafting process. While every offering is inevitably different, a general timeframe from beginning to drafting the offering documents to qualification with the SEC is between three and six months for an issuer engaging in its first Regulation A+ offering.[1] This encom-passes approximately one-two months for due diligence, structuring and drafting the initial disclosure documents, and an additional two-four months following initial filing of the offering statement to complete SEC review.

While we discuss this more a bit later in this chapter, marketing activities through "testing-the-waters" material may begin prior to the submission of the first filing with the SEC and may continue throughout the pendency of qualification, although issuers must take care with their marketing materials as they are subject to the antifraud laws and rules of the federal securities' regime.

For many offerings, qualification with the SEC will not end the regulatory pro-cess. Regulation A+ permits offerings to be made on a continuous or delayed basis (for up to three years under one offering statement, and indefinitely if new offering statements are filed). As a result of the smaller nature of the companies expected to use Regulation A+ and the lack of a current public trading market for Regulation A+ securities, most Regulation A+ offerings are not expected to be firmly underwritten. As a result, most will be made on a continuous basis until they terminate or until their maximum amounts are reached.

During these continuous offerings, an issuer must file an offering statement amendment to update the audited financials at least every 12 months, and must also file an amendment to reflect any facts or events arising subsequent to qualification that would represent a fundamental change in the offering

[1]For issuers engaging in follow-on Regulation A+ offerings, there's some likelihood that the SEC review time will be reduced or eliminated based on the SEC's treatment of follow-on offerings to initial registered offerings.

statement. For lesser changes, including the inclusion of pricing information for offerings pricing post qualification, the issuer may file an offering circular supplement with the SEC. An offering circular supplement containing pricing information must be filed within two business days of pricing or its first use, whichever is earlier. An offering circular supplement containing substantive changes to the offering circular, but not pricing information, must be filed within five business days of its first use.

Exhibit: Regulation A+ Offering Process/Sample Timeline (Tier 2)

Provided here is a hypothetical timeline for a well-run Tier 2 offering, utilizing an underwriter or managing placement agent to form a selling group of broker-dealers to sell the securities in order to illustrate the process to be expected:

- *Assembling the team:* Securities counsel and auditors should be a priority.

  Week 1

- *Letter of intent with underwriter/managing placement agent:* Selecting an underwriter/managing placement agent (if one is to be used) is formalized pursuant to a "letter of intent" outlining the investment bank's fees, the size of the offering, the price ranges, and other parameters. These deals are currently conducted on a "best-effort" basis.

  Commissions and fees to the distribution element reside between 7-10% currently. The investment bank/managing placement agent will retain 1-2% on total raise, and re-allow the bulk of the balance to the retail members of the syndicate (discussed later in this section).

  Week 1

- *Reviewing and restating the financials:* If the company or issuer has a financial history, those financial statements should be carefully reviewed and, if necessary, restated by the company's current accounting resources to comply with Generally Accepted Accounting Principles (GAAP). This will be necessary for the audited financial presentations required for Tier 2.

  Week 1–3

- *Selection of transfer agent and printer:* The printer will handle electronic formatting and filing; the transfer agent is necessary for proper record keeping of the securities.

Week 1–2

- *Preparing the financials:* Financials are presented and audited in conformance with small reporting company reporting requirements of Regulation SX.

Week 2–4

- *Drafting the offering statement:* The securities lawyers begin the process of preparing the "offering statement". Lawyers will draft the narrative part of the statement and the accountants will prepare financial statements. Both work together to ensure that the prose and financials "marry" and comply with requirements under Tier 2.

Weeks 1–4

- *Due diligence:* Counsel for the company, as well as perhaps the issuer's investment bank and accountants, will perform a detailed "due-diligence investigation" of the company. It is likely that information discovered in the due-diligence investigation will result in changes being made to the statement.

Weeks 1–4

- *Finalizing the marketing plan:* Determining which materials will be made available to investors and during what period of this process is critical. Your lawyers and the investment bank/managing placement agent must understand any regulatory issues now resulting from marketing activities.

Week 1–4

- *Filing the offering statement and SEC review:* The initial draft of the offering statement is filed with the SEC. It is also submitted to FINRA for review of the compensation associated with distribution by FINRA member firms. This commences a process with the SEC where they provide comments to the offering statement related primarily to the disclosure in the offering statement. In turn, this will likely result in changes to the offering statement to accommodate those comments. At the end of this process, the offering is "qualified" as an exempt security with the SEC and is registered as required in the target states.

Weeks 4–16

- *Syndicate:* After the offering statement has been prepared and filed with the SEC, the underwriter/managing placement agent (if one is to be used) will begin the process of assembling a "syndicate" or "selling group" consisting of other investment banks, financial advisors, and broker-dealers who will commit to selling the offering to investors. The assembly of the syndicate often generates useful information as to the market and perhaps changes in structure or the investment proposition, which could further affect the amendments to the offering statement. During this period, the underwriter/managing placement agent should identify any changes that need to be factored into an amendment to the statement.

Weeks 3–16

- *Marketing:* Marketing program to investors may include mailings or other forms of mass media marketing, seminars, and meetings with prospective investors. The goal is to identify as much as possible the subscribing audience for the offering.

Weeks 3–16

- *Finalizing the offering statement:* The offering statement must be revised in accordance with the comments of the SEC. When the SEC declares the offering "qualified," the company can seek to close subscriptions by investors.

Disclosure and Due Diligence

Fundamental to the filing process for Reg A + and similar other offerings is the requirement for full disclosure of materials facts by the issuer—both good and bad. These disclosures are not only to the benefit of potential investors but also protect the issuer against liability claims that may come about if material facts are omitted or misstated.

Some Initial Concepts

An issuer's primary disclosure documents in a Regulation A+ offering, whether engaging in a Tier 1 or Tier 2 offering, will be the issuer's offering statement filed with the SEC on Form 1-A, and the offering circular included therein. Additionally, a Regulation A+ issuer may use marketing materials describing its offering, including the testing-the-waters materials, to enhance the issuer's sales efforts. All materials used in offering and selling securities in a Regulation A+ offering will be subject to the anti-fraud provisions of the federal securities laws, including Sections 12(a)(2) and 17 of the Securities Act and Section 10(b) (and Rule 10b-5 promulgated there under) of the Exchange Act.[2]

Merely complying with the requirements of Form 1-A and completing the review and qualification process with the SEC does not ensure that an issuer has made adequate disclosure under these anti-fraud provisions. Critically, the Regulation A+ issuer and its counsel must review the issuer's business and financial plans and ensure that all material facts have been disclosed and that no material misstatements or omissions have been made in the issuer's offering materials. Per Rule 10b-5, a fact is material if there is a substantial likelihood that an average prudent investor ought to be reasonably informed before buying or selling securities. Putting it another way, the investor would attach importance in making a decision because the fact would significantly alter the "total mix" of available information.

To ensure that all of the material facts make their way into the offering materials, as well as to provide the information necessary to meet the requirements of Form 1-A, the issuer and its counsel should engage in a robust due-diligence process. Typically, counsel will prepare a due-diligence checklist containing requests for documents and narratives from the issuer, and will also prepare a questionnaire for the issuer's management personnel to complete. While counsel can assist in the due-diligence process, ultimately the burden is on the issuer and its management to provide all documents. If the issuer has engaged an underwriter or placement agent, it is likely that the underwriter or placement agent and its counsel will also be heavily involved in the due-diligence process.

Documents Related to the Issuer and the Securities Offered

While the breadth of change or creation necessary in a Regulation A+ issuer's organic or security documents will vary greatly from issuer to issuer, many issuers will require moderate to significant work done to their organic documents to create the securities intended to be offered. Startup entities making equity offerings will likely need entirely new entity documents drafted and adopted as they embark on their first serious fundraising efforts, whereas seasoned companies with prior investors may be required to achieve prior investor or equity holder approval before the proposed Regulation A+ securities may be issued. All entity documents for the issues, such as Articles

---

[2]Federal Register 17 CFR 230.255 and 17 CFR 270.8b-2(g)

of Incorporation, Organization or Limited Partnership, Bylaws, Partnership Agreements, and Operating Agreements will be required exhibits to the offering statement.[3] Any additional documents that create rights of the holders of the offered securities, such as option agreements, warrants, promissory notes, indentures, etc., must also be filed.

Additionally, the issuer's legal counsel will be required to opine as to the legality of equity securities and the legality and binding nature of any debt securities. So, it is critical that the governing documents of the issuer, and, in the case of a debt offering, the notes, indentures, or other agreements used to offer the debt, are thoroughly vetted early in the offering process to ensure that a clean legal opinion is delivered.

The Offering Statement

A Regulation A+ offering statement on Form 1-A consists of three parts:

- *Part I – Notification*
- *Part II – Offering Circular*
- *Part III – Exhibits*

Part I

Part I contains basic identifying information regarding the Regulation A+ issuer, including name, address, Central Indexing Key (CIK) classification, and jurisdiction of formation. Part I also requires certain basic financial information regarding the issuer, which differs slightly if the issuer is in the banking or insurance industries. Among other descriptive information, an issuer must identify whether it is engaging in a Tier 1 or Tier 2 offering, indicate whether its financial statements are audited, identify any underwriters or placement agents, and indicate whether it is engaging in a firmly underwritten or best efforts offering.

Additionally, the issuer must confirm that it is eligible for Regulation A+ and that there are no bad actors involved in its offering. Finally, the issuer must indicate any unregistered securities it or any affiliated issuer[4] has issued in the last year and provide a description of the applicable transaction and exemption from registration.

---

[3]See a further description of the exhibits to the offering statement under "The Offering Statement- Part III" later in this chapter.

[4]Note: In the adopting release for new Regulation A+, the SEC indicated that "affiliated issuer" means only affiliates of the issuer *who are issuing securities in the same Regulation A+ offering*, so this should not be confused with the much more broadly defined term "affiliates" generally applied to the Securities Act.

Part I must be placed into XML format and submitted on EDGAR with each revised submission of Parts II and III.

The chief purpose of Part I is to allow an issuer to determine whether they may be eligible to conduct a Reg A+ offering.

Part II

Part II of Form I-A is the offering circular and it comprises the primary sales document in a Regulation A+ offering. In comparing a Regulation A+ offering to a registered offering, the offering circular is to the offering statement as a prospectus is to a registration statement.

Part II grants flexibility as to the form an offering circular may take, permitting issuers to utilize the instructions set forth in Form I-A, or use Parts I of Forms S-I or S-II, to the issuer's discretion and as applicable to the issuer. This is provided that the financial disclosure in a Regulation A+ offering complies with Part F/S of Part II. As the authors are confident that thorough descriptions of Forms S-I and S-II exist outside the confines of this book (also provided at Appendix B of this book), the rest of this description focuses on the instructions set forth in Part II of Form I-A.

The offering circular consists of two parts: narrative disclosure and financial statements.

Narrative Disclosure

The requirements of the narrative disclosure portion of the offering circular are nearly identical whether the issuer is engaging in a Tier I or Tier 2 offering. Form I-A divides the required disclosures into 14 items, which, generally, may be interchanged as to placement in the offering circular so long as such movement does not obscure any required information. However, certain items, such as the cover page, table of contents, and risk factors are fixed as to their placement. Here is a brief description of each of the 14 items.

- *Item I—Cover page:* Limited to one page only. Basic information about the issuer and the offering, including (i) identification of any underwriters and disclosure of any underwriting discounts, commissions, and other items of compensation; (ii) identification of any minimum and maximum offering amounts and any escrow or trust arrangements; and (iii) the offering termination date in a best efforts offering.

- *Item 2—Table of contents:* Must immediately follow the cover page.

- *Item 3–Summary and risk factors:* If the issuer desires to use an offering summary, it must be placed directly after the table of contents and prior to the risk factors. The summary may not repeat in detail information found later in the offering circular. Risk factors that make the offering speculative or substantially risky must be placed directly after the summary. These risk factors must be specific to the issuer.

- *Item 4–Dilution:* Material disparities between the public offering price and the effective cash costs for shares acquired by insiders during the past year.

- *Item 5–Plan of distribution:* The issuer must describe how it plans to sell its offered securities, including providing descriptions of any underwriting and/or placement arrangements and compensation associated therewith. Any arrangements with underwriters to restrict the resale of securities sold in the offering or otherwise stabilize a market in the securities must be included. Additionally, if any of the issuer's existing security holders are selling in the offering, tabular disclosure regarding such selling security holders must be provided.

- *Item 6—Use of proceeds:* This describes in columnar and numerical format how the capital raised will be used.

- *Item 7–Description of business:* A narrative description of the business operations of the issuer for the prior three fiscal years (or, if in existence for fewer than three years, since its inception).[5]

- *Item 8–Description of Property:* The issuer must describe its principal properties and physical plants, and any encumbrances on them.

- *Item 9–Management's discussion and analysis of financial condition and results of operations:* Commonly referred to as the "MD&A," this is a discussion and analysis of the issuer's liquidity and capital resources and results of operations through the eyes of management, covering the two most recently completed fiscal years and interim periods, if required. For issuers that have not received revenue from operations during each of the three fiscal

---

[5]Note: The SEC's industry guides are applicable to Form 1-A and so may impact disclosure.

years immediately before the filing of the offering statement (or since inception, whichever is shorter), the plan of operations for the 12 months following qualification of the offering statement, including a statement about whether the issuer anticipates that it will be necessary to raise additional funds within the next six months.

- *Item 10—Directors, executive officers, and significant employees:* Identification of directors, executive officers, and significant employees with a discussion of any family relationships within that group, business experience during the past five years, and involvement in certain legal proceedings during the past five years. Some of this information must be presented in tabular format.

- *Item 11—Compensation of directors and executive officers:* Group-level executive compensation disclosure for the most recent fiscal year for the three highest paid executive officers or directors with Tier 2 requiring individual disclosure of the three highest paid executive officers or directors. This disclosure must be provided in tabular format. Additionally, the issuer must disclose any future compensation plans for directors and executive officers.

- *Item 12—Security ownership of management and certain security holders:* Beneficial ownership of voting securities by executive officers, directors, and 10% owners, to be presented in tabular format.

- *Item 13—Interest of management and others in certain transactions:* Transactions with related persons, promoters, and certain control persons.

- *Item 14—Securities being offered:* The material terms of the securities.

The following table provides a summary of these items and how they apply to Tier 1 and Tier 2.

Form 1-A Required Disclosures

Disclosure Item	Tier 1 Issuers	Tier 2 Issuers
	Part I	
1) Cover Page	Basic issuer information, disclosure of underwriters and related discounts and commissions, offering amounts, escrow or trust arrangements, termination date	Same
2) Table of Contents	Must be included and follow cover page	Same
3) Summary and Risk Factors	Significant risk factors that make the offering substantially risky or speculative	Same
4) Dilution	Significant disparities between the public offering price and the effective price paid for shares acquired by insiders during the past year	Same
5) Plan of Distribution	Description of how issuer plans to sell its securities including underwriting and placement arrangements. Also disclosure of any planned sales by existing security holders	Same
6) Use of Proceeds	Principal purposes for which net proceeds are intended to be used	Same
7) Description of Business	Description of up to the three past years of business operations	Same
8) Description of Property	Description of principal properties and physical plants including any encumbrances on them	Same
9) Management's Discusssion and Analysis of Financial Condition and Results of Operation	Discussion of issuer's liquidity and capital resources and results of operations covering the most recently completed fiscal years including a statement about whether the issuer anticipates that it will be necessary to raise additional funds within the next six months	Same
10) Directors, Executive Officers and Significant Employees	Identification of directors, executive officers and significant employees with a discussion of any family relationships within that group, business experience and involvement in certain legal proceedings during the past five years.	Same
11) Compensation of Directors and Executive Officers	Group-level executive compensation disclosure for the most recent fiscal year. Additionally, the issuer must disclose any future compensation plans for directors and executive officers.	Covering three highest paid executives or directors
12) Security Ownership of Management and Certain Security Holders	Beneficial ownership of voting securities by executive officers, directors, and 10% owners, to be presented in tabular format	Same
13) Interest of Management and Others in Certain Transactions	Transactions with related persons, promoters and certain control persons	Same
14) Securities Being Offered	Material terms of securties being offered	Same

Additional information beyond the requirements of these items may, and in some cases will, be required. For example, any offering statement for a tax-advantaged investment, such as a real estate investment trust, Subchapter-S corporation, or entity taxed as a partnership will need significant tax disclosure (as well as a tax opinion from counsel).

Primary responsibility for the narrative portion of the offering circular will fall on the issuer and its counsel. If counsel is involved, it will likely control the document and engage in the bulk of the substantive drafting; however, certain pieces, most notably Item 9 (affectionately known as the MD&A), will fall squarely on the issuer. The efficiency of the due-diligence process described previously will materially impact counsel's ability to quickly draft the offering circular. Should the issuer engage an underwriter, its counsel may also be involved in the drafting process for the offering circular and will likely concern itself with the offering due diligence, especially in the context of any opinion(s) to be delivered at closing.

Part F/S—Your Financial Presentation

Form 1-A requires the same financial statements regardless of the form of disclosure chosen by the issuer relative to the narrative disclosure. Regardless of whether the issuer is engaging in a Tier 1 or Tier 2 offering, if the issuer is a U.S. company, its financial statements must be prepared in accordance with U.S. Generally Accepted Accounting Principles (GAAP). If the issuer is a Canadian company, its financial statements may be prepared either in accordance with U.S. GAAP or the International Financial Reporting Standards.

The instructions to financial statements to be filed in a Tier 1 offering are included in Form 1-A, and provide that, generally, the Tier 1 financial statements need not be audited and do not have to conform to Regulation S-X. However, if the issuer has audited financials for other reasons (including state qualification requirements) and that audit complies with required auditing standards and the auditors are independent in accordance with Rule 2-01 of Regulation S-X, then that audit must be filed. Additionally, while Regulation S-X is generally inapplicable, the instructions often refer to Article 8 of Regulation S-X, including with respect to financial statement requirements for business combinations or acquisitions of real estate operations.

Financial statements for a Tier 2 offering must be audited, and must, generally comport with Article 8 (Financial Reporting for Smaller Reporting Companies) of Regulation S-X, except with respect to the timing of filing of interim financial statements.

Regardless of the offering tier, the issuer must present financial statements for its last two fiscal years, provided that if its filing occurs within three months of its fiscal year end, the issuer may present financial statements for its two immediately preceding fiscal years. If the issuer files its offering statement (or an amendment thereto) more than nine months following its fiscal year end, then, in addition to the financial statements for its most recent two fiscal years, the issuer must file interim semi-annual financial statements. The interim financial statements are not required to be audited whether engaging in a Tier 1 or Tier 2 offering.

The required yearly financial statements are: (i) a consolidated balance sheet; (ii) consolidated income statement; (iii) consolidated statement of cash flows; and (iv) consolidated statement of changes in stockholders' (or other equity holders in the case of non-corporate issuers) equity. When filing interim statements, the changes in equity statement may be omitted.

If the issuer has engaged in a significant acquisition of a business or real estate operations,[6] then the issuer will be required to present additional financial statements for the business or real estate operations acquired. Additionally, if the acquisition of a business has occurred since the end of the last fiscal year for which financial statements are filed, then the issuer must file pro forma financial statements in accordance with Rule 8-05 of Regulation S-X.

The preparation of the financial statements will fall first on the issuer itself. In order to maintain independence, as required in order to issue a report under Rule 2-01 of Regulation S-X, the auditors cannot assist the issuer in the preparation of the financial statements they are to audit. Therefore, issuers that do not have significant in-house accounting and financial capacity will likely need additional outside accounting assistance beyond their auditors.

Part III

Form 1-A provides a list of exhibits that must filed with the offering statement. These include: (i) underwriting or placement agreements; (ii) the issuer's organic documents; (iii) instruments containing the rights of the purchasers in the offering; (iv) any subscription agreement being used; (v) material contracts; (vi) legal opinion(s); (vii) consents of experts named in the offering circular, among others; and (viii) any testing-the-waters material.

---

[6]As determined under Rules 8-04 and 8-06 of Regulation S-X, respectively.

Ancillary Information

If the issuer is using an underwriter, the offering statement must also include a statement as to whether or not the amount of compensation to be allowed or paid to the underwriter has been cleared with the Financial Industry Regulatory Authority (FINRA). Additionally, any expert reports referenced or provided for external use from the offering circular must be filed with the SEC.

Filing on EDGAR

The offering statement must be electronically filed through the SEC's EDGAR system. To do so, an issuer must first create its EDGAR identity by submitting a Form ID to the SEC. Once in EDGAR, an issuer, or more likely its agents, may make filings that comply with EDGAR's formatting requirements. Getting into the EDGAR format will require the services of a financial printer who will take the draft offering statement in document format and transform it into a format compatible with EDGAR. Typically an issuer will want to transmit the offering statement to the printer a few days prior to the anticipated filing date in order to give time for a final review and to correct any errors occurring in the "EDGARization" process.

An offering statement must be signed by the issuer, its principal executive, accounting and financial officers,[7] and a majority of the issuer's board of directors. Once the offering statement is executed, the financial printer will file it on command.

SEC Review Process

Following submission of the initial Form 1-A, the SEC will take approximately 30 days to review the offering statement and to generate initial comments. Absent extraordinary circumstances, an issuer engaging in its first Regulation A offering should expect to receive a comment letter from the SEC. Once the initial comment letter is received, the process with the SEC becomes much more fluid. The issuer and its counsel (and in some cases accountants) must provide specific responses to each SEC comment, or must revise the offering statement, pursuant to an offering statement amendment, to respond to the comment letter. Offering statement amendments are made on the same form as the offering statement and will be labeled a Form 1-A/A.

---

[7]These could be all one person.

The SEC will review responses to their initial comments and any subsequent comments, as well as any new information in the issuer's offering statement, and may provide additional comment letters.[8] Following the initial comment letter, the SEC will typically generate comments on a much quicker timeline with respect to amendments and responses to their comments; however, the exact timeframe is highly dependent on the breadth of initial comments and the current workload of the SEC's staff.

Fortunately, under the new Regulation A+ rules including EDGAR filings, the paper filing requirements of old Regulation A+ have finally given way to electronic filing, which eliminates the time-intensive shipping and intake processes with the SEC.[9]

Ultimately, if a Regulation A+ issuer and its counsel are diligently responding to the SEC's comments, and absent any extraordinary issues with the SEC, the issuer should expect the SEC process to take roughly three-four months. Of course, if business or other reasons result in the issuer delaying responses to the SEC's comments, then this process may take a significantly longer period of time. The SEC may declare an offering statement that has not been qualified or amended within the last nine months to be abandoned, so an issuer should be aware not to take too long to respond to SEC comments without communicating with the SEC.

Once all SEC comments are resolved and the issuer and its counsel are comfortable with the offering statement, the issuer must request qualification of the offering statement with the SEC. The SEC staff typically requires 48-hour notice to process a request for qualification. Once qualified, the issuer may complete sales of its securities.

Marketing

New Regulation A+, in both its Tier 1 and Tier 2 forms, permits broad public marketing of securities offering in reliance on the Regulation A+ exemption from registration. However, similar to the requirements of a public registration, there are limits and requirements surrounding the marketing of a Regulation A+ offering to which an issuer must adhere.

---

[8]The SEC also reserves the right to comment on disclosure it has previously reviewed.
[9]In the experience of the authors, the paper-filing requirements of old Regulation A+ generated three-four days of delay surrounding each amendment of Form 1-A. That delay will be predominantly eliminated in new Regulation A+, making the SEC process in new Regulation A+ much more efficient, especially in the latter stages of the SEC review process when multiple amendments making very few changes are commonplace.

A Regulation A+ issuer's marketing requirements differ across the three periods of the Regulation A+ qualification process delineated by the SEC: (i) prefiling; (ii) post-filing and pre-qualification; and (iii) post-qualification.

Pre-Filing

Prior to making the initial filing of its offering statement on Form 1-A, an issuer cannot make offers of the securities, but can engage in "testing the waters," meaning an issuer may solicit interest in a proposed offering (and ask for communication of that interest, or not) from the public via oral or written communication. These types of communication prior to filing must include disclaimers indicating that: (i) no money or other consideration is being solicited or will be accepted; (2) an indication of interest is no obligation to purchase; and (3) no offers to buy the securities will be accepted or money taken until the qualification of the offering statement. Any offer to buy the securities may be withdrawn at any time prior to the issuer's postqualification acceptance of the offer. All written testing-the-waters materials must be filed with the SEC once you file for a Regulation A+ offering and, like all other offering materials, testing-the-waters materials are subject to the SEC's anti-fraud rules, so a Regulation A+ issuer must carefully review any statements regarding its offering or business being made before release testing-the-waters materials. Additionally, if the terms of the offering or fundamentals of the business described in testing-the-waters materials change prior to the closing of the offering, the issuer will be obliged to recirculate revised materials and file them with the SEC.

Post-Filing

Once the issuer has filed its initial Form 1-A but prior to its qualification, the marketing opportunities expand. An issuer may now make oral offers without complying with the testing-the-waters regulations (i.e.: providing the disclaimers but, of course, these remain subject to anti-fraud), and may also make offers using the preliminary offering circular, which is the Regulation A+ equivalent of the red herring in a public registration. Additionally, issuers may continue to make written communications under the testing-the-waters regulations (including disclaimers), provided that they add information to their materials indicating how to request a preliminary offering circular, or a URL to the current preliminary offering circular.

Post-Qualification

Following qualification, offers may be made in a generally unfettered manner (subject again to the anti-fraud rules), but any written offer must be accompanied or preceded by delivery of the most up-to-date offering circular qualified with the SEC. The new Regulation A+ rules provide generally for an "access equals delivery" model for final offering circulars, so issuers and their intermediaries can meet their delivery burdens relative to making written offers post-qualification (and closing sales with investors with whom a pre-qualification preliminary offering circular was used) by providing investors with the URL location of the final offering circular.

There are a couple of additional critical questions regarding marketing compliance, as follows:

- *When does the pre-filing period begin?* Generally, it begins 30 days prior to the first filing of the offering statement. Communications prior to that period will generally not be considered offers, unless they refer specifically to the proposed offering. However, if those communications would be considered offers during the 30-day period, the issuer must take reasonable steps to prevent their further distribution or publication during that 30-day period. Any communication referencing a proposed securities offering, even before the 30-day period directly prior to the filing of the offering statement, may be considered an offer by the SEC and should be reviewed by counsel.

- *What is an "offer"?* The definition of offer as used in U.S. securities laws is much broader than the everyday definition of offer, and the SEC has indicated that any publicity that may "contribute to conditioning the public mind or arousing the public interest" in an offering may be considered an offer. However, the SEC has indicated that the regular dissemination of factual business information that does not include predictions or projections regarding the issuer's business or valuation of its securities will not constitute an offer for the purposes of Regulation A+. This is consistent with the SEC's approach in registered offerings. Ultimately, once an issuer has determined it is moving forward with a Regulation A+ offering, all public communications should be vetted by counsel.

FINRA Members

Issuers who have engaged or are seeking to engage one or more FINRA members (i.e., securities broker-dealers) to market their offerings must be mindful of a few additional points. First, an issuer's negotiations with an underwriter, or negotiations among underwriters, regarding the terms of the offering are exempt from the definition of "offer". Secondly, materials used by the underwriters or other FINRA members to form an offering syndicate (referred to as "BD only materials") are generally not subject to the regulatory requirements surrounding marketing materials described previously (although they should certainly be reviewed for factual accuracy). Finally, to the extent a FINRA member(s) will be involved in public communications using testing the waters, the issuer must work carefully with the FINRA member, and its counsel, to ensure compliance with the FINRA rules governing a member's communications with the public. These FINRA rules are far more burdensome than the requirements for testing the waters under Rule 255 of Regulation A+.

Closing/Investor Intake

The SEC has adopted an "access equals delivery" approach to the requirements for providing the offering circular disclosure to the investor. This is similar to what you would see in a traditional registered offering. Physical delivery of the circular is not required if a notice is provided as to where the final circular, and all previous filings, can be obtained on the EDGAR site at the SEC at the time subscription is made. The investor then has 48 hours to rescind the order, ostensibly giving time for review and the ability to withdraw if they change their mind.

The subscription form(s) related to a security offered under Regulation A+ can be very basic. Many of the representations related to investment intent and disclosures—legends related to the securities being restricted and certifications and informational requests related to accredited investors status such as are found in Regulation D offerings—are not required in the Regulation A+ context. Tier 1 securities, because of the state regulatory aspects associated with them, will typically have some representation to comply with the state securities requirements, such as prescribed legends and suitability representations. But for Tier 2 offerings, the form can really be very basic—outlining the amount subscribed for and a representation that the investor complies with the rules related to investment caps (discussed in Chapter 5).

The process of physically bringing the investor in as a stockholder, member, limited partner, or noteholder (to name a few) can be very straightforward or complicated by such considerations as facilitating trading or holding the securities in "street name." However, the latter situations would require the use of broker-dealers, and many of the complexities of intake in those situations will be designed and handled by them. The most important things for the issuer to remember is clear communication of orders by the broker-dealer to the issuer, and making sure a copy of the order intake forms are received so that the issuer has evidence of the investment cap compliance representations.

Transfer Agents/Escrow

Two other critical aspects of your offering and intake will be establishing an escrow for the offering and selecting a transfer agent for securities going forward.

If you have contingencies to closing on funds—such as a minimum to be reached, or investments being closed upon at only certain time intervals—an escrow is mandatory for broker-dealers if you are using them to sell. Even if you are not, it's a wise choice in the circumstances to ensure that funds to which you do not necessarily have a right as yet are properly accounted for until closed. Remember that the subscriber has a 48-hour period to withdraw, so, again, it's important to make sure no mistakes are made.

A transfer agent is a regulated entity that is charged with essentially keeping records of how the securities of an issuer are held—by whom and in what amounts. They may provide other services related to the securities, but this is their core function, and it is essential when dealing with tradeable securities. A transfer agent is selected in the creation of your offering and will be an integral part of intake to ensure accurate records going forward of securities ownership.

Post-Closing /Post-Qualification Obligations

For Tier 1, issuers don't have any obligations post closing, other than they will be required to provide certain information about their Regulation A+ offerings on a new form, Form 1-Z. This is informational to the SEC, however, and will not affect the validity of the qualification.

Tier 2 issuers, however, will be subject to an ongoing reporting regime and would be required to file:

- Annual reports on Form 1-K
- Semi-annual reports on Form 1-SA

- Current reports on Form 1-U

- Special financial reports on Form 1-K and Form 1-SA

- Exit reports on Form 1-Z

Form 1-K is required to be filed within 120 calendar days of the issuer's fiscal year end and would require disclosures:

- Relating to the issuer's business and operations for the preceding three fiscal years (or since inception if in existence for fewer than three years)

- Related party transactions

- Beneficial ownership

- Executive officers and directors

- Executive compensation

- MD&A

- Two years of audited financial statements

The semi-annual report is required to be filed within 90 days after the end of the first six months of the issuer's fiscal year and is similar to a Form 10-Q, although it's subject to scaled disclosure requirements.

A current report on Form 1-U must be filed within four business days of the triggering event and will be required to announce:

- Fundamental changes in the issuer's business

- Entry into bankruptcy or receivership proceedings

- Material modifications to the rights of security holders

- Changes in accountants

- Non-reliance on audited financial statements

- Changes in control

- Changes in key executive officers

- Sales of 10% or more of outstanding equity securities in exempt offerings

An exit report on Form 1-Z is required to be filed within 30 days after the termination or completion of a Regulation A+ exempt offering.

Raising the Capital through an Underwriter

Chapter 4 discussed the use of portals and crowdfunding in the context of Reg A+. While these may be ultimately very effective methods to raise capital, they are yet to be proven, and questions remain as to whether they can drive traffic to their sites. Furthermore, for issuers looking to create liquidity, sources of market expertise are a must. Therefore, issuers must consider seriously the use of an underwriter in their offering process.

This chapter summarizes the roles and responsibilities of the underwriter in assisting a firm to raise capital and in setting the stage for successful post-offering share performance.

Underwriters, also known as *investment banks*, are firms or individuals employed by companies (or *issuers*) that are seeking assistance to sell their shares to third-party investors. For larger firms, the buyers of an issuer's shares may in fact initially be the underwriting firm itself, which will resell the shares to others, thereby earning a *spread* between what it paid the issuing firm for its shares and what it subsequently receives when reselling its shares.

Smaller firms, such as those contemplating Reg A+ IPOs, will most likely utilize smaller underwriters, who will act as intermediaries and directly sell the firms' shares to predominantly retail investors who are clients of financial advisory broker–dealer firms. In some cases, a lead underwriter will enter into agreements with other broker–dealers to *syndicate* the offering (i.e., create a selling group of multiple brokerage firms) in order to generate more visibility and create greater demand for the shares.

■ **Tip** The underwriting procedures and processes discussed in this chapter are those typically encountered by smaller firms, which are the most likely to benefit from Regulation A+.

Selecting a suitable underwriting firm has been likened to the process of finding a new spouse inasmuch as the relationship between the issuer and the underwriter may likely continue for many years into the future and, like a normal marriage, have its ups and downs. While there are fact-based criteria that are employed to select underwriters—such as relevant industry experience and number of successful deals done with similar firms as yours—there are also considerations of chemistry, compatibility, commitment, and other more qualitative and even emotional reasons that will need to be evaluated.

Similarly, underwriters, especially good ones, have no shortage of firms seeking their assistance and will be selective in evaluating and finalizing relationships with their clients. Like talent agents, underwriters are careful to enter only into relationships that are likely to enhance, rather than tarnish, their reputations. The process of winning over a good underwriter to a deal is much like attracting a top investor. Issuers are well advised not to attempt to attract underwriters until they are fully prepared to present a compelling story to gain their interest.

Role of the Underwriter

Prior to identifying potential investors, the underwriter will conduct due diligence on the issuer firm and confirm that all regulatory requirements have been fulfilled, including completing all required filings, paying filing fees, and making all disclosures required by securities regulations and risk considerations.

Following the substantial completion of due diligence, the underwriter will reach out to groups representing retail investors to obtain feedback on open questions, general suitability, potential pricing, and to assess overall demand.

For smaller issues, underwriters are typically only willing to commit to raise funds on a *best-efforts* basis. In contrast to a firm commitment to purchase shares, which is more common with larger issues in traditional IPOs that have higher demand, this type of arrangement will not guarantee that the underwriter will be able to raise the full amount of sought-after funds. While best efforts are not as attractive to an issuer as a firm commitment, it is the sort of arrangement that should be expected for smaller, lower-priced issues.

But there is a silver lining in that the risk of falling short of fundraising objectives in a best-efforts arrangement encourages the underwriter to syndicate the offering in order to increase the number of potential investors who might be exposed to the offering. The downside is that the issuing firm cannot rely solely on the efforts of the underwriter to source all the funds.

As for the attainment of many key objectives in a smaller firm, the CEO in particular should remain deeply immersed and be constantly active in reaching out to all possible appropriate sources of funds until the fundraising objectives have been satisfied. Often investors who were not interested in investing at the beginning of the fundraising process will step up when they see other investors committing to the deal and momentum building. Also, early investors should be approached before the round closes in an effort to raise more money from them due to growing interest.

Finding an Appropriate Underwriter

Smaller Reg A+ offerings are not likely to attract the interest of larger underwriters such as Goldman Sachs and Morgan Stanley. These firms have business models that reflect their established Wall Street positions and overheads to cover that make it impractical for them to consider working with smaller firms. The entrepreneur contemplating a Reg A+ offering must focus on finding smaller underwriters who are more flexible and willing to work with smaller firms.

While IPO attorneys, CPAs, and other service firms that deal with smaller public offerings can often provide good referrals, we recommend that the entrepreneur begin their search efforts by researching firms that have successfully underwritten similar-size deals in similar market segments. Fortunately, this research can be accomplished quickly and relatively inexpensively using the Internet.

Begin by visiting sites that summarize IPO-related information.[1] There you can find names of underwriters who have been engaged by other firms, and through further research you should be able to easily develop a good target list.

Once you have identified potential underwriters, it is best that you obtain an introduction from a warm referral source—such as a CPA, lawyer, or broker–dealer who has worked with the firm—to an appropriate contact within the firm. Cold calls or e-mails are not likely to achieve the desired results and may actually backfire by creating a less-than-optimum first impression that causes consideration of your firm to go no further.

[1] One of our favorites is http://www.renaissancecapital.com.

As you begin to collect more data on potential underwriters, keep the following areas in mind:

- Past performance with similar-sized offerings

- Knowledge of your market

- Target investors and distribution channels

- Aftermarket support

- Compatibility with your firm's objectives and with you and your key executives

Although all five of these areas are important, compatibility often becomes the most important discriminator when comparing firms with similar track records. Your relationship with the underwriter will likely last far beyond the first fundraising event and you need to have mutual respect and trust along with lots of patience to achieve optimal results.

You should exhaustively check out all references for each underwriter who makes your short list—those provided by the underwriter, as well as those that you seek out without their introduction. CEOs and CFOs who have recently been through an IPO are often easy to contact and will usually be glad to answer your questions about their experiences. Here are some questions that you must ask:

- Did the firm fully meet your expectations? If not, where did they fall short? (No firm will obtain a perfect score on this question—so don't overweigh negative responses unless they disclose a strategic weakness that you are likely to face.)

- How do you assess their knowledge of your products and market?

- What was their methodology in determining your offering share price and was it sound?

- What was their distribution plan? Did they use other firms and, if so, who were they?

- Describe their road show.[2]

- Which specific people did you work with and did they deliver the expected results? Any communication issues?

---

[2]Prior to an offering it is common to go on a grueling whirlwind cross-country tour to visit various broker–dealers and sometimes large direct potential investors and give presentations on your firm to attract investments. These road shows are orchestrated by the underwriter.

- How much of your stock performance is attributable to their contributions?

- Describe their current efforts to support your firm in the aftermarket.

- All things considered, would you have selected them if you knew then what you know now?

The underwriting firm will likely insist on one or more face-to-face meetings. Take full advantage of these opportunities and bring your top executives along as appropriate. While the CEO often is the center of attention in these meetings, it can be very helpful to expose other key executives to this process for both practical and political reasons.

On the practical side, you want to get buy-in from your inner circle that you are selecting the best firm for the job and utilize the combined brain power of your top execs to evaluate the many options and trade-offs that you will confront. You also may want to show off a superstar who might be able to further generate investor interest and make the job of the underwriter a bit easier.

On the political side, most top executives want to be intimately plugged into discussions with underwriters due to their perception that these decisions may impact the valuation of their equity positions. To maintain harmony and trust with your executive team, include them when appropriate.

The Letter of Intent

Once you have settled on an underwriter, you will need to finalize the details of your engagement. This process starts with receipt of a *letter of intent* (LOI) from the underwriting firm that details the nature of your relationship with the firm as well as the terms and conditions of your offering. An LOI typically includes the following sections:

- *Legal Representatives*: Identifies attorneys representing the underwriter and the issuing firm.

- *SEC Filing*: Confirms the specific filing that will be submitted.

- *Duties of Underwriter's Counsel*: Summarizes areas that the underwriter's counsel will complete, including specific state and federal filings and related fees.

- *Offering*: Summarizes decisions reaching on the type of security to be offered, number of shares (min/max), and anticipated price range of the shares. Also covers the nature of the underwriter's performance commitment (e.g., best efforts or firm commitment) and the anticipated offering date and extension details, and identifies the transfer and escrow agents.

- *Percentage Ownership*: Details the number of shares to be offered and the anticipated min/max range of post-offering stock ownership.

- *Offering Commencement*: Typically states that the public offering will be made by the underwriter within three business days of the effective date of the qualification.

- *Future Sales*: The issuer affirms that they will not sell any additional securities without approval of the underwriter for a specified period of time—typically 12 months from the effective date.

- *Mutual Indemnification*: Provides for mutual indemnification by the underwriter and the issuer covering potential liabilities under the Securities Act of 1933.

- *Questionnaire*: Details required information to be provided by the issuer to the underwriter.

- *Notice of Litigation*: Underwriter and issuer mutually agree to inform each other of any litigation or suspension actions that may be initiated by regulators.

- *State Filings*: Sets forth states in which required documents will be filed.[3]

- *Adverse Change*: Provides that the underwriter may withdraw efforts if there is an adverse material change in the issuer's business conditions or in the equity markets.

- *Underwriter Fees*: Discloses the range of fees that will be paid to the underwriter.

- *Expense Allowance*: Sets the amount of expense reimbursement to be paid by the company to the underwriter.

- *Underwriter Warrants*: Details the number of warrants that will be given to the underwriter and related terms, if any.

---

[3]While Reg A+ is exempt from state blue sky filings, notice filings may still be required.

- *Right of Refusal:* Sets forth the right of the underwriter to participate in future fundraising activities.

- *Registration:* Specifies any registrations that the firm must complete.

- *Miscellaneous:* Summarizes any material details not covered in the previous sections. Can include commitments by the issuer to not sell assets, change board positions, disclose revenue figures, and so on.

- *Formal Agreement Contemplated:* Confirms that the parties agree that a final agreement will be concluded and executed prior to the proposed offering date.

The underwriting agreement LOI will also include sections on Reps and Warranties, and Covenants.

Reps and Warranties covers guarantees by the issuer that the information that is provided to the underwriter is true and accurate as of the date of the agreement and that it has completed all of its obligations to file required documents and pay related feeds.

The Covenants section contains guarantees by the issuer that they will *lock up*—that is, that they will not sell shares for a set period of time (usually 180 days) after the initial offering date (see "The Lock-Up Period" below).

The Final Underwriting Agreement

The final underwriting agreement will closely mirror the items detailed in the LOI and, if firmly underwritten, will also include final stock pricing and the number of shares to be issued. Technically, the issuer has the right to back out of the offering until the point that the final underwriting agreement is signed. In most instances, however, accrued expenses owed the underwriter would still need to be paid.

Pricing the Offering

Unlike larger firms, which can often significantly influence the pricing of their shares, the smaller firms that pursue a Reg A+ public offering will need to accept pricing that is largely set by market receptivity—i.e., how effectively the strength of their story drives demand for their shares. Regardless of the desires, wishes, and needs that the issuing firm may have, the pricing process will be controlled by the underwriting firm and its interpretation of feedback from its client base on share prices that are most likely to result in a successful IPO—i.e., one that meets the issuing firm's minimum fundraising objectives.

The process of setting a share price is often called *book building* and refers to efforts by the underwriter to gather feedback from broker–dealers, intermediaries, and key investors to determine a share price that will be most likely to raise minimum amount of funds sought by the issuing firm.

While it may sound intuitive that a higher initial price is better than a lower price, there is a downside to setting a share price that is too high. The risks are higher that 1) the total funds raised will actually be less since not as many shares will be purchased and 2) the stock price may drop in the aftermarket, thereby weakening the perceived attractiveness of the firm for some time.

A good example of this that still sticks in the minds of many investors was the overpricing of Facebook's IPO in 2012. Within 90 days of its IPO, share prices had dropped from an opening price of $38/share to $18.75/share—a loss of over 50% and billions of dollars of value. While Facebook stock has since positively corrected, this huge loss of value (dubbed the "Faceplant") still haunts perceptions of the firm.

Drawing an analogy from the traditional IPO market, most entrepreneurs and investors wish to see their stock rise after an IPO, and the common wisdom is therefore to set an opening price at the lower end of the anticipated trading range even if that means that "something is left on the table."

■ **Tip** When liquidity and equity appreciation are significant objectives of your Reg A+ offering, the ability of the underwriter firm to consistently realize its share price expectations is one of the most important areas that should be investigated when you conduct due diligence. Similarly, an entrepreneur should not select an underwriter solely on the basis of the share price that the underwriter suggests it could deliver.

The Lock-Up Period

A universal provision in the underwriting agreement for offerings of tradable securities is the requirement that employees and executives refrain from selling their shares until a sufficient amount of time passes to allow the share price to stabilize in the secondary market. In traditional IPOs, the minimum lock-up period required is 90 days but can be as long as two years. Many investors closely watch the end of the lock-up period for new issues in an actual IPO, because a significant increase in selling by insiders frequently takes place immediately after the lock-up period ends, causing the share price to decline—sometimes significantly. The conditions for this dynamic apply in the Reg A+ world, as well. Such price declines are often temporary, and good forward planning can mitigate a decline by timing the release of good news (e.g., strong earnings) just ahead of the end of the lock-up.

Aftermarket Pricing

The Reg A+ secondary market is still developing, but many of the considerations applicable to truly public smaller companies with lower trading volumes may be extrapolated to Reg A+ issuers. Smaller companies face significant challenges in obtaining third-party coverage to attract investors to purchase shares of their stock. Also, because the number of traded shares of a smaller firm will represent relatively low amounts of value, even moderately sized buy/sell orders can swing the price quite significantly, creating undesirable volatility in the firm's stock price. This is not an easy problem to solve and requires that the issuing firm have a solid financial public relations plan in place prior to going public. The primary objective of this public relations plan is to release ongoing information about the firm that will aid in maintaining and increasing the value of the firm's shares.

This is a complex topic to address, and a comprehensive discussion of the effective strategies used to bolster share prices of smaller firms is outside the scope of this book. Here, however, are some generalities:

- Once a smaller firm completes its offering, the CEO must devote more time to investor relations and plan to invest efforts each week to reach out to analysts, intermediaries, and other outside parties who can positively influence favorable interest from retail investors to purchase the firm's stock. Many CEOs fall short of the challenges of effectively communicating with outside parties. They should seek critical inputs from their financial PR firm to make sure that adequate energies are being expended.

- Once a firm completes a Tier 2 offering, it will be required to file public reports of its ongoing operations and financial performance. The issuer shall consider whether the CEO will deliver a summary of the past reported performance and provide guidance to interested parties, including current investors, broker–dealers, and industry analysts, among others. The worst thing to report on during these conference calls is a "miss" in achieving expected financial objectives. Meeting or beating expectations should therefore be the top priority in order to keep share prices in a desired range.

- The use of the Internet should be fully exploited to enhance the public image of the firm. This starts by having and (very importantly) maintaining a current web site that looks at least as good as your top competitor's. It also includes extensive use of social media, including Facebook, Twitter, LinkedIn, and so on. News articles on the site need to be plentiful and up to date. Having a blog that covers both company and industry topics will help the web site move up the rankings of search engines. Effective search engine optimization strategies should be employed to ensure that web searches on topics related to the firm will tend to pull up the firm page's URL. Finally, coordinate content that is published on your web site with legal reporting and compliance so that all updates are current and comply with the law.

The Dutch Auction

Noted venture capitalist Bill Hambrecht has updated and revamped an alternative method for setting stock prices that merits consideration.

Originally conceived as a means of selling tulips in Holland, the *Dutch auction* has been successfully utilized by Hambrecht's firm, WR Hambrecht, to raise public funds for firms ranging from Boston Beer to Google.

Hambrecht's form of the Dutch auction, branded as "OpenIPO", starts in a manner similar to what is described in "The Letter of Intent" section earlier in this chapter, such that an investment banker prepares much of the legal documentation along with an analysis of a potential pricing range. However, the final pricing of the public offering is set by the marketplace and not by the investment banker. In contrast to a traditional auction in which pricing starts low and gradually increases due to competitive bidding, the Dutch auction begins with setting the highest expected price. Interested investors then place online bids for a specified number of shares at prices that are lower than the opening price. Bidding is closed when the full amount of capital is raised and all bidders ultimately pay the same lowest per share price that is required to raise the desired equity.

Proponents of the Dutch auction argue that firms can save additional monies that would otherwise be paid to investment bankers. Bankers typically earn 7% of the amount of the offering for selling a deal to their clients, so these selling fees can be very significant. Another argument is that a Dutch auction minimizes the price swings that often occur during the first days of trading relative to large swings that occur when prices are set by investment bankers. Average first day gains for 25 of Hambrecht's IPOs utilizing the Dutch auction averaged 3.1%.[4] By contrast, first-day gains for traditionally-priced firms tend to be much higher. For example, prices were up 73% on Twitter's first day and 109% on LinkedIn's first day. Dutch auction supporters point out that because such gains in the secondary market largely go to investors and not to the issuers, they may be considered as funds that could have been realized by the issuing firms if they had utilized the Dutch auction.

Fans of the traditional investment banker approach emphasize that their process results in more orderly price setting and also better educates investors on the merits of the firm's offering, its competition, and long-term prospects. More than 99% of all IPOs are completed using traditional price-setting processes utilized by investment bankers. The Dutch auction and other novel methods of fundraising clearly face an uphill battle to gain more adherents. Still, for smaller companies that have an established track record and a client base that may be interested in investing in them, the Dutch auction is worth some exploration.

---

[4]http://www.cnbc.com/2014/08/19/es-took-off-but-the-auction-didnt.html

Post-IPO Activities

After filing a Reg A+ mini-IPO, a company needs to address additional respon-sibilities in the areas of accounting, reporting, and investor relations. This chapter covers the basics of what lies ahead after the funds have been raised, including a number of best practices that we have observed in smaller firms.

Accounting and Reporting

Firms that have raised funds under Tier 2 of Reg A+ need to prepare for greater financial and reporting scrutiny that will be required by investors and governmental entities. Failure of firms to comply with regulations in a timely and complete manner can lead not only to a loss of credibility with investors but can (i) jeopardize many of the benefits of Tier 2 (e.g., carve-outs from Rule 12) or their ability to conduct further Reg A+ offerings; and (ii) substantially and negatively impact the market value of the securities held by investors. Any sloppiness or lack of attention to detail needs to be identified and eliminated so that a disciplined process can be established that becomes part of the firm's culture. Ideally, the processes that must be in place after a successful Reg A+ fundraising effort were planned and anticipated as part of the overall fundrais-ing strategy. The key accounting and reporting areas that need to be reviewed and improved as needed include the following:

- Tracking and reporting financial changes per SEC guidelines.
- Closing period financials in a timely and complete manner.

- Ensuring that the firm has experienced personnel who fully understand steps that need to be taken to comply with SEC accounting and reporting requirements.

- Assessing whether the organization has adequate capabilities to accurately project future expectations so that the firm's executives will not lose credibility with investors and analysts.

- Making sure that adequate IT infrastructure is in place to prevent loss of critical data.

At a minimum, the firm must have access to a qualified CPA who understands GAAP financial statements and the reporting requirements under Reg A+. This is not a job to be delegated to a bookkeeper or a recent graduate. Several best practices include:

- Use professional financial software systems such as QuickBooks rather than Excel.

- Institute frequent reviews by the management and the CPA of financial operations and statements to catch errors and omissions.

- Organize all financial data in an electronic repository that can be quickly accessed and has adequate backup protections in case of infrastructure failures.

- Move to a professional payroll service and pay all required payroll taxes on time.

- Keep close track of any required sales taxes, registration, and regulatory fees. Failure to remain current on these items can result in personal liability to management and impact investors' value.

- Document all critical decisions and contracts—no more handshake agreements.

- Keep detailed minutes of all board meetings and keep corporate counsel aware of all significant corporate actions and decisions.

Many small firms may also need to hire a chief finance officer (CFO) who has prior experience with required SEC reporting and filings. Rather than hiring a full-time CFO to supervise new accounting and reporting activities, firms might retain a part-time CFO to avoid the added costs of an additional full-time executive. In most larger metro areas, there are placement agencies that specialize in assisting firms to locate part-time finance executives who have adequate experience.[1]

Dos and Don'ts of Shareholder Recordkeeping

The opportunities created by the JOBS Act are exciting for issuers seeking to raise capital, but its provisions provide additional shareholder recordkeeping challenges for the issuers.

Reg A+ provisions permit an issuer to avail itself of the exemptions afforded by the Securities Act of 1933, but only if the issuer stays within float or revenue limitations and—more importantly for this discussion—employs a professional transfer agent registered with the Securities and Exchange Commission under Section 17A of the Exchange Act.

Accurate records of shareholder ownership and the efficient processing of transactions are essential for investors. An issuer's failure to accurately record or maintain shareholder records (including address changes) or to prevent fraudulent transfers can have the same devastating effect on an investor as if his or her savings were stolen or misdirected through fraud. It is for this reason that Congress and the SEC have continued to recognize the essential importance of registered transfer agents for public securities.

In recent years, changes in the regulatory landscape have significantly expanded the recordkeeping burden. New IRS reporting requirements—most notably those associated with *cost basis reporting*, passed as part of the Emergency Economic Stabilization Act of 2008 and effective since the 2011 tax year—have created a virtual minefield of obstacles for issuers and investors. Now issuers and shareholders must keep cost basis information on a lot-by-lot basis for all securities purchased and sold and report it to the IRS.

Moreover, issuers and their record keepers must comply with the relevant abandoned property/escheatment laws of all 50 states. Issuers are required to keep track of all contacts (such as letters, address changes, telephone contacts, deposited checks, and returned mail) for each and every holder. All contacts must be noted to the shareholder's account. In three-year states such as California and New York, the issuer must mail notification to any holder with whom no contact has been noted for three years that the shareholder's shares or funds will be escheated to the state as abandoned unless the shareholder updates the account.

---

[1]The URLs of some representative agencies that place CFOs include www.thebrennergroup.com, go.expert360.com, www.cfogrowthadvisors.com, and thecfoconnection.com.

So the question arises: What is an issuer to do when confronted with the daunting task of keeping shareholder records compliant with IRS reporting rules and the abandoned property rules of all 50 states? The simple and correct answer is that the issuer must hire a professional transfer agent with the systems and expertise to manage its records. The customary rule in the industry is that if an issuer has more than 75–100 holders of record, then the account should be serviced by a transfer agent.

Professional transfer agents have sophisticated systems, software, and personnel who are expert in all facets of recordkeeping. Stock ledger recordkeeping is a highly technical and specialized area. Small issuers often try to utilize their lawyers or accountants for this task, but that is very unwise. Lawyers and accountants do not have the expertise to handle the task, and they are likely to cost $100–500 per hour (even for paralegal time). By contrast, professional transfer agents typically charge small private companies $200–300 per month for supplying expert services in this very complicated field.

In the normal course of their everyday handling tasks, professional transfer agents keep and update individual shareholder accounts (including name, address, social security number, number of shares, certificate number, date of issuance, cost basis by lot, seasonal addresses, and restrictions on transfer), and they keep company-wide records, including geographical records, share range analysis, restricted shares, and plan shares. Professional transfer agents also track abandoned property rules of the 50 states as they apply to all shareholders, and they will do the requisite lost-shareholder due diligence searches and ultimately escheat property to all 50 states. Transfer agents do all this in the normal course, and they do so efficiently and economically. Lawyers and accountants do not.

The costs associated with not having a professional transfer agent as an issuer's recordkeeper are likely to be very high. First, errors in an issuer's records can lead to the wrong person receiving a record owner's shares; or the record owner may receive the wrong number of shares altogether. Such errors may expose the issuer to significant monetary liability and litigation risk, including legal fees. This is particularly problematic when companies undergo forward or reverse splits, which may obscure errors and magnify exposure. Second, poor recordkeeping and shoddy communications with core investors expose the issuer to reputational risk. Third, confidential shareholder information, including address and social security number, may be disclosed unwittingly or may be vulnerable to data breaches when the records are not held in the secure environment that is provided by a highly regulated registered transfer agent, particularly a bank agent.

An issuer's shareholder records, if not properly secured, will subject the issuer to the liability associated with identity theft of its shareholders. Both federal and state "red flag" laws impose significant restrictions and penalties for data breaches resulting in identity theft of shareholders' personal information. This exposure is far from hypothetical: the news media over the past five years have reported innumerable data breaches costing public companies untold billions of dollars. The dangers are real and can prove very painful and damaging to an emerging company.

Titles II and III of the JOBS Act have already incorporated a requirement that issuers and funding portals use "banks" or registered brokers as escrow agents to ensure proper recordkeeping and minimize the risk of defalcation. Likewise, Title II and III issuers must certify to funding platforms that they have established adequate means to maintain accurate records, and the funding platform must have a "reasonable basis" to believe the same. The commission's recent release of the Reg A+ rules goes one step further for Tier 2 offerings: issuers for Tier 2 offerings must use a registered transfer agent to be exempt from registration under Section 12 of the Exchange Act. The message for JOBS Act issuers is clear: retain a professional agent where required and proceed at your own peril if you decide not to do so where not specifically required, as with Tier 1 offerings.

Digitized Recordkeeping

As market professionals are aware, there has been a concerted effort since the 1980s to move away from certificated shares and ownership to electronic recordkeeping a book-entry ownership. This process has been called *dematerialization* or *demobilization* and has been a central tenet of the SEC's move to make the Clearance and Settlement System more efficient and less subject to risk.

The creation and expansion of the Depository Trust Company (DTC) has led to dematerialization of all shares held for shareholders by banks and brokers ("street name shares"), which now comprise well more than 80% of all shares held in U.S. publicly traded securities. The remaining 20% or less are shares registered on the books of the issuer—either certificated or book-entry—and registered in the name of the owner.

The push for dematerialization of publicly-traded shares has come from both the SEC and DTC on behalf of its bank and broker ownership. Indeed, book-entry eligibility of all U.S. exchange traded issues became mandatory in January 2009, under a system called *mandatory DRS*. As a result, all such securities were dematerialized so that book-entry statements were henceforth issued to holders in lieu of physical stock certificates. Book-entry ownership has also been the default position for all dividend reinvestment plans and employee stock option plans for many years.

In this dematerialized environment, both "street" holders and "registered" holders are accustomed to receiving book-entry statements reflecting their share ownership and can engage in purchases and sales just as they would in a certificated environment—only more efficiently. Accordingly, both institutional holders and individual investors have been used to book-entry ownership for many years.

Why then, you might ask, have many (if not most) private companies—even those high-tech companies originating in Silicon Valley—continued to issue stock certificates to investors rather than moving to book-entry ownership? This is strange indeed given that these titans of tech are often promoting technology companies whose investors include well-known venture funds and private equity titans. While some of these companies (and their lawyers and accountants) have seen the light, most still issue physical stock certificates to investors, which seems an anachronistic and archaic practice.

Certificated shares make no sense at all in this day and age, and the concept of keeping paper stockholder records is inconsistent with Reg A+, which is philosophically focused on reducing barriers for smaller firms. Certificated shares have the following major disadvantages: they lead to lost certificates, which can be difficult and expensive to replace; they must be called in and re-presented to the issuer for reverse splits or other recapitalization events; and they must be called in for re-legending of Securities Act legends, affiliate legends, or other contractual restrictions that must be affixed to the securities.

In the case of lost certificates, replacement generally requires the shareholder of record to submit an affidavit of loss and indemnity and often a surety bond, which can cost 2–3% of the value of the lost securities. This is often a significant hassle and can lead to confrontations and complaints from key early-stage investors. All of these issues simply disappear with a book-entry statement, which can be easily replaced without any of these requirements.

Digitized, book-entry positions mimic tried-and-true models that have been used by the most advanced and sophisticated public companies in the DRS settlement system as well as DRP and DSPP models. They are used every day by tens of millions of records and beneficial owners. It makes absolutely no sense for emerging companies, many in the high-tech world, to issue physical stock certificates rather than book-entry positions. Using book-entry also sends the right message to key investors and to market professionals, and will facilitate as well any ultimate-exit strategy, whether it be a sale or an IPO.

In getting ready for a Reg A+ mini-IPO, the well-prepared issuer will not only move to book-entry ownership, but they should likely outsource their record-keeping to a professional stock transfer agent with the expertise and systems to assist them. A transfer will likely cost far less than lawyers' and accountants' time, and they will ensure that your records are kept in a secure and digitized environment. This will make the transition from a private company to a public company via an IPO a seamless one—no last-minute panic attacks, calling in old certificates, processing recaps and stock splits, or affixing restrictive legends. A foresighted company will have digitized and outsourced its records to avoid such last-minute nightmares.

An additional significant advantage of book-entry prior to an IPO is that selling shareholders and their attorney-in-fact will not have to hunt for certificates and replace lost securities. Book-entry avoids all of that needless hassle and confusion, and selling shareholders—often key employees and early-stage investors—will be well served.

For private companies that grow large but choose to remain private (such as Uber, Dropbox, Xiaomi, and Airbnb), the move to digitized recordkeeping and a professional transfer agent is equally important, if not more so. Companies such as these often have raised capital in many rounds or series of offerings. They also generally have many employees and executives who are equity owners because their compensation is often based in significant part on stock options and grants as well as restricted stock units. The recordkeeping for these highly capitalized private companies is often kept by lawyers, stock plan administrators, and in-house personnel. However, whether you use a professional transfer agent or a combination of lawyers, stock plan administrators, and in-house personnel, the records should absolutely be maintained in a secure, digitized, and book-entry environment.

A centralized book-entry platform will allow investors, including venture firms and private equity firms, to access their holdings via the Internet 24/7 using a simple PIN code. For venture and private equity firms that have many portfolio companies or investments in many private issuers, the use of one centralized book-entry platform—i.e., one stock transfer agent—will allow them to access all of their holdings anytime and anywhere. No more certificates being held in the venture of PE firm's vault, and no more needless audits. Digitized, book-entry recordkeeping is clearly the right answer for these large private companies and their investors.

Additionally, one of the great hopes for the JOBS Act is that a secondary trading market will develop for Reg A+ issuers. Once Reg A+ secondary trading markets do indeed develop and succeed, you can be sure that they will operate in a totally digitized and book-entry environment. If that is the case, any and all private (or public) issuers who wish to trade on these exchanges will benefit greatly if they have planned ahead and moved to book-entry at the earliest possible stage.

Moreover, when secondary trading markets develop, the ultimate hope is that such markets would link to the brokerage community via a Depository Trust and Clearing Corporation (DTCC) interface. In this way, the buy side and the sell side could be truly linked together in a functional way to allow for full monetization and ease of processing. That is the hope. Whether it comes to pass remains to be seen.

Regardless of the success or failure of secondary trading markets, the advantages of digitized, book-entry recordkeeping for all private companies are clear and obvious, as laid out. A forward-thinking private issuer as well as its lawyers, accountants, and other advisors should move to such an environment as soon as possible to minimize risk and promote efficiency and connectivity in line with current technological advances.

Having covered important basics related to accounting, reporting, and record keeping, let us now shift to how small firms should plan to interact with their investors and other key industry groups to maintain interest and value in their shares.

Investor Relations for Reg A+ Firms

One of the most challenging aspects of raising public funds for a small company is the need to maintain appropriate communications with the firm's investors after funds have been raised. The opinions that investors hold about firms in which they have committed capital can be as important as perceptions that customers have about the firm's products and services. Investors who become unhappy with a firm's performance can publish unfavorable comments on any number of financial web sites that can be just as damaging to a firm's reputation as negative comments from customers.

Furthermore, unhappy investors can make it much more difficult for a firm to raise future funds, as new investors can be expected to look at past performance before committing fresh funds. Unfortunately, we see too many small firms forgetting about investors after they have obtained funding and succumbing to the temptation to focus solely on the challenges of growing the business rather investing appropriate time communicating with investors.

The remainder of this chapter covers a number of techniques used by smaller firms to develop and maintain good investor relations. At the onset it is worth noting that smaller firms have significantly greater challenges than larger firms, owing to the much smaller number of outside parties who may have interest in writing about ongoing developments. If you put the name of a larger firm such as Apple, Facebook, or Tesla into a daily Google search, you will find many articles and comments from third parties. By contrast, smaller firms rarely receive mention from third parties and instead need to rely almost solely on the communications that are directly developed by the firm's executives or their investor relations firm.

While we know of many CEOs who are excellent communicators and can easily compose content about their companies, we believe that smaller firms can benefit by hiring a third-party investor relationships (IR) specialist. A good IR specialist can institute a disciplined approach that can allow a firm to allocate and balance resources between the needs of growing the business and of communicating with investors. He or she will also provide the firm with valuable insights on the practices of competitors and introductions to key centers of influence that can further build the firm's reputation.

Investor versus Customer Communication

It is natural and common for key executives to develop skills for communicating with customers. Indeed, the top executives in a small firm and especially the CEO are often the most effective sales people. The skills and techniques used for selling products and services to customers are in many ways similar to communicating with investors, but they differ in a number of important respects. Selling is fundamentally about convincing customers that they will derive benefits in acquiring products and services that are perceived to be more valuable than the funds used to make the purchase. The foundation of good investor relations is primarily about how effectively the firm performs in meeting or exceeding previously set financial expectations.

Many executives who are skilled in selling products fall short when they are put in a position to communicate and are held accountable for financial objectives. While it is common and even acceptable for a sales pitch to contain some level of exaggerated claims of benefits and hyperbolic language ("This is insanely great!"), this style will quickly destroy investor communications.

In contrast to selling, investor communications need to be tempered and unemotional, emphasizing facts and accomplishments and setting future guidance on reasonable extrapolations of past results. Let's break down the critical components of a comprehensive IR communication, beginning with those areas that are similar to the points emphasized during the fundraising process.

Strategy

Investors prefer that a firm's strategy remain consistent unless new facts come to light that can result in greater success through modest course corrections. Sudden unexpected changes in direction cause investors to become nervous and lose confidence. Strategy changes should be announced by first restating the former strategy and then describing the new facts that require changes. Strategy changes are best explained in terms of new data that has been uncovered, as opposed to admissions that the firm's executives made mistakes in setting forth the previous strategy. While there are many wise sayings that praise the virtue of admitting one's mistakes, investors will lose faith in a CEO who too frequently admits he or she was mistaken.

To summarize: be consistent, make only incremental changes based on new facts, and go easy on admitting mistakes.

Track Record

Once investors contribute capital to an enterprise they will tend to focus more on how actual results compare with previous expectations and less on future expectations. Examples of this abound during earnings announcements for publicly traded companies. An earnings shortfall of even a few pennies can sometimes have a large negative impact on stock values, even in spite of what the firm says about positive expectations for the next quarter. CEOs who consistently miss expectations can expect to have short job tenure unless they possess unusually strong offsetting skills and abilities.

A good IR strategy includes ongoing messages in the form of "here is what we said we would do, and here is what we actually did that met or bettered previously set expectations." In other words, foster a corporate culture and style of communication whereby you strive to undercommit and overdeliver.

Profits Matter

While operational successes such as product releases, new customers, awarded patents, clinical trials, approvals, and certifications are all very important, a firm's financial results are even more important to investors, and profit growth is the most important number. Firms that have not yet become profitable must strive to disclose plans and results that demonstrate how their financial performance is trending toward breakeven and beyond to profitability.

While there are extended cycles when investors are swayed by nonfinancial metrics such as eyeballs, users, subscribers, and likes, such ebullient times are always followed by market corrections that cause investors to refocus on fundamentals. And making profits—or at least making tangible progress in that direction—is the most important fundamental that investors care about.

The ability of a firm to achieve a breakeven cash flow position is most critical for smaller firms. Investors will face a dilution of their interests if cash runs out and a new round of capital is needed. Unless earlier investors are willing to contribute additional funds, new investors in a subsequent funding round will gain ownership at the expense of the previous investors. While seed investors will typically expect that additional funds will need to be raised to achieve growth objectives, later-round investors will typically expect their capital to be the last capital needed to take a firm to breakeven.

Most CEOs—especially if their core competency is in nonfinancial areas such as engineering—are well advised to have their CFOs involved in key investor-related communications. A tag-team CEO–CFO approach when communicating with investors has the added benefit of demonstrating solidarity among top executives in the firm's vision and direction.

Corporate Web Site

Today the corporate web site is the most common and important means of establishing and maintaining a corporate identity and, for better or worse, it creates strong impressions that influence investor perceptions. A top objective in your IR strategy is to create and maintain a very professional and current web site. The days of "set-it-and-forget-it" web sites have long passed, and modern web sites must be constantly maintained and updated (at least monthly) with the latest news and other content, often including a blog in which the CEO can provide content in a more conversational and informal style. The web site also should include a discrete "For Investors" area containing links to the firm's public disclosures and contain other information appropriate for investors.

Reg A+ allows electronic filings to EDGAR, a web site hosted by the SEC where investment disclosures are posted for public viewing. Links to these documents on the EDGAR web site are often added to the "For Investors" section of the firm's web site.

The content on the corporate web site as well as postings made to social media such as Facebook, Twitter, LinkedIn, and YouTube may be subject to numerous SEC regulations. As an example, Regulation FD, often referred to as the *Fair Disclosure Regulation*, requires that whenever issuers disclose material nonpublic information to certain individuals or entities—such as securities market professionals, stock analysts, or groups that may trade the firm's stock based on the disclosed information—the issuer must make a full public disclosure of that information. Regulation FD aims to promote the full and fair disclosure to minimize special advantages that certain groups or entities can gain over average investors who may otherwise not have access to the same information.

Due to the many regulations that govern public disclosures, many firms as a best practice have their corporate counsels review content before posting online to ensure compliance.

Media Relations

In addition to frequent direct communication to investors, an effective IR strategy must utilize mass communications via print and electronic media, as well as ongoing communications and interactions with various trade and industry organizations. Organizing this effort is the primary role of an investor relations firm, and a good firm will develop a detailed calendar of activities that can fully take advantage of key media opportunities.

It is very important to develop and stick to a discipline of investing some time each week to leverage media channels to deliver information about your firm. Like many ideas that start with the best of intentions only to run out of steam, small firms must attend to the important job of cultivating media exposure in order to build interest in their firm that will ultimately lead to higher values for its traded shares.

CEOs of smaller firms would be especially well advised to attend investment conferences where similar companies deliver presentations about their plans and progress to groups of brokers and bankers.[2] Some well-known conferences for smaller firms are hosted by the following organizations:

www.sidoti.com
www.redchip.com
www.marcumllp.com
www.ldmicro.com
www.onemedconferences.com

Smaller firms are usually charged a fee of several thousands of dollars to present at these conferences—and individuals representing brokers, banks, or investors are often allowed to attend at very low or no cost. This encourages a larger audience for the presenting firms and a greater likelihood that firms will have success in meeting interested parties who can help them attain financial objectives. There is merit in attending these conferences even as an observer if you feel you are not yet ready to present; you will learn a great deal about the networking process and be able to make a better showing when you are ready.

Cultivate Analysts

An important milestone is reached when third parties begin to take an interest in publishing reports about a firm. It is not uncommon that the value of small firm's stock can take a significant jump when a professional analyst announces that they are beginning to cover or periodically report on the firm. Many firms struggle with locating and then cultivating relationships with professional analysts. The easiest way to learn who to target is first to identify all larger firms similar to your own and then determine which analysts are covering them. If you do not find any initially, just keep looking for firms that are larger in sales volume and you will soon learn who to go after. Attending industry conferences—particularly those that attract investment bankers and venture capitalists—can also provide excellent networking opportunities and increase your odds of establishing a relationship with a qualified analyst. Obviously, also seek introductions from attorneys, accountants, and other industry executives with whom you have good relations.

---

[2]Some well-known conferences for smaller firms are hosted by the following organizations: www.sidoti.com, www.redchip.com, www.marcumllp.com, www.ldmicro.com, and www.onemedconferences.com.

In parallel to efforts to reach professional analysts, smaller firms should invest time developing a following among lesser-known industry analysts, due diligence providers, and commentators who publish on the web part-time as an avocation rather than on a full-time professional basis. Perhaps the best source of locating these individuals is the web site www.SeekingAlpha.com. This site attracts thousands of individuals and industry experts who write about mostly smaller firms. The quality of the content varies considerably but, at its best, many of these writers provide commentaries that equal those produced by full-time professional analysts. We have direct experience proving that a favorable commentary on SeekingAlpha can have a significant impact on stock value.

Summary

A successful Reg A+ fundraising effort is not an end in itself but the beginning of a new phase of business operations that should be considered as a step forward toward a full-blown IPO. No matter whether a firm ultimately lists on a national exchange, gets acquired, or remains status quo, once funds are raised, the company must adopt a public company mindset and take all appropriate actions needed to meet compliance issues as well as the greater responsibilities that come with having outside investors and key third parties that can influence the value of the firm's shares.

Having highlighted a number of best practices in this chapter, we would like to close by reinforcing perhaps the best way of learning how to develop optimum post-IPO processes and procedures. Make a concerted effort to meet with companies that have already graduated to the next step and are similar enough to your firm that you can clearly see what they have done to meet the added challenges that come with accepting funds from outsiders and dealing with regulators.

If you determine that your firm comes up short in needed internal talent, consider adding experienced personnel to your board of directors, hiring a part-time CFO, or seeking out needed resources from consulting organizations. If you look earnestly, you will find many helping hands who may willing to assist and who perhaps would be willing to take a portion of their compensation in stock.

Having real stock that has the potential of being tradable is a major benefit of Reg A+ and can provide added incentives to encourage talented and experienced people to join with you to help realize your objectives.

Secondary Markets and Regulation A+ Securities

We discuss throughout this book that one of the great potential advantages of Reg A+ securities is the ability to freely trade shares. However, beyond isolated, negotiated trades between brokers or investors, the development of the infrastructure of a real secondary market is still nascent and has a lot of room to grow. In this chapter—to give context and to help you understand the needs of a vibrant secondary market and how new trading options may develop for Reg A+ shares—we discuss the history of the development of exchanges, dynamics of the current stock market and, in particular, those dynamics when investing in "small-cap" companies. We also discuss venture exchanges as an analog to secondary markets and conclude by reviewing a couple of market options that are currently available to facilitate trading of Reg A+ shares.

History of Stock Exchanges

The concept of a market is as old as civilization itself. The act of trading goods and services was one of the driving factors in creating organized society. From the early civilizations of Mesopotamia, to the Incan empire, the market has always been the focal point of a society. Generally considered to be the economic driver of trade, the market has taken many forms, trading foodstuffs, spices, and other commodities throughout history.

A stock market or equity market is the aggregation of buyers and sellers (a loose network of economic transactions, not a physical facility or discrete entity) of stocks (also called shares); these may include securities listed on a stock exchange as well as those only traded privately.

While the first stock market is something that has been debated among historians, debt instruments and the idea of interest bearing investments go back to the beginning of known civilization, with scholars finding clay tablets recording interest-bearing loans from Mesopotamia. The concept of stock, or an equity interest in an enterprise, is something that evolved much later. There is little consensus among scholars as to when corporate stock was first traded. Some link the first equity-based stock to the Dutch East India Company's founding in 1602,[1] while others point to earlier developments. Economist Ulrike Malmendier of the University of California at Berkeley argues that a share market existed as far back as the Roman Republic.[2] Regardless of the timing of the first stock market, almost immediately thereafter, a regulatory body was established to implement controls to prevent market manipulation and fraudulent activity.

Historians have found evidence of trade unions several hundred years before the Roman Empire, in which contractors or leaseholders would perform temple-building or other services on behalf of the government. Participants in these organizations held shares that could be considered close to what we would consider partnership or equity interest today. The orator Cicero has been quoted saying that these "shares that had a very high price at the time," indicating that these interests could be bought and sold, and may well have been traded on the first secondary market for stocks. Despite the existence of such an exchange, these markets did not persist due to both political and economic changes brought on by the shift from a republic to an empire.

---

[1]https://en.wikipedia.org/wiki/Dutch_East_India_Company
[2]https://en.wikipedia.org/wiki/Stock_exchange

The first tradeable bonds as a commonly used security were a more recent innovation that was first seen during the Renaissance period in the Italian city-states of Florence and Venice. The Italian city-states, ruled by a council of citizens as opposed to a monarch, were the first governments to issue government securities. In the middle of the 13th Century, Venetian bankers began to trade in government securities, which then led to the first regulation of the market, when in 1351 the Venetian government outlawed spreading rumors intended to lower the price of government funds.

Italian companies were also the first to issue shares, with companies from England and the Netherlands soon to follow suit.

The first true stock exchange, the one we are familiar with today, was founded in Amsterdam when the Dutch East India Company was the first joint-stock company to get a fixed capital stock that allowed for continuous trading of company stock. Shortly thereafter, a number of derivatives, options, and other contracts appeared on the Amsterdam market. The Dutch were also the first to engage in short selling, which led the Dutch authorities to ban the practice as early at 1610.

The Amsterdam trader, Joseph de la Vega, also known as Joseph Penso de la Vega, wrote the first book on the inner workings of a stock market, Confusion of Confusions, in 1688. The book described a market that was sophisticated but also prone to excesses.

The markets evolved in 1693 when King William of England used government bonds to finance the country's wars, and the Bank of England was set up the following year. This allowed for English joint-stock companies and facilitated the first English public offerings.

Despite the existence of the Royal Exchange, brokers of the joint-stock companies were banned from participating, and rather they conducted their business in local coffee shops. One broker, John Castaing, posted regular lists of stock and commodity prices, which became the foundation of the London Stock Exchange.

One of the driving forces behind the London Stock Exchange was the trading companies that were established to exploit the opportunities of the new world, such as The South Sea Company and the Mississippi Company. Investor appetite for these new offerings was considerable, and led to one of the first bubbles in the market. At the height of the New World-driven bubble, in 1720, blind pool companies were even being offered.

Shortly thereafter, it became clear that expectations of imminent wealth from the Americas were overblown, and share prices collapsed, forcing the government to act. Parliament passed the Bubble Act, mandating that only royally-chartered companies could issue public shares, greatly reducing the size and scope of the public markets for some time. This opened the door for the first stock markets in the newly established United States of America in the 1790s.

The Markets of Today

The financial system in most developed countries is considerably more complex today, with the introduction of electronic trading systems replacing human trading and the disintermediation of banks from the savings and lending business. Traditionally, local banks played a larger role in financing, using bank deposits of its customers to place funds into securities. Today, market participants can directly access investment banking products, trade in dark pools, and actively manage their portfolios without the need to use a direct intermediary. Additionally, the public is an active participant with more pension plans, retirement accounts, and mutual funds placing capital directly into the markets.

With the introduction of electronic trading, the markets are considerably more vulnerable to systemic risks associated with programs and algorithms that react to overall market movements. As such, in recent market crashes, electronic trading can effectively remove buyers from the market during these swings.

There have been famous stock market crashes that have caused billions of dollars in losses and global wealth destruction. The most notable crashes include the Wall Street Crash of 1929, 1973-4, Black Monday of 1987, the dot-com bubble of 2000, the Housing Bubble crash of 2008, and the Flash Crash of 2015.

In the crash of 1929, the Dow Jones Industrial Average lost 50% of its value, leading to the start of the Great Depression. Black Monday began with the market in Hong Kong but quickly affected all markets globally. At the bottom of the crash, the Hong Kong market had crashed 45.5%, Spain 31%, the UK 26.4%, the United States 22.7%, and Canada 22.5%. Notably, Black Friday was the biggest one-day drop in the stock market, with the Dow Jones losing 22.6% in a single trading session.

One of the mysteries of Black Friday is the lack of a major new event or other indicator to cause the immediate selloff. Rather, the crash has caused a number of academics and economists to propose various new theories of market dynamics, including irrational human behavior, efficient markets, and even the underlying assumption that markets are rational.

As a result of the largest single-day crash, regulators introduced a number of new market controls that were designed to prevent such significant losses again in the future. These included halting the markets when large drops occurred and other measures designed to allow for more holistic reviews of market activities.

One adoption following Black Friday was the introduction of electronic trading. Rather than stocks trading via human callers, software was introduced that performed the duties of matching buyers and sellers. Computers could handle larger trading volumes and the thinking was that this should prevent large market crashes due to inefficiencies in human trading.

Additionally, the SEC in the United States increased the margin requirements, in an attempt to remove blatant speculation from the markets.

Trading vs. Capital Formation

While the stock markets were initially envisioned to match buyers and sellers, or direct participants, in actuality, the markets have created a new breed of participant, traders. These traders are generally not party to the underlying transaction, i.e., a future contract for the delivery of a barrel of oil, and have no long-term interest in the underlying security other than using it to be able to profit from the trading of the note. Traders participate in the market in many ways, and they are allowed to participate in the market because of the idea that they create market liquidity. However, some individuals believe that excessive trading is one of the reasons that markets no longer offer the same advantages as they once did.

The cost of going public has risen steadily, and early capital formation has become an expensive endeavor reserved for only large-cap companies. The idea of going public for early stage companies is no longer cost effective and exposes issuers to trader, market makers and other third parties that can greatly affect a firm's stock.

Trading Strategies

Traders in the market can employ a number of strategies to profit off the securities markets, some of which can have an underlying detrimental impact on the underlying security, or in other cases the issuing company. One such strategy is called *short selling*, in which a trader "borrows" a stock from a broker and then sells it in the market with the idea that the price of the stock will decrease. If the stock does in fact decrease, the trader can then purchase the stock at a lower price and repay the loan, pocketing the difference in price between the time the stock was borrowed and the new price, only paying the broker interest on the transaction.

Another similar strategy involves creating a financial *derivative*, in which a contract is written allowing a trader to control a large amount of shares without actually owning the underlying security. Both short selling and derivatives pose significant risk to the issuers and defeats the underlying purpose of public markets. Generally, these strategies benefit few individuals, but are legal under the guise of market liquidity. In reality, smaller issuers see no benefit from traders in their shares, and would be better served with less liquidity in their stocks.

Short selling is especially dangerous to thinly traded shares because a rogue trader can manipulate a stock with very little capital risk. This has led to markets either preventing short selling or placing market capitalization restrictions on the practice. In the United States, while some of these restrictions have been implemented, the practice still occurs.

The opposite of shorting a stock is called *going long*. In this case, a trader borrows money from a brokerage and uses it to purchase shares. If and when the stock increases in value, the trader can sell the shares to cover the loan, pocketing the difference in price minus the interest payment. In the event that that stock decreases in price, the brokerage may ask for repayment of the loan, known as a *margin call*. Most markets have placed restrictions on the amount of margin buying allowed. In the United States, traders are required to hold 50% of the trade value in cash in their brokerage account to be able to trade on margin.

Margin trading regulations were introduced after the 1929 market crash, prior to which there were very low margin restrictions, with brokers allowing traders to have 10% in cash to enter into a long position.

Another strategy that has since been outlawed, and is similar in practice to kiting checks, is known as *free riding*. This is when a trader purchases shares and then sells them before having paid for the initial trade. Settlement of trading generally takes three days and if a trader believes that shares are going increase in price, he or she could place a buy order and sell the shares within the three days and pocket the difference.

All of these strategies, while potentially profitable, have been largely frowned upon by regulators and contradict the underlying purpose of the markets to provide liquidity for securities.

Regulators have attempted to remove a great majority of speculation from the market; however, traders have continued to develop new ways to profit from the existence of the markets.

Issues with Today's Market Structure

Traders today are no longer just individuals: computer programs are also actively participating and manipulating the markets. High-frequency computerized stock trading now controls more than half the market.[3]

---

[3]https://en.wikipedia.org/wiki/High-frequency_trading

Recently, the New York attorney general and the federal government have opened up investigations into this type of trading in response to a book published by Michael Lewis, called *Flash Boys*. In it, Lewis argues that the stock market is now rigged to benefit a group of insiders that have made tens of billions of dollars exploiting computerized trading. In his book, Lewis outlines how, in his words, the "United States stock market, the most iconic market in global capitalism, is rigged by a combination of these stock exchanges, the big Wall Street banks, and high-frequency traders." Lewis argues that the high-frequency traders are essentially front running stock orders and driving prices up for traditional investor based on insider information that is available to them before the general public becomes aware of information.

This front running happens because stocks are no longer traded on floors of stock exchanges, but by computers. The NYSE ceased to be the center of U.S. financial activity years ago, and exists today mostly as a photo op. Today, most of the trades take place at more than 60 public and private exchanges, where billions of dollars in stock change hands every day with little or no public documentation. The trades are being made by thousands of robot computers without human interaction. These programs were also thought to be the cause of the August 2015 market crash.

Lewis states, "Humans have been completely removed from the marketplace."

"Fast" is the operative word. Machines with secret programs are now trading stocks in tiny fractions of a second, way too fast to be seen or recorded on a stock ticker or computer screen. Faster than the market itself. High-frequency traders, big Wall Street firms, and stock exchanges have spent billions to gain an advantage of a millisecond for themselves and their customers, just to get a peek at stock market prices and orders a flash before everyone else, along with the opportunity to act on it.

This form of front running means that high-frequency traders can identify an investor's desire, for example, to buy shares in Microsoft and buy them before the investor and sell them back to the investor at a higher price. In other words, it's like you wanted to buy a hamburger at McDonalds and rather than give your order to the cashier, you give it to the person in front of you in line. He then buys the hamburger and turns around and sells it to you for more than he paid, making a tiny profit, just by standing in front of you in line. This front running happens in infinitesimally small periods of time, but it still allows for traders to act.

Brad Katsuyama, a trader at the Royal Bank of Canada, realized that high-frequency trading was occurring when he tried to understand why none of his trades were being completely filled. Upon investigation, he uncovered that when his order was placed on one exchange, high-frequency traders were beating his order to other exchanges and buying his stocks in front of him. To combat this, he started his own trading platform that is attempting to remove high-frequency traders from the market.

Katsuyama uncovered that the methodology that allowed for this to occur was a direct result of the logistics of how traders are processed and routed on the Internet. A new exchange started by Katsuyama called the IEX,[4] or the investor's exchange, was launched quietly in September 2013 with the support of some of the biggest players on Wall Street. And it comes with built-in speed bumps to eliminate the advantage of high-speed predators.

Large Cap vs. Small Cap

When characterizing equities, the market capitalization of a company plays a significant impact on the capability of the issuer to be able to withstand public markets. Equities are generally characterized by their market capitalization. "Capitalization" refers to the size of a company, calculated by multiplying its current stock price by the number of shares outstanding. The biggest companies are considered mega-cap, which are those with market capitalization of over $100B dollars. Large-cap companies are considered those with $10B in market capitalization. mid-cap stocks are generally companies between $2 and $10B; small-cap are from $300M to $2B; micro-caps are from $50 to $300M; and nano-cap stocks are under $50M in capitalization. Most new Reg A+ stocks would therefore be considered micro- or nano-cap stocks.

From an investment perspective, market capitalization can have a large impact on the growth of a security. From an issuer perspective, market capitalization is generally a good indicator of public market sophistication, meaning that smaller companies are less likely to have the capability of investor protections and investor relations' functionality. As a result, the markets for trading shares of smaller-cap companies have been either disappearing or going private to protect themselves from the public markets.

Historically, despite the significantly higher volatility of smaller cap stocks, they have generally outperformed large-cap stocks. From the crash in 1929 to today, smaller capitalized stock have averaged an annual return of over 12%, while larger capitalized stocks have returned just over 10% according to MorningStar. The issue behind this is that larger-cap companies are generally market leaders in their fields and do not have the same growth prospects. Larger companies do not have the same capability to expand their markets. As a result, larger-cap companies tend to be active participants in acquiring companies that can add growth capability. The companies generally targeted are smaller-caps, making investment into these companies additionally beneficial.

---

[4]https://en.wikipedia.org/wiki/IEX

Reg A+ should increase the number of smaller-cap companies available to non-accredited investors, allowing for the general public to participate in the largest component of wealth creation in the United States today.

Positive Features of a Functional Stock Market

A properly functioning stock market is one of the main drivers of a sound economy. A functioning market will provide a direct barometer of the economic health of an economy, provide for ample supply and demand, ensure that listing companies have been fully vetted and are not fraudulent actors, provide a large enough secondary market to support capital formation and continued investment in the economy, provide ample transparency to provide comfort for market participants, provide a managed process for third-party traders to facilitate liquidity without harming market function, and provide a savings and investment vehicle for the society at large.

Existing Venture Exchanges

Several larger global exchanges, including the London Exchange and the Singapore Exchange, have developed secondary markets for earlier stage companies, commonly referred to as *venture exchanges*. One such exchange, the Alternative Investment Market (AIM), was developed to provide earlier access to the capital markets for younger companies.[5] A recent study on the AIM was conducted to identify how the exchange functioned for listing companies, in addition to the quality of the market as a whole. Since 1995, over 2,300 British and 400 foreign companies have listed on the AIM, raising almost $79B in new capital.

The study found that some of the key benefits of the AIM and venture exchanges are specialized regulation designed for smaller companies, wide investor attraction, strong secondary market performance, low failure rates, and strong liquidity for larger companies, all characteristics needed for a vibrant market. The AIM has been in existence for 20 years, and it proves that the venture exchange model can work and assist with capital formation for growth-stage companies.

---

[5]https://en.wikipedia.org/wiki/Alternative_Investment_Market

Case Studies

Back in the early 70s and 80s, the markets served smaller companies and facilitated early capital formation for some of the most notable companies of today. One of the biggest success stories of the late 20th Century is the story of Intel. The firm was established in Mountain View, California in 1968 by Gordon E. Moore (of "Moore's Law" fame), and Robert Noyce, a physicist and co-inventor of the integrated circuit. While the firm has some initial venture capital, the firm accesses the public markets very early on in the company's development. Prior to going public, the company had revenues of $3,978,000 and profit before extraordinary items of $93,000. Intel went public, just two years after its founding, with a common stock underwriting of 350,000 shares at $23.50 per share, for a total of $8.225M and for a post-money value of $58M. This offering included 42,000 shares for selling shareholders.

The size and scale of Intel's IPO was common in the 70s. On April 18, 1972, Datascope, a firm with $973,000 in revenue, went public with an offering of 105,000 shares at $19 per share, raising $2,011,000 of which $977,000 went to selling shareholders. Datascope's post-money value was $9M. Datascope was sold in 2009 for $865M. Also in the 70s, Storage Technology went public at a market cap of $13M; Four Phase Systems raised $15M; Cray Research raised $10M; and Tandem Computers raised $9.4M. In 1980, Sci-Tex raised $6.8M from initial offerings. Even Adobe went public with a small offering raising $6M in 1986. It would have been impossible for any of these companies to go public in today's environment. Virtually all the buyers of these securities were individuals, as opposed to institutional investors, who make up the majority of the market today.

While the size of Intel's IPO may be surprising by today's standards of $100M + IPOs, the most interesting part of the IPO was that there were 64 underwriters in the selling group. Of the 64, only five are still in existence today. Such a small offering, with the number of brokers in the selling group, would all but be impossible today due to the new restrictions and regulations implemented by the SEC following the dot-com and housing bubble crashes. Intel benefited from easy access to the public markets and was able to raise much needed capital. Today, smaller market companies do not have this option and are forced to raise capital from the private markets, a much slower and harder process. With the passage of the JOBS Act, there is hope in the marketplace that the public markets will reopen for smaller companies.

The JOBS Act and Secondary Trading

The future of crowdfunding and early capital formation depends on a vibrant and active secondary market for the new Reg A+ securities. While the JOBS Act has provided a mechanism for early-stage public capital formation, the Act does not actively address the need for secondary market liquidity. There has been some talk by the SEC as well as by prominent members of existing exchanges as to how these new venture exchanges should operate to provide liquidity and investor protections.

As discussed in previous chapters, Reg A+ securities are freely tradeable, meaning that they can trade on any registered exchange or trading platform. However, by definition, the Reg A+ companies are earlier stage micro-caps, meaning that they are less likely to be prepared for public markets and the various trader issues.

Existing early-stage exchanges have had success in overseas markets, such as the SIM VSE in Australia and the CSE in Canada. They have shown that venture exchanges can function and provide market liquidity; however, these exchanges do not actively address the key issues with early-stage and thinly-traded securities. Currently in the United States, micro-cap companies generally lack market support either in the form of active market makers, or low shareholder count, thus allowing for uncertain market pricing and market manipulation.

Unlike private-placement securities, Reg A+ securities are freely tradeable, meaning that initial investors can easily trade their shares. Without a purpose-defined marketplace, it becomes difficult for holders of Reg A+ securities to trade.

Current Market Options: ASMX

The ASMX was developed to provide liquidity for Reg A+ securities, but also provide a safe environment for trading of these new securities. For issuers, it is important that their stock price cannot be actively manipulated by a single rogue trade or via market activists.

The ASMX is a primary and secondary trading platform that harkens back to the early days of a stock exchange, where buyers and sellers met face to face. On the ASMX, trading is done by appointment, similar to online auction sites like eBay.

Buyers or sellers can list their intentions for buying or selling shares, the price they are willing to accept or pay, and how long to keep their order open. The ASMX will aggregate all orders each day and provide matching services. Unlike the NYSE or NASDAQ, there is a single settlement each day in which all orders are sorted and shares allocated, providing a managed system for the buyer and seller.

The platform developed by the ASMX provides unparalleled transparency, allowing for early-stage investor attraction. Issuers can access a broad network of broker-dealers who can sell their primary offerings through their existing networks as well, very similar to existing markets, such as the NASDAQ.

The ASMX platform is designed specifically to prevent short selling by mandating that sellers be verified owners of shares before they can be listed on the platform. Additionally, the matching system means that there are no broker-dealer market makers needed. As a pure matching service, liquidity is still provided, but immediate settlement cannot be guaranteed.

The trading by appointment auction system can prevent high-frequency trading by definition, excluding flash traders from the marketplace.

As a dedicated early-stage trading platform, the ASMX has lower compliance and regulatory costs when compared with other exchanges. The ASMX bridges the gap between a company's private placements with angels or venture capital and a full public offering, at a fraction of the cost of a formal public listing.

Additional information can be found at TheASMX.com.

Current Market Options: OTC

Regulation A+ Tier 2 offerings will be a source of new securities traded on the OTC markets. Upon completion of a Regulation A+ Tier 2 offering, non-affiliate shareholders will have publicly tradable shares in companies that are subject to continuing Regulation A+ disclosure, but are not necessarily fully SEC reporting. The OTCQX® Best and OTCQB® Venture markets operated by OTC Markets Group Inc. ("OTC Markets Group")—as well as any newly developed secondary markets designed for Regulation A+ securities—will provide secondary markets for those shareholders and other interested investors.

Existing U.S. and Canadian companies traded on OTCQX and OTCQB that are not SEC reporting, and those that are considering deregistering from the SEC, may utilize Regulation A+ as an additional attractive option for raising money in a public securities offering. Additional shares issued by these companies in a Regulation A+ transaction will trade along with the companies' existing secondary markets on the OTCQX and OTCQB markets.

OTC Markets Group has developed a Regulation A+ "on-ramp," which includes new OTCQX and OTCQB market rules specifically designed for companies using Regulation A+ to go public and develop their secondary trading markets.

The OTCQX Best Market

The OTCQX U.S. market is the top level of the United States over the counter market, divided into OTCQX U.S. and, for the highest-level companies, OTCQX U.S. Premier. To qualify for OTCQX, U.S. companies must meet high financial standards, demonstrate compliance with U.S. securities laws, be current in their disclosure, and be sponsored by a third-party advisor. OTCQX securities are quoted by FINRA member broker-dealers on OTC Link® ATS, an SEC-registered alternative trading system.

The OTCQB Venture Market

The OTCQB Venture Market is for entrepreneurial and development stage U.S. and international companies that are unable to qualify for OTCQX. To be eligible, companies must be current in their reporting and undergo an annual verification and management certification process. These standards provide a strong baseline of transparency, as well as the technology and regulation to improve the information and trading experience for investors. Companies must meet a minimum $0.01 bid price test and may not be in bankruptcy. OTCQB securities are quoted by FINRA member broker-dealers on OTC Link® ATS.

Trading Regulation A+ Securities on OTCQX and OTCQB

In June of 2015, OTC Markets Group updated its OTCQX rules for U.S. companies and its OTCQB standards to create a Regulation A+ reporting standard that streamlines the qualification process for companies issuing securities under Regulation A+.

OTCQX

Most significantly, OTCQX rules for U.S. companies now allow a company to use its required disclosure under Regulation A+ to help meet the initial and ongoing OTCQX disclosure requirements. To qualify for OTCQX, a company using the Regulation A+ reporting standard must file all reports required to be filed on the SEC's EDGAR system pursuant to Regulation A+, as well as quarterly disclosure and certain current information.

Under the initial disclosure obligations, a Regulation A+ reporting company must have filed all reports required to be filed on EDGAR. The most recent financial statements required to be audited under Regulation A+ must be audited by an independent public accountant registered with the PCAOB.

Under the ongoing disclosure obligations, a Regulation A+ reporting company must file, on an ongoing basis, all annual, semi-annual, and other interim reports required to be filed on EDGAR under Regulation A+. Also, within 45 days of the end of each fiscal quarter, it must publish on EDGAR through Form 1-U quarterly disclosures, including all information required in the company's semi-annual report. Each annual report must include financial statements audited by an independent public accountant registered with the PCAOB. Companies seeking to trade on OTCQX U.S. Premier must publish, on EDGAR through SEC Form 1-U, copies of all proxies, proxy statements, and all other material mailed by the company to its shareholders with respect thereto, within 15 days of the mailing of such material.

Summary

Developing secondary markets for Reg A+ securities, proprietors of these trading systems have a lot of experience and analogs from which to draw in developing effective marketplaces for trading in these securities. Promising options are already popping up. With greater use of Regulation A+ as a channel to obtain capital and grow value these options should mature into viable and attractive venues for investors.

Final Thoughts

Reg A+ Guide for Entrepreneurs and Investors

In summary, the key benefits of Regulation A+ include:

- Investment opportunities for ~100M plus non-accredited and ~8M accredited investors in attractive pre-IPO companies

- Unrestricted advertising of offerings on the Internet, in print, on the radio and TV to reach investors

- Immediate liquidity with potential of full trading of stock in a secondary market after initial raise

- Higher pricing per share and lower cost for raising capital compared to other alternatives

- Ability to raise up to $50M in any 12-month period

- Applicable to most U.S. and Canadian businesses with very few exceptions

Reasons for entrepreneurs to consider Regulation A+ include:

- Raise growth capital for early- and mid-stage companies

- Provide liquidity for current investors

- Raise equity/debt for new discrete projects, e.g. real estate development

- As an alternative to Reg D in order to access both accredited and non-accredited investors via public solicitation

Reg A+ provides small, existing companies who have been operating for a number of years a realistic means of raising additional capital and providing liquidity for current investors. As discussed in Chapters 1 and 2, there are thousands of businesses that cannot attract additional private capital and do not qualify for an M&A or a big IPO on Wall Street.

As discussed in Chapter 3, thousands of companies over the past 20-30 years have raised the majority of their capital by utilizing exemptions provided under Regulation D of the securities laws. The JOBS Act introduced several new fundraising options, including Reg A+, that can be helpful in raising needed capital depending on the need and choices made by each company. Each option requires careful evaluation before a decision can be made.

Start-Up Funding and Growth Capital

Most companies go through 3–4 stages of capital raises in their lifetime.

Seed Stage

The *seed stage* typically requires up to $1M to prove the new product or business concept with a prototype model. This is generally the most difficult capital to raise because it has the highest risk for investors. These funds are either invested by entrepreneurs themselves or through friends and family. Depending on the long-term potential and the strength of the management team, some VCs may also invest, especially if team members have a track record of successes. Investors and VCs typically sign a contract with a convertible note with some accrued interest on this investment to be converted into Series A stock during a formal first round of funding.

Recently many new Internet-based portals such as www.kickstarter.com have successfully helped entrepreneurs raise initial capital to develop concepts. However, in many of these portals, investors cannot share in the ownership equity or future profits of the company. Instead of obtaining an ownership position, investors are permitted to make donations or gifts to the company. Individuals give money due to their personal passion for the idea or to promote an exciting concept. Sometimes companies will provide discounts on future goods or services in exchange for contributions. As an example, one entrepreneur was able to raise up to $7M for an Internet-based watch concept on Kickstarter.

Due to the lower cost of raising funds through Internet portals such as Kickstarter, entrepreneurs seeking seed capital should fully explore this option in addition to other non-equity sources such as bank loans, credit cards, etc. These options minimize the amount of ownership that may need to be sacrificed to attract the needed capital.

First Stage (Series A)

The first stage or *Series A* funding is the first formal round of capital. It's usually raised when the product/business concept is introduced to a select group of customers for first revenues. This round is still quite risky for investors, as total long-term cost of building the enterprise and the profit model are still not fully established. This stage typically requires less than $5M and VCs or experienced angels can be the most effective investors since they not only provide the required capital but also help the company with many introductions to manufacturers, customers, and key employees. Due to the risk of success, investors in this round will likely seek a significant ownership position for their investments. This can be as high as 50% of the company.

■ **Tip**   Reg A+ is not ideal for raising seed capital or very early stage funds. The added costs and time required to obtain SEC approval for a Reg A+ are not a good match for a very young company that will likely be cash strapped and wanting to move quickly on a new idea. Use of Reg D for very early funding generally remains a better option.

Second Stage (Series B)

The second stage or *Series B* is termed "growth stage" capital and raised funds are typically used to increase revenues, scale manufacturing, and hire additional employees to build a larger and profitable business. Since this funding is generally sought after the firm has been successful in generating repeat revenues, the risk of an investment in this round is often less than in earlier stages. This funding round may also require significantly more capital (in the range of $5–25M, depending on the nature of the business). For the last 10–15 years prior to the JOBS Act, this was a key period where growth capital simply was scarce. That is, unless the company was perceived as being a hot start-up with a potential to deliver a 100-times or more return and could generate interest from VCs.

Reg A+ is an option that should be explored at this stage since the firm is now far enough along to have some degree of operating history and has added financial resources to cover the required legal and filing costs. The ability to access a wider pool of investors and raise up to $50M annually via public solicitation that is permitted under Reg A+ can be a good option to achieve funding objectives at this stage.

Later Stages (Series C/D)

The later stages or *Series C/D* funding rounds typically have a primary objective to raise sufficient capital to provide liquidity to a firm's investors, preferably through a full IPO on a national exchange, such as the NASDAQ. If a company has raised previous funds via Reg A+, a later stage company can raise additional funds by qualifying for listing on a secondary exchange and thereby provide liquidity to its investors. Alternatively, a company can seek to obtain liquidity and added investment through being acquired or merging with a larger company. To the extent that the previous rounds established share prices (which may be easier to achieve under Reg A+), the valuation of the firm for either acquisition or merger can be more objectively set.

Liquidity for Current Investors of Private Firms

Most small companies are initially funded by private investors and friends and family utilizing Regulation D. The vast majority of smaller firms remain private for an extended period and therefore their investors have limited options to sell their ownership positions since their shares are not freely tradable. Even for companies that are generally growing well and producing revenue and profits, investors still may not be able to get their profits or original capital back for many years until an IPO or a cash acquisition happens. Most investors who invest in small companies therefore end up stuck in an illiquid investment and become reluctant to invest in other small firms even if they have means and/or desire to do so.

Regulation A+ can help these small companies. If the capital required is $50M or less, companies may use Regulation A+ to raise new capital up to $50M in a private or public offering at a much lower cost than a traditional IPO. In addition to $50M, existing investors can sell up to 30% of their current equity or $15M in secondary sales or a maximum of 30% with initial offering or during the next 12-month period. This allows current investors to get liquidity for their equity that may have been locked up for many years.

One-Off Projects

There are many business opportunities having specific short-term objectives where the principals do not intend to establish a long-term ongoing company. Examples include real estate development projects, movies, and limited term investment vehicles such as a Delaware Statutory Trust.[1] These projects typically have a 3-10 year horizon to completion. Most real estate projects also seek leverage through seeking loans for a large portion of the total capital requirement. Loans are available for such projects because they have real assets as collateral, plus the borrower may elect to take some loan guarantees as well provide added security for the debt. Therefore the equity portion of the total capital requirement is relatively small but can still range from $5–$50M, depending on the size of the project. This equity portion is a higher risk investment relative to the debt since the lender usually has a priority to recover the loan balance against the assets of the project before investors can receive their original equity and profits.

Most of the required equity for these types of one-off projects has been raised under Reg D offerings, with capital provided by accredited retail investors and private equity funds. Reg A+ provides another choice now, by allowing options to raise equity for these types of projects through public offerings in which both accredited and non-accredited investors can participate.

How to Fundraise

In order to choose the target investors and reach them for fundraising, some of the key considerations are the amount of funds being raised, time allowed to raise capital, legal costs, auditing and other costs, including filing fees. Lastly, but importantly, you need to consider the need for secondary trading by investors after the initial raise.

Typically most companies want to complete the fundraising process in less than six months. If they have access to existing investors, it may be possible to complete the process more quickly. Assuming an approximate timeline of six months, there are two main options to consider:

- Although in its infancy, online fundraising may be a very realistic option to raise amounts of up to $5M (e.g., Kickstarter).

- For higher amounts up to $50M, it may be better to seek help from qualified broker-dealers, who have a focus and willingness to use Reg A+ as a platform to raise capital.

Online fundraising is expected to explode as companies and retail investors recognize the potential to participate in opportunities that were previously only available to an exclusive club of accredited high net worth investors (HNI). As early evidence of the success of online fundraising, in the three years since the approval of Title II of JOBS Act, over 200 online portals have emerged to

---

[1]https://en.wikipedia.org/wiki/Delaware_statutory_trust

help Reg D investors raise capital online under the newly approved Regulation D 506(c) exemption. By some estimates, these portals have been able to raise several $100M in the last 2–3 years. As the Reg A+ potential is recognized, many of these portals are expected to add Reg A+ offerings and the amount of funds via online portals is expected to dramatically rise in the years ahead.

New broker-dealers will likely emerge to take advantage of the disruptive opportunity created by Reg A+ and will have a greater focus on utilizing online platforms with lower cost structures to investors than is currently offered by traditional securities firms. Online portals that are established by registered broker-dealers can engage in a much broader range of activities to distribute securities than portals who are not similarly licensed and registered. Therefore, it is likely that more portals will be established by broker-dealers and that the range of offerings will expand accordingly.

Selection Guide

Table 9-1 summarizes guidelines to assist entrepreneurs in determining which funding options may best fit with specific investment objectives.

Table 9-1. Regulation A Selection Guide

QUICK SELECTION GUIDE FOR ENTREPREUNERS

Category	Reason for Capital raise	Amount of Funding required	Donations: Internet	Crowd funding Title III/ Friends Family	Crowd funding (syndicated Portals, 506 c)	Venture Capital (VCs)/ Reatail Broker-dealers	Current Investors/ Private equity Funds	Title IV Tier 1	Title IV Tier 2	National Exchanges	Comments
			Donations	**Private Equity (Reg D)**				**Private/Public (Reg A Mini IPO)**		**Public (IPO)**	
Existing Operating Companies	Liquidity	No new funds, List current stock									Listing w/o new capital is not a good idea usually
		$5-25M							XXX	X	This is where Reg A can be most effective
		$25M-50M							XX	XX	Both Reg A or IPO can be effective case by case
		$50M++								XXX	If Company can afford the cost and need high amount of capital, traditional IPO is still the best option
	Distress					XX	XXX				Most new investors shy away from this situation
New Companies	Seed to prove concept	Up to $1M	X	X	X	X					
		$1-2M		XX	XX	XXX					This is the most difficult area of funding due to very high risk VCs and angels are a better choice as they can often provided aded asstance and guidance to the company
	Scale to first revenue	$2-5M			X	XXX					
	Growth	$5-25M				XX			XXX	X	
		$25M-50M				X			XX	XX	
		$50M++								XXX	
Fixed Life Projects/Companies	Life less than 3 years	$1-5M		X	XX	XXX					
		$5M++				XX					
	Life more than 3 years	$5-25M							XXX	X	
		$25M-50M							XX	XX	
		$50M++								XXX	

X- May work
XX- Good potential
XXX-Recommended

So Where Do We Go from Here?

It's important to remember that everything discussed in this book is within the context of changes in the law that are likely to continue to evolve over time. There is no question that Reg A+ in and of itself has been a *big* step forward in diversifying channels to source capital.

For its full potential as an economic and job creation engine to be realized, a number of further developments need to happen at both the private and public level. From the private perspective, growth in the use of Reg A+ will foster the development of secondary markets, as well as attract professional services essential to transparency and efficiency in a secondary market, including analytical coverage. That will attract more brokerages and issuers, thus fostering competition. This will, in turn, create "best practices" and industry standards to bolster confidence in investment in these securities and lead to increased demand.

Of course, from the public level, there needs to be further examination of many of the issues previously discussed in this book to attract more and diverse financial service firms as well as issuers to this market.

Reconciliation of State Blue Sky Laws

In previous chapters we discussed the interplay of state securities laws with Regulation A+. Tier 1 still remains subject to state registration requirements, and the preemption from state registration for Tier 2 securities does not cover secondary trading in those securities, although various exemptions apply in that context. Reg A+ securities can attract capital without state registration, but secondary trading of the Reg A+ shares remains subject to state registration under Blue Sky laws.

Admittedly, the vast majority of states have agreed to a "coordinated" review process to try to alleviate the logistical and time burdens associated with state registration of Tier 1 offerings. But this is only an effort to streamline the process of registration and does not deal with the chief concern of the market, which is merit review by the states. Merit review means that many states can assess substantively an issuer's offering based on pre-established guidelines adopted by those states to determine if the offering should be allowed to be sold in those states. (See Appendix E for more information on the Coordinated Review Program and exemplars of these guidelines.)

A big question remains for much of the private market as to the practicality of trying to comply with these guidelines, especially for those who are planning to raise funds in all 50 states. Many in the private sector have expressed concerns that this process will invite invasiveness outside of the coordinated review process by regulators or result in states trying to impose impractical deal terms on the issuer. Proponents of further exemptions from Blue Sky registration requirements often quote the Commonwealth of Massachusetts's refusal to register Apple's IPO (conducted prior to federal exemptions of listed securities) in that state because they felt it presented undue risk to the public…Apple!

As previously stated, even though initial issuances are pre-empted from state registration requirements, that does not necessarily hold true for secondary transactions in those securities. A number of exemptions exist for secondary activity, but most of these apply to "isolated" transactions by shareholders not otherwise affiliated with the issuer. They are not, generally speaking, trading for purposes of arbitrage activity, i.e., affecting or exploiting swings in price through buying and selling securities in volume. For the time being, this is likely not too much of an issue for issuers and investors alike, since the bulk of investors will be retail in nature and be motivated by yield or fundamentals of the company rather than market trends, as this market is still very immature. But market maturation will ultimately require that larger, more sophisticated brokerages and investment houses come to this market.

In part, their motivation to sophisticate this market will come from the potential to profit from the dynamics of the market. The debate as to what extent these players can or should be able to arbitrage Reg A+ securities will go on for some time, but one thing appears to be clear—the secondary market for Reg A+ shares cannot move too far beyond merely a reliable venue for the pricing and transfer of these securities on an episodic basis without addressing the layers of complexity that current state requirements pose.

Finally, several states require that a broker-dealer registered in that state be affiliated with a Regulation A+ offering, or the issuer must register as a broker there. While not a terribly large obstacle to conduct as part of the offering, this can pose a problem when issuers are using portals and aren't intending to use a broker-dealer for their offering.[2] Much is still to be learned about how the SEC will treat portals not licensed as brokers that facilitate these offerings, but this issue points to the fact that a number of issues still need to

---

[2]Issuers can directly solicit investors without being registered as broker-dealers. As an example, start-up executives frequently attend investor events e.g., angel forums, in an effort to directly solicit funds—yet do not need to be registered as broker-dealers since they are regarded being exempt to their position as a principal and not an intermediary. Unlike intermediaries who must be registered, principals are prohibited from taking a commission on any funds that they raise.

be addressed in order to provide greater regulatory clarity to facilitate the growth of this offering type.

Raise Caps

Title IV of the JOBS Act requires the SEC to reevaluate regularly the caps on the amount that can be raised under Reg A in a 12-month period. During the process of adopting rules to implement Reg A+, the SEC heard from many commentators suggesting that the cap should already be raised to $100M.

$50M on a public basis presents a huge leap forward for a very large number of companies out there, but a large number of companies—for example, those in real estate investment or development—can exhaust $50M in capital quickly. Furthermore, for many sophisticated or larger investment houses, "float" is an issue. Float represents the number of securities of an issuer in the marketplace at a given time. Typically, brokerages look at this to try to determine what volume of trading can be expected in order to drive price. That becomes even more important if you are dealing with a security that is held by investors who will only buy/sell on an episodic basis. You need a lot more of the securities out there to make up for the volume typically achieved by investors seeking to arbitrage the security.

If the amount to be raised is revised, the carve-out from 12(g) will also need to be revised to account for the larger issuances.

But these issues as well as others will be dealt with in due course. Lawyers, investment bankers, brokers, innovators, and entrepreneurs are wading into the waters of Reg A+, and this will certainly facilitate discourse and debate needed to resolve them.

Summary

But even with its present flaws, business owners and entrepreneurs have a powerful new tool to reach a broader investing audience. A broader investing audience has access to a more diverse range of products and opportunities for income or wealth appreciation. They can also take some comfort that the regulatory regime provides for transparency, thus requiring business owners to succeed on the merits of how their business performs in the market. Finally, those business owners have new options for monetizing their success in growing their operations.

Hopefully, this book has helped you begin the journey to discover dynamic and diverse methods and channels for sourcing capital, finding investing success, and building your "American dream."

Afterword

This book is an important educational milestone that will help advance entrepreneurial access to capital.

My colleague Ed Kim and I (our work is cited in the book) discovered and documented the collapse in the small IPO market and the decline in the number of NASDAQ- and NYSE-listed companies. We linked this drop to the loss of millions of jobs in the U.S. economy. Congress responded and gave rise to the JOBS Act. I had the distinct honor of helping to draft Regulation A+ and to testify in support of it in Congress. I was in the Rose Garden when President Obama signed the JOBS Act into law. And, while the SEC's final Regulation A+ rules took three years to become effective, we are now "off to the races".

I commend Messrs. Getty, Gupta, and Kaplan for their timely book that will help educate entrepreneurs, companies, investment banks, portals, and securities counsels on how to apply these new regulations to access capital.

Reg A+ is major step forward. However, we must not rest on our laurels: This great country of ours averaged over 500 IPOs in the years preceding the dot-com bubble. Regulatory changes dropped the number of corporate IPOs to an average of only 150 IPOs per year in the post-dot-com era. Worse, had the United States not changed its stock market model, we would likely be enjoying the economic fruits of 950 IPOs a year after adjusting for today's much larger economy. That estimated "loss" of 800 corporate IPOs is, in our view, one of the primary causes of today's lackluster economy. Regulation A+ may help begin to breathe new life into capital formation.

We also hope that this book will help inspire entrepreneurs and their investors to take their fight to Washington. The United States must jettison what SEC Chair White and we have called, "one-size-fits-all markets". The United States deserves a new form of stock exchange to serve the very different after-market support and capital access needs of small capitalization companies and their investors. Today's one-size-fits-all markets only work for innately visible and naturally liquid stocks. For the rest of the economy, they have been a disaster. It is time to have your voices heard.

We congratulate the authors for bringing together many of the elements needed to help corporations and their investors take advantage of Reg A+ in a simple and easy-to-understand guide.

The U.S. IPO markets were once the envy of IPO markets throughout the world. This book is another step in clawing our way back to a new age of American prosperity. Join the fight and help bring back the "land of opportunity" for which we were all once so proud.

—David Weild IV
Founder and CEO, Weild & Co.
Former Vice Chairman of NASDAQ
"Father" of the JOBS Act

Current Legal Authority

Appendix A contains the operative provisions of Federal law discussed in this book. First, the text of Title IV of the Jumpstart Our Business Start-Ups Act which requires changes to Section 3(b) of the Securities Act of 1933, as amended, to mandate the reform of Regulation A. Then, the text of Section 3(b) as changed by Title IV. Finally, the new Regulation A+ itself, with changes to the Regulations mandated by Section 3(b) and further changes by the SEC under the regulatory authority to implement the same.

H.R.3606 Jumpstart Our Business Startups Act (Enrolled Bill [Final as Passed Both House and Senate] - ENR)

Title IV—Small Company Capital Formation Sec. 401. Authority to Exempt Certain Securities

(a) In General- Section 3(b) of the Securities Act of 1933 (15 U.S.C. 77c(b)) is amended—

(1) by striking (b) The Commission and inserting the following:

(b) Additional Exemptions-

(1) SMALL ISSUES EXEMPTIVE AUTHORITY-
The Commission; and

(2) by adding at the end the following:

(2) ADDITIONAL ISSUES- The Commission shall by rule or regulation add a class of securities to the securities exempted pursuant to this section in accordance with the following terms and conditions:

(A) The aggregate offering amount of all securities offered and sold within the prior 12-month period in reliance on the exemption added in accordance with this paragraph shall not exceed $50,000,000.

(B) The securities may be offered and sold publicly.

(C) The securities shall not be restricted securities within the meaning of the Federal securities laws and the regulations promulgated thereunder.

(D) The civil liability provision in section 12(a)(2) shall apply to any person offering or selling such securities.

(E) The issuer may solicit interest in the offering prior to filing any offering statement, on such terms and conditions as the Commission may prescribe in the public interest or for the protection of investors.

(F) The Commission shall require the issuer to file audited financial statements with the Commission annually.

(G) Such other terms, conditions, or requirements as the Commission may determine necessary in the public interest and for the protection of investors, which may include—

(i) a requirement that the issuer prepare and electronically file with the Commission and distribute to prospective investors an offering statement, and any related documents, in such form and with such content as prescribed by the Commission, including audited financial statements, a description of the issuers business operations, its financial condition, its corporate governance principles, its use of investor funds, and other appropriate matters; and

(ii) disqualification provisions under which the exemption shall not be available to the issuer or its predecessors, affiliates, officers, directors, underwriters, or other related persons, which shall be substantially similar to the disqualification provisions contained in the regulations adopted in accordance with section 926 of the Dodd-Frank Wall Street Reform and Consumer Protection Act (15 U.S.C. 77d note).

(3) LIMITATION- Only the following types of securities may be exempted under a rule or regulation adopted pursuant to paragraph (2): equity securities, debt securities, and debt securities convertible or exchangeable to equity interests, including any guarantees of such securities.

(4) PERIODIC DISCLOSURES- Upon such terms and conditions as the Commission determines necessary in the public interest and for the protection of investors, the Commission by rule or regulation may require an issuer of a class of securities exempted under paragraph (2) to make available to investors and file with the Commission periodic disclosures regarding the issuer, its business operations, its financial condition, its corporate governance principles, its use of investor funds, and other appropriate matters, and also may provide for the suspension and termination of such a requirement with respect to that issuer.

(5) ADJUSTMENT- Not later than 2 years after the date of enactment of the Small Company Capital Formation Act of 2011 and every 2 years thereafter, the Commission shall review the offering amount limitation described in paragraph (2)(A) and shall increase such amount as the Commission determines appropriate. If the Commission determines not to increase such amount, it shall report to the Committee on Financial Services of the House of Representatives and the Committee on Banking, Housing, and Urban Affairs of the Senate on its reasons for not increasing the amount.

(b) Treatment as Covered Securities for Purposes of NSMIA- Section 18(b)(4) of the Securities Act of 1933 (as amended by section 303) (15 U.S.C. 77r(b)(4)) is further amended by inserting after subparagraph (C) (as added by such section) the following:

(D) a rule or regulation adopted pursuant to section 3(b)(2) and such security is—

  (i) offered or sold on a national securities exchange; or

  (ii) offered or sold to a qualified purchaser, as defined by the Commission pursuant to paragraph (3) with respect to that purchase or sale;

(c) Conforming Amendment- Section 4(5) of the Securities Act of 1933 is amended by striking section 3(b) and inserting section 3(b)(1).

SEC. 402. STUDY ON THE IMPACT OF STATE BLUE SKY LAWS ON REGULATION A OFFERINGS

The Comptroller General shall conduct a study on the impact of State laws regulating securities offerings, or Blue Sky laws, on offerings made under Regulation A (17 CFR 230.251 et seq.). The Comptroller General shall transmit a report on the findings of the study to the Committee on Financial Services of the House of Representatives, and the Committee on Banking, Housing, and Urban Affairs of the Senate not later than 3 months after the date of enactment of this Act.

15 U.S. Code § 77c - Classes of Securities Under this Subchapter

(b) Additional exemptions

(1) Small issues exemptive authority

The Commission may from time to time by its rules and regulations, and subject to such terms and conditions as may be prescribed therein, add any class of securities to the securities exempted as provided in this section, if it finds that the enforcement of this subchapter with respect to such securities is not necessary in the public interest and for the protection of investors by reason of the small amount involved or the limited character of the public offering; but no issue of securities shall be exempted under this subsection where the aggregate amount at which such issue is offered to the public exceeds $5,000,000.

(2) Additional issues

The Commission shall by rule or regulation add a class of securities to the securities exempted pursuant to this section in accordance with the following terms and conditions:

- **(A)** The aggregate offering amount of all securities offered and sold within the prior 12-month period in reliance on the exemption added in accordance with this paragraph shall not exceed $50,000,000.

- **(B)** The securities may be offered and sold publicly.

- **(C)** The securities shall not be restricted securities within the meaning of the Federal securities laws and the regulations promulgated thereunder.

- **(D)** The civil liability provision in section 77l (a)(2) of this title shall apply to any person offering or selling such securities.

- **(E)** The issuer may solicit interest in the offering prior to filing any offering statement, on such terms and conditions as the Commission may prescribe in the public interest or for the protection of investors.

- **(F)** The Commission shall require the issuer to file audited financial statements with the Commission annually.

(G) Such other terms, conditions, or requirements as the Commission may determine necessary in the public interest and for the protection of investors, which may include—

    (i) a requirement that the issuer prepare and electronically file with the Commission and distribute to prospective investors an offering statement, and any related documents, in such form and with such content as prescribed by the Commission, including audited financial statements, a description of the issuer's business operations, its financial condition, its corporate governance principles, its use of investor funds, and other appropriate matters; and

    (ii) disqualification provisions under which the exemption shall not be available to the issuer or its predecessors, affiliates, officers, directors, underwriters, or other related persons, which shall be substantially similar to the disqualification provisions contained in the regulations adopted in accordance with section 926 of the Dodd-Frank Wall Street Reform and Consumer Protection Act (15 U.S.C. 77d note).

(3) Limitation

Only the following types of securities may be exempted under a rule or regulation adopted pursuant to paragraph (2): equity securities, debt securities, and debt securities convertible or exchangeable to equity interests, including any guarantees of such securities.

(4) Periodic disclosures

Upon such terms and conditions as the Commission determines necessary in the public interest and for the protection of investors, the Commission by rule or regulation may require an issuer of a class of securities exempted under paragraph (2) to make available to investors and file with the Commission periodic disclosures regarding the issuer, its business operations, its financial condition, its corporate governance principles, its use of investor funds, and other appropriate matters, and also may provide for the suspension and termination of such a requirement with respect to that issuer.

(5) Adjustment

Not later than 2 years after April 5, 2012, and every 2 years thereafter, the Commission shall review the offering amount limitation described in paragraph (2)(A) and shall increase such amount as the Commission determines appropriate. If the Commission determines not to increase such amount, it shall report to the Committee on Financial Services of the House of Representatives and the Committee on Banking, Housing, and Urban Affairs of the Senate on its reasons for not increasing the amount.

Regulation A—Conditional Small Issues Exemption

AUTHORITY: Secs. 230.251 to 230.263 issued under 15 U.S.C. 77c, 77s.

SOURCE: 57 FR 36468, Aug. 13, 1992, unless otherwise noted.

§230.251 Scope of Exemption

(a) *Tier 1 and Tier 2.* A public offer or sale of eligible securities, as defined in Rule 261 (§230.261), pursuant to Regulation A shall be exempt under section 3(b) from the registration requirements of the Securities Act of 1933 (the "Securities Act") (15 U.S.C. 77a *et seq.*).

 (1) *Tier 1.* Offerings pursuant to Regulation A in which the sum of all cash and other consideration to be received for the securities being offered ("aggregate offering price") plus the gross proceeds for all securities sold pursuant to other offering statements within the 12 months before the start of and during the current offering of securities ("aggregate sales") does not exceed $20,000,000, including not more than $6,000,000 offered by all selling securityholders that are affiliates of the issuer ("Tier 1 offerings").

 (2) *Tier 2.* Offerings pursuant to Regulation A in which the sum of the aggregate offering price and aggregate sales does not exceed $50,000,000, including not more than $15,000,000 offered by all selling securityholders that are affiliates of the issuer ("Tier 2 offerings").

(3) *Additional limitation on secondary sales in first year.* The portion of the aggregate offering price attributable to the securities of selling securityholders shall not exceed 30% of the aggregate offering price of a particular offering in:

    (i) The issuer's first offering pursuant to Regulation A; or

    (ii) Any subsequent Regulation A offering that is qualified within one year of the qualification date of the issuer's first offering.

NOTE TO PARAGRAPH (a). Where a mixture of cash and non-cash consideration is to be received, the aggregate offering price must be based on the price at which the securities are offered for cash. Any portion of the aggregate offering price or aggregate sales attributable to cash received in a foreign currency must be translated into United States currency at a currency exchange rate in effect on, or at a reasonable time before, the date of the sale of the securities. If securities are not offered for cash, the aggregate offering price or aggregate sales must be based on the value of the consideration as established by bona fide sales of that consideration made within a reasonable time, or, in the absence of sales, on the fair value as determined by an accepted standard. Valuations of non-cash consideration must be reasonable at the time made. If convertible securities or warrants are being offered and such securities are convertible, exercisable, or exchangeable within one year of the offering statement's qualification or at the discretion of the issuer, the underlying securities must also be qualified and the aggregate offering price must include the actual or maximum estimated conversion, exercise, or exchange price of such securities.

(b) *Issuer.* The issuer of the securities:

(1) Is an entity organized under the laws of the United States or Canada, or any State, Province, Territory or possession thereof, or the District of Columbia, with its principal place of business in the United States or Canada;

(2) Is not subject to section 13 or 15(d) of the Securities Exchange Act of 1934 (the "Exchange Act") (15 U.S.C. 78a *et seq.*) immediately before the offering;

(3) Is not a development stage company that either has no specific business plan or purpose, or has indicated that its business plan is to merge with or acquire an unidentified company or companies;

(4) Is not an investment company registered or required to be registered under the Investment Company Act of 1940 (15 U.S.C. 80a-1 *et seq.*) or a business development company as defined in section 2(a)(48) of the Investment Company Act of 1940 (15 U.S.C. 80a-2(a)(48));

(5) Is not issuing fractional undivided interests in oil or gas rights, or a similar interest in other mineral rights;

(6) Is not, and has not been, subject to any order of the Commission entered pursuant to Section 12(j) of the Exchange Act (15 U.S.C. 78*l*(j)) within five years before the filing of the offering statement;

(7) Has filed with the Commission all reports required to be filed, if any, pursuant to Rule 257 (§230.257) during the two years before the filing of the offering statement (or for such shorter period that the issuer was required to file such reports); and

(8) Is not disqualified under Rule 262 (§230.262).

(c) *Integration with other offerings.* Offers or sales made in reliance on this Regulation A will not be integrated with:

(1) Prior offers or sales of securities; or

(2) Subsequent offers or sales of securities that are:

(i) Registered under the Securities Act, except as provided in Rule 255(e) (§230.255(e));

(ii) Exempt from registration under Rule 701 (§230.701);

(iii) Made pursuant to an employee benefit plan;

(iv) Exempt from registration under Regulation S (§§230.901 through 203.905);

(v) Made more than six months after the completion of the Regulation A offering; or

(vi) Exempt from registration under Section 4(a)(6) of the Securities Act (15 U.S.C. 77d(a)(6)).

NOTE TO PARAGRAPH (c). If these safe harbors do not apply, whether subsequent offers and sales of securities will be integrated with the Regulation A offering will depend on the particular facts and circumstances.

(d) *Offering conditions—*(1) *Offers.* (i) Except as allowed by Rule 255 (§230.255), no offer of securities may be made unless an offering statement has been filed with the Commission.

(ii) After the offering statement has been filed, but before it is qualified:

(A) Oral offers may be made;

(B) Written offers pursuant to Rule 254 (§230.254) may be made; and

(C) Solicitations of interest and other communications pursuant to Rule 255 (§230.255) may be made.

(iii) Offers may be made after the offering statement has been qualified, but any written offers must be accompanied with or preceded by the most recent offering circular filed with the Commission for such offering.

(2) *Sales.* (i) No sale of securities may be made:

(A) Until the offering statement has been qualified;

(B) By issuers that are not currently required to file reports pursuant to Rule 257(b) (§230.257(b)), until a Preliminary Offering Circular is delivered at least 48 hours before the sale to any person that before qualification of the offering statement had indicated an interest in purchasing securities in the offering, including those persons that responded to an issuer's solicitation of interest materials; and

(C) In a Tier 2 offering of securities that are not listed on a registered national securities exchange upon qualification, unless the purchaser is either an accredited investor (as defined in Rule 501 (§230.501)) or the aggregate purchase price to be paid by the purchaser for the securities (including the actual or maximum estimated conversion, exercise, or exchange price for any underlying securities that have been qualified) is no more than ten percent (10%) of the greater of such purchaser's:

(1) Annual income or net worth if a natural person (with annual income and net worth for such natural person purchasers determined as provided in Rule 501 (§230.501)); or

(2) Revenue or net assets for such purchaser's most recently completed fiscal year end if a non-natural person.

NOTE TO PARAGRAPH (d)(2)(i)(C). When securities underlying warrants or convertible securities are being qualified pursuant to Tier 2 of Regulation A one year or more after the qualification of an offering for which investment limitations previously applied, purchasers of the underlying securities for which investment limitations would apply at that later date may determine compliance with the ten percent (10%) investment limitation using the conversion, exercise, or exchange price to acquire the underlying securities at that later time without aggregating such price with the price of the overlying warrants or convertible securities.

(D) The issuer may rely on a representation of the purchaser when determining compliance with the ten percent (10%) investment limitation in this paragraph (d)(2)(i)(C), provided that the issuer does not know at the time of sale that any such representation is untrue.

   (ii) In a transaction that represents a sale by the issuer or an underwriter, or a sale by a dealer within 90 calendar days after qualification of the offering statement, each underwriter or dealer selling in such transaction must deliver to each purchaser from it, not later than two business days following the completion of such sale, a copy of the Final Offering Circular, subject to the following provisions:

(A) If the sale was by the issuer and was not effected by or through an underwriter or dealer, the issuer is responsible for delivering the Final Offering Circular as if the issuer were an underwriter;

(B) For continuous or delayed offerings pursuant to paragraph (d)(3) of this section, the 90 calendar day period for dealers shall commence on the day of the first bona fide offering of securities under such offering statement;

(C) If the security is listed on a registered national securities exchange, no offering circular need be delivered by a dealer more than 25 calendar days after the later of the qualification date of the offering statement or the first date on which the security was bona fide offered to the public;

(D) No offering circular need be delivered by a dealer if the issuer is subject, immediately prior to the time of the filing of the offering statement, to the reporting requirements of Rule 257(b) (§230.257(b)); and

(E) The Final Offering Circular delivery requirements set forth in paragraph (d)(2)(ii) of this section may be satisfied by delivering a notice to the effect that the sale was made pursuant to a qualified offering statement that includes the uniform resource locator ("URL"), which, in the case of an electronic-only offering, must be an active hyperlink, where the Final Offering Circular, or the offering statement of which such Final Offering Circular is part, may be obtained on the Commission's Electronic Data Gathering, Analysis and Retrieval System ("EDGAR") and contact information sufficient to notify a purchaser where a request for a Final Offering Circular can be sent and received in response.

(3) *Continuous or delayed offerings.* (i) Continuous or delayed offerings may be made under this Regulation A, so long as the offering statement pertains only to:

(A) Securities that are to be offered or sold solely by or on behalf of a person or persons other than the issuer, a subsidiary of the issuer, or a person of which the issuer is a subsidiary;

(B) Securities that are to be offered and sold pursuant to a dividend or interest reinvestment plan or an employee benefit plan of the issuer;

(C) Securities that are to be issued upon the exercise of outstanding options, warrants, or rights;

(D) Securities that are to be issued upon conversion of other outstanding securities;

(E) Securities that are pledged as collateral; or

(F) Securities the offering of which will be commenced within two calendar days after the qualification date, will be made on a continuous basis, may continue for a period in excess of 30 calendar days from the date of initial qualification, and will be offered in an amount that, at the time the offering statement is qualified, is reasonably expected to be offered and sold within two years from the initial qualification date. These securities may be offered and sold only if not more than three years have elapsed since the initial qualification date of the offering statement under which they are being offered and sold; provided, however, that if a new offering statement has been filed pursuant to this paragraph (d)(3)(i)(F), securities covered by the prior offering statement may continue to be offered and sold until the earlier of the qualification date of the new offering statement or 180 calendar days after the third anniversary of the initial qualification date of the prior offering statement. Before the end of such three-year period, an issuer may file a new offering statement covering the securities. The new offering statement must include all the information that would be required at that time in an offering statement relating to all offerings that it covers. Before the qualification date of the new offering statement, the issuer may include as part of such new offering statement any unsold securities covered by the earlier offering statement by identifying on the cover page of the new offering circular, or the latest amendment, the amount of such unsold securities being included. The offering of securities on the earlier offering statement will be deemed terminated as of the date of qualification of the new offering statement. Securities may be sold pursuant to this paragraph (d)(3)(i)(F) only if the issuer is current in its annual and semiannual filings pursuant to Rule 257(b) (§230.257(b)), at the time of such sale.

(ii) At the market offerings, by or on behalf of the issuer or otherwise, are not permitted under this Regulation A. As used in this paragraph (d)(3)(ii), the term *at the market offering* means an offering of equity securities into an existing trading market for outstanding shares of the same class at other than a fixed price.

(e) *Confidential treatment.* A request for confidential treatment may be made under Rule 406 (§230.406) for information required to be filed, and Rule 83 (§200.83) for information not required to be filed.

(f) *Electronic filing.* Documents filed or otherwise provided to the Commission pursuant to this Regulation A must be submitted in electronic format by means of EDGAR in accordance with the EDGAR rules set forth in Regulation S-T (17 CFR part 232).

§230.252 Offering Statement

(a) *Documents to be included.* The offering statement consists of the contents required by Form 1-A (§239.90 of this chapter) and any other material information necessary to make the required statements, in light of the circumstances under which they are made, not misleading.

(b) *Paper, printing, language and pagination.* Except as otherwise specified in this rule, the requirements for offering statements are the same as those specified in Rule 403 (§230.403) for registration statements under the Act. No fee is payable to the Commission upon either the submission or filing of an offering statement on Form 1-A, or any amendment to an offering statement.

(c) *Signatures.* The issuer, its principal executive officer, principal financial officer, principal accounting officer, and a majority of the members of its board of directors or other governing body, must sign the offering statement in the manner prescribed by Form 1-A. If a signature is by a person on behalf of any other person, evidence of authority to sign must be filed, except where an executive officer signs for the issuer.

(d) *Non-public submission.* An issuer whose securities have not been previously sold pursuant to a qualified offering statement under this Regulation A or an effective registration statement under the Securities Act may submit a draft offering statement to the Commission for non-public review by the staff of the Commission before public filing, provided that the offering statement shall not be qualified less than 21 calendar days after the public filing with the Commission of:

(1) The initial non-public submission;

(2) All non-public amendments; and

(3) All non-public correspondence submitted by or on behalf of the issuer to the Commission staff regarding such submissions (subject to any separately approved confidential treatment request under Rule 251(e) (§230.251(e)).

(e) *Qualification.* An offering statement and any amendment thereto can be qualified only at such date and time as the Commission may determine.

(f) *Amendments.* (1)(i) Amendments to an offering statement must be signed and filed with the Commission in the same manner as the initial filing. Amendments to an offering statement must be filed under cover of Form 1-A and must be numbered consecutively in the order in which filed.

> (ii) Every amendment that includes amended audited financial statements must include the consent of the certifying accountant to the use of such accountant's certification in connection with the amended financial statements in the offering statement or offering circular and to being named as having audited such financial statements.

> (iii) Amendments solely relating to Part III of Form 1-A must comply with the requirements of paragraph (f)(1)(i) of this section, except that such amendments may be limited to Part I of Form 1-A, an explanatory note, and all of the information required by Part III of Form 1-A.

(2) Post-qualification amendments must be filed in the following circumstances for ongoing offerings:

> (i) At least every 12 months after the qualification date to include the financial statements that would be required by Form 1-A as of such date; or

(ii) To reflect any facts or events arising after the qualification date of the offering statement (or the most recent post-qualification amendment thereof) which, individually or in the aggregate, represent a fundamental change in the information set forth in the offering statement.

§230.253 Offering Circular

(a) *Contents.* An offering circular must include the information required by Form 1-A for offering circulars.

(b) *Information that may be omitted.* Notwithstanding paragraph (a) of this section, a qualified offering circular may omit information with respect to the public offering price, underwriting syndicate (including any material relationships between the issuer or selling securityholders and the unnamed underwriters, brokers or dealers), underwriting discounts or commissions, discounts or commissions to dealers, amount of proceeds, conversion rates, call prices and other items dependent upon the offering price, delivery dates, and terms of the securities dependent upon the offering date; provided, that the following conditions are met:

(1) The securities to be qualified are offered for cash.

(2) The outside front cover page of the offering circular includes a bona fide estimate of the range of the maximum offering price and the maximum number of shares or other units of securities to be offered or a bona fide estimate of the principal amount of debt securities offered, subject to the following conditions:

(i) The range must not exceed $2 for offerings where the upper end of the range is $10 or less or 20% if the upper end of the price range is over $10; and

(ii) The upper end of the range must be used in determining the aggregate offering price under Rule 251(a) (§230.251(a)).

(3) The offering statement does not relate to securities to be offered by competitive bidding.

(4) The volume of securities (the number of equity securities or aggregate principal amount of debt securities) to be offered may not be omitted in reliance on this paragraph (b).

NOTE TO PARAGRAPH (b). A decrease in the volume of securities offered or a change in the bona fide estimate of the offering price range from that indicated in the offering circular filed as part of a qualified offering statement may be disclosed in the offering circular filed with the Commission pursuant to Rule 253(g) (§230.253(g)), so long as the decrease in the volume of securities offered or change in the price range would not materially change the disclosure contained in the offering statement at qualification. Notwithstanding the foregoing, any decrease in the volume of securities offered and any deviation from the low or high end of the price range may be reflected in the offering circular supplement filed with the Commission pursuant to Rule 253(g)(1) or (3) (§230.253(g)(1) or (3)) if, in the aggregate, the decrease in volume and/or change in price represent no more than a 20% change from the maximum aggregate offering price calculable using the information in the qualified offering statement. In no circumstances may this paragraph be used to offer securities where the maximum aggregate offering price would result in the offering exceeding the limit set forth in Rule 251(a) (§230.251(a)) or if the change would result in a Tier 1 offering becoming a Tier 2 offering. An offering circular supplement may not be used to increase the volume of securities being offered. Additional securities may only be offered pursuant to a new offering statement or post-qualification amendment qualified by the Commission.

(c) *Filing of omitted information.* The information omitted from the offering circular in reliance upon paragraph (b) of this section must be contained in an offering circular filed with the Commission pursuant to paragraph (g) of this section; except that if such offering circular is not so filed by the later of 15 business days after the qualification date of the offering statement or 15 business days after the qualification of a post-qualification amendment thereto that contains an offering circular, the information omitted in reliance upon paragraph (b) of this section must be contained in a qualified post-qualification amendment to the offering statement.

(d) *Presentation of information.* (1) Information in the offering circular must be presented in a clear, concise and understandable manner and in a type size that is easily readable. Repetition of information should be avoided; cross-referencing of information within the document is permitted.

(2) Where an offering circular is distributed through an electronic medium, issuers may satisfy legibility requirements applicable to printed documents by presenting all required information in a format readily communicated to investors.

(e) *Date.* An offering circular must be dated approximately as of the date it was filed with the Commission.

(f) *Cover page legend.* The cover page of every offering circular must display the following statement highlighted by prominent type or in another manner:

The United States Securities and Exchange Commission does not pass upon the merits of or give its approval to any securities offered or the terms of the offering, nor does it pass upon the accuracy or completeness of any offering circular or other solicitation materials. These securities are offered pursuant to an exemption from registration with the Commission; however, the Commission has not made an independent determination that the securities offered are exempt from registration.

(g) *Offering circular supplements.* (1) An offering circular that discloses information previously omitted from the offering circular in reliance upon Rule 253(b) (§230.253(b)) must be filed with the Commission no later than two business days following the earlier of the date of determination of the offering price or the date such offering circular is first used after qualification in connection with a public offering or sale.

(2) An offering circular that reflects information other than that covered in paragraph (g)(1) of this section that constitutes a substantive change from or addition to the information set forth in the last offering circular filed with the Commission must be filed with the Commission no later than five business days after the date it is first used after qualification in connection with a public offering or sale. If an offering circular filed pursuant to this paragraph (g)(2) consists of an offering circular supplement attached to an offering circular that previously had been filed or was not required to be filed pursuant to paragraph (g) of this section because it did not contain substantive changes from an offering circular that previously was filed, only the offering circular supplement need be filed under paragraph (g) of this section, provided that the cover page of the offering circular supplement identifies the date(s) of the related offering circular and any offering circular supplements thereto that together constitute the offering circular with respect to the securities currently being offered or sold.

(3) An offering circular that discloses information, facts or events covered in both paragraphs (g)(1) and (2) of this section must be filed with the Commission no later than two business days following the earlier of the date of the determination of the offering price or the date it is first used after qualification in connection with a public offering or sale.

(4) An offering circular required to be filed pursuant to paragraph (g) of this section that is not filed within the time frames specified in paragraphs (g)(1) through (3) of this section, as applicable, must be filed pursuant to this paragraph (g)(4) as soon as practicable after the discovery of such failure to file.

(5) Each offering circular filed under this section must contain in the upper right corner of the cover page the paragraphs of paragraphs (g)(1) through (4) of this section under which the filing is made, and the file number of the offering statement to which the offering circular relates.

§230.254 Preliminary Offering Circular

After the filing of an offering statement, but before its qualification, written offers of securities may be made if they meet the following requirements:

(a) *Outside front cover page.* The outside front cover page of the material bears the caption *Preliminary Offering Circular,* the date of issuance, and the following legend, which must be highlighted by prominent type or in another manner:

An offering statement pursuant to Regulation A relating to these securities has been filed with the Securities and Exchange Commission. Information contained in this Preliminary Offering Circular is subject to completion or amendment. These securities may not be sold nor may offers to buy be accepted before the offering statement filed with the Commission is qualified. This Preliminary Offering Circular shall not constitute an offer to sell or the solicitation of an offer to buy nor may there be any sales of these securities in any state in which such offer, solicitation or sale would be unlawful before registration or qualification under the laws of any such state. We may elect to satisfy our obligation to deliver a Final Offering Circular by sending you a notice within two business days after the completion of our sale to you that contains the URL where the Final Offering Circular or the offering statement in which such Final Offering Circular was filed may be obtained.

(b) *Other contents.* The Preliminary Offering Circular contains substantially the information required to be in an offering circular by Form 1-A (§239.90 of this chapter), except that certain information may be omitted under Rule 253(b) (§230.253(b)) subject to the conditions set forth in such rule.

(c) *Filing.* The Preliminary Offering Circular is filed as a part of the offering statement.

§230.255 Solicitations of Interest and Other Communications

(a) *Solicitation of interest.* At any time before the qualification of an offering statement, including before the non-public submission or public filing of such offering statement, an issuer or any person authorized to act on behalf of an issuer may communicate orally or in writing to determine whether there is any interest in a contemplated securities offering. Such communications are deemed to be an offer of a security for sale for purposes of the antifraud provisions of the federal securities laws. No solicitation or acceptance of money or other consideration, nor of any commitment, binding or otherwise, from any person is permitted until qualification of the offering statement.

(b) *Conditions.* The communications must:

    (1) State that no money or other consideration is being solicited, and if sent in response, will not be accepted;

    (2) State that no offer to buy the securities can be accepted and no part of the purchase price can be received until the offering statement is qualified, and any such offer may be withdrawn or revoked, without obligation or commitment of any kind, at any time before notice of its acceptance given after the qualification date;

    (3) State that a person's indication of interest involves no obligation or commitment of any kind; and

    (4) After the public filing of the offering statement:

        (i) State from whom a copy of the most recent version of the Preliminary Offering Circular may be obtained, including a phone number and address of such person;

        (ii) Provide the URL where such Preliminary Offering Circular, or the offering statement in which such Preliminary Offering Circular was filed, may be obtained; or

        (iii) Include a complete copy of the Preliminary Offering Circular.

(c) *Indications of interest.* Any written communication under this rule may include a means by which a person may indicate to the issuer that such person is interested in a potential offering. This issuer may require the name, address, telephone number, and/or email address in any response form included pursuant to this paragraph (c).

(d) *Revised solicitations of interest.* If solicitation of interest materials are used after the public filing of the offering statement and such solicitation of interest materials contain information that is inaccurate or inadequate in any material respect, revised solicitation of interest materials must be redistributed in a substantially similar manner as such materials were originally distributed. Notwithstanding the foregoing in this paragraph (d), if the only information that is inaccurate or inadequate is contained in a Preliminary Offering Circular provided with the solicitation of interest materials pursuant to paragraphs (b)(4)(i) or (ii) of this section, no such redistribution is required in the following circumstances:

(1) in the case of paragraph (b)(4)(i) of this section, the revised Preliminary Offering Circular will be provided to any persons making new inquiries and will be recirculated to any persons making any previous inquiries; or

(2) in the case of paragraph (b)(4)(ii) of this section, the URL continues to link directly to the most recent Preliminary Offering Circular or to the offering statement in which such revised Preliminary Offering Circular was filed.

(e) *Abandoned offerings.* Where an issuer decides to register an offering under the Securities Act after soliciting interest in a contemplated, but subsequently abandoned, Regulation A offering, the abandoned Regulation A offering would not be subject to integration with the registered offering if the issuer engaged in solicitations of interest pursuant to this rule only to qualified institutional buyers and institutional accredited investors permitted by Section 5(d) of the Securities Act. If the issuer engaged in solicitations of interest to persons other than qualified institutional buyers and institutional accredited investors, an abandoned Regulation A offering would not be subject to integration if the issuer (and any underwriter, broker, dealer, or agent used by the issuer in connection with the proposed offering) waits at least 30 calendar days between the last such solicitation of interest in the Regulation A offering and the filing of the registration statement with the Commission.

§230.256 Definition of "Qualified Purchaser"

For purposes of Section 18(b)(3) of the Securities Act [15 U.S.C. 77r(b)(3)], a "qualified purchaser" means any person to whom securities are offered or sold pursuant to a Tier 2 offering of this Regulation A.

§230.257 Periodic and Current Reporting; Exit Report

(a) *Tier 1: Exit report.* Each issuer that has filed an offering statement for a Tier 1 offering that has been qualified pursuant to this Regulation A must file an exit report on Form 1-Z (§239.94 of this chapter) not later than 30 calendar days after the termination or completion of the offering.

(b) *Tier 2: Periodic and current reporting.* Each issuer that has filed an offering statement for a Tier 2 offering that has been qualified pursuant to this Regulation A must file with the Commission the following periodic and current reports:

(1) *Annual reports.* An annual report on Form 1-K (§239.91 of this chapter) for the fiscal year in which the offering statement became qualified and for any fiscal year thereafter, unless the issuer's obligation to file such annual report is suspended under paragraph (d) of this section. Annual reports must be filed within the period specified in Form 1-K.

(2) *Special financial report.* (i) A special financial report on Form 1-K or Form 1-SA if the offering statement did not contain the following:

(A) Audited financial statements for the issuer's most recent fiscal year (or for the life of the issuer if less than a full fiscal year) preceding the fiscal year in which the issuer's offering statement became qualified; or

(B) unaudited financial statements covering the first six months of the issuer's current fiscal year if the offering statement was qualified during the last six months of that fiscal year.

(ii) The special financial report described in paragraph (b)(2)(i)(A) of this section must be filed under cover of Form 1-K within 120 calendar days after the qualification date of the offering statement and must include audited financial statements for such fiscal year or other period specified in that paragraph, as the case may be. The special financial report described in paragraph (b)(2)(i)(B) of this section must be filed under cover of Form 1-SA within 90 calendar days after the qualification date of the offering statement and must include the semiannual financial statements for the first six months of the issuer's fiscal year, which may be unaudited.

(iii) A special financial report must be signed in accordance with the requirements of the form on which it is filed.

 (3) *Semiannual report.* A semiannual report on Form 1-SA (§239.92 of this chapter) within the period specified in Form 1-SA. Semiannual reports must cover the first six months of each fiscal year of the issuer, commencing with the first six months of the fiscal year immediately following the most recent fiscal year for which full financial statements were included in the offering statement, or, if the offering statement included financial statements for the first six months of the fiscal year following the most recent full fiscal year, for the first six months of the following fiscal year.

 (4) *Current reports.* Current reports on Form 1-U (§239.93 of this chapter) with respect to the matters and within the period specified in that form, unless substantially the same information has been previously reported to the Commission by the issuer under cover of Form 1-K or Form 1-SA.

 (5) *Reporting by successor issuers.* Where in connection with a succession by merger, consolidation, exchange of securities, acquisition of assets or otherwise, securities of any issuer that is not required to file reports pursuant to paragraph (b) of this section are issued to the holders of any class of securities of another issuer that is required to file such reports, the duty to file reports pursuant to paragraph (b) of this section shall be deemed to have been assumed by the issuer of the class of securities so issued. The successor issuer must, after the consummation of the succession, file reports in accordance with paragraph (b) of this section, unless that issuer is exempt from filing such reports or the duty to file such reports is terminated or suspended under paragraph (d) of this section.

(c) *Amendments.* All amendments to the reports described in paragraphs (a) and (b) of this section must be filed under cover of the form amended, marked with the letter A to designate the document as an amendment, e.g., "1-K/A," and in compliance with pertinent requirements applicable to such reports. Amendments filed pursuant to this paragraph (c) must set forth the complete text of each item as amended, but need not include any items that were not amended. Amendments must be numbered sequentially and be filed separately for each report amended.

Amendments must be signed on behalf of the issuer by a duly authorized representative of the issuer. An amendment to any report required to include certifications as specified in the applicable form must include new certifications by the appropriate persons.

(d) *Suspension of duty to file reports.* (1) The duty to file reports under this rule shall be automatically suspended if and so long as the issuer is subject to the duty to file reports required by section 13 or 15(d) of the Exchange Act (15 U.S.C. 78m or 15 U.S.C. 78o).

(2) The duty to file reports under paragraph (b) of this section with respect to a class of securities held of record (as defined in Rule 12g5-1 (§240.12g5-1 of this chapter)) by less than 300 persons, or less than 1,200 persons for a bank (as defined in Section 3(a) (6) of the Exchange Act (15 U.S.C. 78c(a)(6)), or a bank holding company (as defined in section 2 of the Bank Holding Company Act of 1956 (12 U.S.C. 1841)), shall be suspended for such class of securities immediately upon filing with the Commission an exit report on Form 1-Z (§239.94 of this chapter) if the issuer of such class has filed all reports due pursuant to this rule before the date of such Form 1-Z filing for the shorter of:

   (i) The period since the issuer became subject to such reporting obligation; or

   (ii) Its most recent three fiscal years and the portion of the current year preceding the date of filing Form 1-Z.

(3) For the purposes of paragraph (d)(2) of this section, the term *class* shall be construed to include all securities of an issuer that are of substantially similar character and the holders of which enjoy substantially similar rights and privileges. If the Form 1-Z is subsequently withdrawn or if it is denied because the issuer was ineligible to use the form, the issuer must, within 60 calendar days, file with the Commission all reports which would have been required if such exit report had not been filed. If the suspension resulted from the issuer's merger into, or consolidation with, another issuer or issuers, the notice must be filed by the successor issuer.

(4) The ability to suspend reporting, as described in paragraph (d)(2) of this section, is not available for any class of securities if:

    (i) During that fiscal year a Tier 2 offering statement was qualified;

    (ii) The issuer has not filed an annual report under this rule or the Exchange Act for the fiscal year in which a Tier 2 offering statement was qualified; or

    (iii) Offers or sales of securities of that class are being made pursuant to a Tier 2 Regulation A offering.

(e) *Termination of duty to file reports.* If the duty to file reports is suspended pursuant to paragraph (d)(1) of this section and such suspension ends because the issuer terminates or suspends its duty to file reports under the Exchange Act, the issuer's obligation to file reports under paragraph (b) of this section shall:

    (1) Automatically terminate if the issuer is eligible to suspend its duty to file reports under paragraphs (d)(2) and (3) of this section; or

    (2) Recommence with the report covering the most recent financial period after that included in any effective registration statement or filed Exchange Act report.

§230.258 Suspension of the Exemption

(a) *Suspension.* The Commission may at any time enter an order temporarily suspending a Regulation A exemption if it has reason to believe that:

    (1) No exemption is available or any of the terms, conditions or requirements of Regulation A have not been complied with;

    (2) The offering statement, any sales or solicitation of interest material, or any report filed pursuant to Rule 257 (§230.257) contains any untrue statement of a material fact or omits to state a material fact necessary in order to make the statements made, in light of the circumstances under which they are made, not misleading;

(3) The offering is being made or would be made in violation of section 17 of the Securities Act;

(4) An event has occurred after the filing of the offering statement that would have rendered the exemption hereunder unavailable if it had occurred before such filing;

(5) Any person specified in Rule 262(a) (§230.262(a)) has been indicted for any crime or offense of the character specified in Rule 262(a)(1) (§230.262(a)(1)), or any proceeding has been initiated for the purpose of enjoining any such person from engaging in or continuing any conduct or practice of the character specified in Rule 262(a)(2) (§230.262(a)(2)), or any proceeding has been initiated for the purposes of Rule 262(a)(3)-(8) (§230.262(a)(3) through (8)); or

(6) The issuer or any promoter, officer, director, or underwriter has failed to cooperate, or has obstructed or refused to permit the making of an investigation by the Commission in connection with any offering made or proposed to be made in reliance on Regulation A.

(b) *Notice and hearing.* Upon the entry of an order under paragraph (a) of this section, the Commission will promptly give notice to the issuer, any underwriter, and any selling securityholder:

(1) That such order has been entered, together with a brief statement of the reasons for the entry of the order; and

(2) That the Commission, upon receipt of a written request within 30 calendar days after the entry of the order, will, within 20 calendar days after receiving the request, order a hearing at a place to be designated by the Commission.

(c) *Suspension order.* If no hearing is requested and none is ordered by the Commission, an order entered under paragraph (a) of this section shall become permanent on the 30th calendar day after its entry and shall remain in effect unless or until it is modified or vacated by the Commission. Where a hearing is requested or is ordered by the Commission, the Commission will, after notice of and opportunity for such hearing, either vacate the order or enter an order permanently suspending the exemption.

(d) *Permanent suspension.* The Commission may, at any time after notice of and opportunity for hearing, enter an order permanently suspending the exemption for any reason upon which it could have entered a temporary suspension order under paragraph (a) of this section. Any such order shall remain in effect until vacated by the Commission.

(e) *Notice procedures.* All notices required by this rule must be given by personal service, registered or certified mail to the addresses given by the issuer, any underwriter and any selling securityholder in the offering statement.

§230.259 Withdrawal or Abandonment of Offering Statements

(a) *Withdrawal.* If none of the securities that are the subject of an offering statement has been sold and such offering statement is not the subject of a proceeding under Rule 258 (§230.258), the offering statement may be withdrawn with the Commission's consent. The application for withdrawal must state the reason the offering statement is to be withdrawn and must be signed by an authorized representative of the issuer. Any withdrawn document will remain in the Commission's files, as well as the related request for withdrawal.

(b) *Abandonment.* When an offering statement has been on file with the Commission for nine months without amendment and has not become qualified, the Commission may, in its discretion, declare the offering statement abandoned. If the offering statement has been amended, the nine-month period shall be computed from the date of the latest amendment.

§230.260 Insignificant Deviations from a Term, Condition or Requirement of Regulation A

(a) *Failure to comply.* A failure to comply with a term, condition or requirement of Regulation A will not result in the loss of the exemption from the requirements of section 5 of the Securities Act for any offer or sale to a particular individual or entity, if the person relying on the exemption establishes that:

    (1) The failure to comply did not pertain to a term, condition or requirement directly intended to protect that particular individual or entity;

    (2) The failure to comply was insignificant with respect to the offering as a whole, provided that any failure to comply with Rule 251(a), (b), and (d)(1) and (3) (§230.251(a), (b), and (d)(1) and (3)) shall be deemed to be significant to the offering as a whole; and

    (3) A good faith and reasonable attempt was made to comply with all applicable terms, conditions and requirements of Regulation A.

(b) *Action by Commission.* A transaction made in reliance upon Regulation A must comply with all applicable terms, conditions and requirements of the regulation. Where an exemption is established only through reliance upon paragraph (a) of this section, the failure to comply shall nonetheless be actionable by the Commission under section 20 of the Securities Act.

(c) *Suspension.* This provision provides no relief or protection from a proceeding under Rule 258 (§230.258).

§230.261 Definitions

As used in this Regulation A, all terms have the same meanings as in Rule 405 (§230.405), except that all references to *registrant* in those definitions shall refer to the issuer of the securities to be offered and sold under Regulation A. In addition, these terms have the following meanings:

(a) *Affiliated issuer.* An affiliate (as defined in Rule 501 (§230.501)) of the issuer that is issuing securities in the same offering.

(b) *Business day.* Any day except Saturdays, Sundays or United States federal holidays.

(c) *Eligible securities.* Equity securities, debt securities, and securities convertible or exchangeable to equity interests, including any guarantees of such securities, but not including asset-backed securities as such term is defined in Item 1101(c) of Regulation AB.

(d) *Final order.* A written directive or declaratory statement issued by a federal or state agency described in Rule 262(a)(3) (§230.262(a)(3)) under applicable statutory authority that provides for notice and an opportunity for hearing, which constitutes a final disposition or action by that federal or state agency.

(e) *Final offering circular.* The more recent of: the current offering circular contained in a qualified offering statement; and any offering circular filed pursuant to Rule 253(g) (§230.253(g)). If, however, the issuer is relying on Rule 253(b) ((§230.253(b)), the Final Offering Circular is the most recent of the offering circular filed pursuant to Rule 253(g)(1) or (3) (§230.253(g)(1) or (3)) and any subsequent offering circular filed pursuant to Rule 253(g) (§230.253(g)).

(f) *Offering statement.* An offering statement prepared pursuant to Regulation A.

(g) *Preliminary offering circular.* The offering circular described in Rule 254 (§230.254).

§230.262 Disqualification Provisions

(a) *Disqualification events.* No exemption under this Regulation A shall be available for a sale of securities if the issuer; any predecessor of the issuer; any affiliated issuer; any director, executive officer, other officer participating in the offering, general partner or managing member of the issuer; any beneficial owner of 20% or more of the issuer's outstanding voting equity securities, calculated on the basis of voting power; any promoter connected with the issuer in any capacity at the time of filing, any offer after qualification, or such sale; any person that has been or will be paid (directly or indirectly) remuneration for solicitation of purchasers in connection with such sale of securities; any general partner or managing member of any such solicitor; or any director, executive officer or other officer participating in the offering of any such solicitor or general partner or managing member of such solicitor:

    (1) Has been convicted, within ten years before the filing of the offering statement (or five years, in the case of issuers, their predecessors and affiliated issuers), of any felony or misdemeanor:

        (i) In connection with the purchase or sale of any security;

        (ii) Involving the making of any false filing with the Commission; or

        (iii) Arising out of the conduct of the business of an underwriter, broker, dealer, municipal securities dealer, investment adviser or paid solicitor of purchasers of securities;

    (2) Is subject to any order, judgment or decree of any court of competent jurisdiction, entered within five years before the filing of the offering statement, that, at the time of such filing, restrains or enjoins such person from engaging or continuing to engage in any conduct or practice:

        (i) In connection with the purchase or sale of any security;

       (ii) Involving the making of any false filing with the Commission; or

      (iii) Arising out of the conduct of the business of an underwriter, broker, dealer, municipal securities dealer, investment adviser or paid solicitor of purchasers of securities;

(3) Is subject to a final order (as defined in Rule 261 (§230.261)) of a state securities commission (or an agency or officer of a state performing like functions); a state authority that supervises or examines banks, savings associations, or credit unions; a state insurance commission (or an agency or officer of a state performing like functions); an appropriate federal banking agency; the U.S. Commodity Futures Trading Commission; or the National Credit Union Administration that:

      (i) At the time of the filing of the offering statement, bars the person from:

(A) Association with an entity regulated by such commission, authority, agency, or officer;

(B) Engaging in the business of securities, insurance or banking; or

(C) Engaging in savings association or credit union activities; or

      (ii) Constitutes a final order based on a violation of any law or regulation that prohibits fraudulent, manipulative, or deceptive conduct entered within ten years before such filing of the offering statement;

(4) Is subject to an order of the Commission entered pursuant to section 15(b) or 15B(c) of the Securities Exchange Act of 1934 (15 U.S.C. 78o(b) or 78o-4(c)) or section 203(e) or (f) of the Investment Advisers Act of 1940 (15 U.S.C. 80b-3(e) or (f)) that, at the time of the filing of the offering statement:

      (i) Suspends or revokes such person's registration as a broker, dealer, municipal securities dealer or investment adviser;

      (ii) Places limitations on the activities, functions or operations of such person; or

       (iii) Bars such person from being associated with any entity or from participating in the offering of any penny stock;

(5) Is subject to any order of the Commission entered within five years before the filing of the offering statement that, at the time of such filing, orders the person to cease and desist from committing or causing a violation or future violation of:

       (i) Any scienter-based anti-fraud provision of the federal securities laws, including without limitation section 17(a)(1) of the Securities Act of 1933 (15 U.S.C. 77q(a)(1)), section 10(b) of the Securities Exchange Act of 1934 (15 U.S.C. 78j(b)) and 17 CFR 240.10b-5, section 15(c)(1) of the Securities Exchange Act of 1934 (15 U.S.C. 78o(c)(1)) and section 206(1) of the Investment Advisers Act of 1940 (15 U.S.C. 80b-6(1)), or any other rule or regulation thereunder; or

       (ii) Section 5 of the Securities Act of 1933 (15 U.S.C. 77e).

(6) Is suspended or expelled from membership in, or suspended or barred from association with a member of, a registered national securities exchange or a registered national or affiliated securities association for any act or omission to act constituting conduct inconsistent with just and equitable principles of trade;

(7) Has filed (as a registrant or issuer), or was or was named as an underwriter in, any registration statement or offering statement filed with the Commission that, within five years before the filing of the offering statement, was the subject of a refusal order, stop order, or order suspending the Regulation A exemption, or is, at the time of such filing, the subject of an investigation or proceeding to determine whether a stop order or suspension order should be issued; or

(8) Is subject to a United States Postal Service false representation order entered within five years before the filing of the offering statement, or is, at the time of such filing, subject to a temporary restraining order or preliminary injunction with respect to conduct alleged by the United States Postal Service to constitute a scheme or device for obtaining money or property through the mail by means of false representations.

(b) *Transition, waivers, reasonable care exception.* Paragraph (a) of this section shall not apply:

(1) With respect to any order under §230.262(a)(3) or (5) that occurred or was issued before June 19, 2015;

(2) Upon a showing of good cause and without prejudice to any other action by the Commission, if the Commission determines that it is not necessary under the circumstances that an exemption be denied;

(3) If, before the filing of the offering statement, the court or regulatory authority that entered the relevant order, judgment or decree advises in writing (whether contained in the relevant judgment, order or decree or separately to the Commission or its staff) that disqualification under paragraph (a) of this section should not arise as a consequence of such order, judgment or decree; or

(4) If the issuer establishes that it did not know and, in the exercise of reasonable care, could not have known that a disqualification existed under paragraph (a) of this section.

NOTE TO PARAGRAPH (b)(4). An issuer will not be able to establish that it has exercised reasonable care unless it has made, in light of the circumstances, factual inquiry into whether any disqualifications exist. The nature and scope of the factual inquiry will vary based on the facts and circumstances concerning, among other things, the issuer and the other offering participants.

(c) *Affiliated issuers.* For purposes of paragraph (a) of this section, events relating to any affiliated issuer that occurred before the affiliation arose will be not considered disqualifying if the affiliated entity is not:

(1) In control of the issuer; or

(2) Under common control with the issuer by a third party that was in control of the affiliated entity at the time of such events.

(d) *Disclosure of prior "bad actor" events.* The issuer must include in the offering circular a description of any matters that would have triggered disqualification under paragraphs (a)(3) and (5) of this section but occurred before June 19, 2015. The failure to provide such information shall not prevent an issuer from relying on Regulation A if the issuer establishes that it did not know and, in the exercise of reasonable care, could not have known of the existence of the undisclosed matter or matters.

§230.263 Consent to Service of Process

(a) If the issuer is not organized under the laws of any of the states or territories of the United States of America, it shall furnish to the Commission a written irrevocable consent and power of attorney on Form F-X (§239.42 of this chapter) at the time of filing the offering statement required by Rule 252 (§230.252).

(b) Any change to the name or address of the agent for service of the issuer shall be communicated promptly to the Commission through amendment of the requisite form and referencing the file number of the relevant offering statement.

§§230.300-230.346 [Reserved]

ATTENTION ELECTRONIC FILERS

THIS REGULATION SHOULD BE READ IN CONJUNCTION WITH REGULATION S-T (PART 232 OF THIS CHAPTER), WHICH GOVERNS THE PREPARATION AND SUBMISSION OF DOCUMENTS IN ELECTRONIC FORMAT. MANY PROVISIONS RELATING TO THE PREPARATION AND SUBMISSION OF DOCUMENTS IN PAPER FORMAT CONTAINED IN THIS REGULATION ARE SUPERSEDED BY THE PROVISIONS OF REGULATION S-T FOR DOCUMENTS REQUIRED TO BE FILED IN ELECTRONIC FORMAT.

Current Guidance from SEC

Appendix B provides critical information on how the SEC intends to apply Regulation A in everyday scenarios. Often, federal regulatory agencies provide detailed rules like we see with Regulation A, but, given their complexity and interplay with other regulations, agencies will also provide informal guidance as to how they read their rules or intend to apply them.

Compliance and Disclosure Interpretations – Securities Act Rules; Regulation A[1]

Section182. Rules 251 to 263 [June 23, 2015]

Question 182.01

Question: Where an issuer elects to nonpublicly submit a draft offering statement for staff review pursuant to Rule 252(d) of Regulation A before publicly filing its Form 1A, Item 15 (Additional Exhibits) of Part III (Exhibits) to Form 1A requires issuers to file as an exhibit to the publiclyfiled offering statement: (1) any nonpublic, draft offering statement previously submitted pursuant to Rule 252(d), and (2) any related, nonpublic correspondence submitted by or on behalf of the issuers. Would an issuer that elects to make the nonpublic, draft offering statements public on the EDGARLink submissions page of EDGAR (see Chapter 7 (Preparing and Transmitting EDGARLink Online Submissions) of Volume II of the EDGAR Filer Manual, *available at*: http://www.sec.gov/info/edgar/edmanuals.htm) at the time it publicly files its Form 1A also be required to refile such material as an exhibit pursuant to Item 15 of Part III?

Answer: No. If, at the time it first files the offering statement publicly, the issuer makes public on the EDGARLink submissions page all prior nonpublic, draft offering statements, the offering statements will no longer be nonpublic and the issuer will not be required to file them as exhibits. The issuer is still required to file as an exhibit any related, nonpublic correspondence submitted by or on behalf of the issuer regarding nonpublic draft offering statements submitted pursuant to Rule 252(d).

Question 182.02

Question: If an issuer elects to submit a draft offering statement for nonpublic staff review before public filing pursuant to Rule 252(d), and, as part of that process, submits correspondence relating to its offering statement, what must it do if it wants to protect portions of that correspondence from public release?

Answer: During the review of the draft offering statement, the issuer would request confidential treatment of any information in the related correspondence pursuant to Rule 83, in the same manner it would during a typical review of a registered offering. It would submit a redacted copy of the

---

[1]http://www.sec.gov/divisions/corpfin/guidance/securitiesactrules-interps.htm

correspondence via EDGAR, with the appropriate legend indicating that it was being submitted pursuant to a confidential treatment request under Rule 83. At the same time, it would submit an unredacted paper version to the SEC, in the manner required by that rule. When the issuer makes its public filing of the offering statement, it will be required to file as an exhibit to the electronically filed offering statement any previously submitted nonpublic correspondence related to the non public review. Since that correspondence will be information required to be filed with the SEC, the issuer must redact the confidential information from the filed exhibit, include the required legends and redaction markings, and submit in paper format to the SEC's Office of the Secretary an application for confidential treatment of the redacted information under Rule 406. The staff will consider and act on that application in the same manner it would with any other application under Rule 406 for other types of filed exhibits. As with registered offerings, the review staff will act on Rule 406 confidential treatment applications before the offering statement is qualified. For the requirements a registrant must satisfy when requesting confidential treatment, see Division of Corporation Finance Staff Legal Bulletin No. 1 (with Addendum).

Question 182.03

Question: Would a company with headquarters that are located within the United States or Canada, but whose business primarily involves managing operations that are located outside those countries be considered to have its "principal place of business" within the United States or Canada for purposes of determining issuer eligibility under Regulation A?

Answer: Yes, an issuer will be considered to have its "principal place of business" in the United States or Canada for purposes of determining issuer eligibility under Rule 251(b) of Regulation A if its officers, partners, or managers primarily direct, control and coordinate the issuer's activities from the United States or Canada.

Question 182.04

Question: Is a company that was previously required to file reports with the Commission under Section 15(d) of the Exchange Act, but that has since suspended its Exchange Act reporting obligation, an eligible issuer under Rule 251(b)(2) of Regulation A?

Answer: Yes. A company that has suspended its Exchange Act reporting obligation by satisfying the statutory provisions for suspension in Section 15(d) of the Exchange Act or the requirements of Exchange Act Rule 12h3 is not considered to be subject to Section 13 or 15(d) of the Exchange Act for purposes of Rule 251(b)(2) of Regulation A.

Question 182.05

Question: Is a voluntary filer under the Exchange Act an eligible issuer for purposes of Rule 251(b)(2) of Regulation A?

Answer: Yes. A voluntary filer is not subject to Exchange Act Section 13 or 15(d) because it is not obligated to file Exchange Act reports pursuant to either of those provisions.

Question 182.06

Question: Is a private whollyowned subsidiary of an Exchange Act reporting company parent eligible to sell securities pursuant to Regulation A?

Answer: Yes, although the Exchange Act reporting company parent could not be a guarantor or co issuer of the securities of the private whollyowned subsidiary.

Question 182.07

Question: Can Regulation A be relied upon by an issuer for business combination transactions, such as a merger or acquisition?

Answer: Yes. The final rules do not limit the availability of Regulation A for business combination transactions, but, as the Commission (SEC Rel. No. 339497) indicated, Regulation A would not be available for business acquisition shelf transactions, which are typically conducted on a delayed basis.

Question 182.08

Question: May a recently created entity choose to provide a balance sheet as of its inception date?

Answer: Yes, as long as the inception date is within nine months before the date of filing or qualification and the date of filing or qualification is not more than three months after the entity reached its first annual balance sheet date. The date of the most recent balance sheet determines which fiscal years, or period since existence for recently created entities, the statements of comprehensive income, cash flows and changes in stockholders' equity must cover. When the balance sheet is dated as of inception the statements of comprehensive income, cash flows and changes in stockholders' equity will not be applicable.

Question 182.09

Question: Can an issuer solicit interest (or "test the waters") in a Regulation A offering on a platform that limits the number of characters or amount of text that can be included, thereby preventing the inclusion in such communication of the information required by Rule 255?

Answer: Yes. The staff will not object to the use of an active hyperlink to satisfy the requirements of Rule 255 in the following limited circumstances:

- The electronic communication is distributed through a platform that has technological limitations on the number of characters or amount of text that may be included in the communication;

- Including the required statements in their entirety, together with the other information, would cause the communication to exceed the limit on the number of characters or amount of text; and

- The communication contains an active hyperlink to the required statements that otherwise satisfy Rule 255 and, where possible, prominently conveys, through introductory language or otherwise, that important or required information is provided through the hyperlink.

Where an electronic communication is capable of including the entirety of the required statements, along with the other information, without exceeding the applicable limit on number of characters or amount of text, the use of a hyperlink to the required statements would be inappropriate.

Question 182.10

Question: Are state securities law registration and qualification requirements preempted with respect to resales of securities purchased in a Tier 2 offering?

Answer: No. State securities law registration and qualification requirements are only preempted with respect to primary offerings of securities by the issuer or secondary offerings by selling securityholders that are qualified pursuant to Regulation A and offered or sold to qualified purchasers pursuant to a Tier 2 offering. Resales of securities purchased in a Tier 2 offering must be registered, or offered or sold pursuant to an exemption from registration, with state securities regulators.

Question 182.11

Question: When is an issuer required to engage the services of a registered transfer agent before being able to avail itself of the conditional exemption from mandatory registration under Section 12(g) of the Exchange Act described in Exchange Act Rule 12g51(a)(7)?

Answer: An issuer that seeks to rely on the conditional exemption from mandatory registration under Section 12(g) of the Exchange Act must at the time of reliance on the conditional exemption satisfy the requirements of Rule 12g51(a)(7).

Amendments to Regulation A: A Small Entity Compliance Guide*, June 18, 2015[2]

Table of Contents

This compliance guide is divided into the following parts:

- Summary of Regulation A
- Scope of Exemption
- Offering Statement
- Solicitation of Interest Materials
- Ongoing Reporting
- Bad Actor Disqualification
- Relationship with State Securities Law
- Transition Issues
- Other Resources
- Contacting the SEC

1. Summary of Regulation A

On March 25, 2015, the Securities and Exchange Commission (the "Commission") adopted final rules to implement Section 401 of the Jumpstart Our Business Startups (JOBS) Act by expanding Regulation A into two tiers: Tier 1, for securities offerings of up to $20 million in a 12-month period; and Tier 2, for securities offerings of up to $50 million in a 12-month period. An issuer of $20 million or less of securities can elect to proceed under either

---

[2]http://www.sec.gov/info/smallbus/secg/regulation-a-amendments-secg.shtml

Tier 1 or Tier 2. The final rules for offerings under Tier 1 and Tier 2 build on current Regulation A and preserve, with some modifications, existing provisions regarding issuer eligibility, offering circular contents, testing the waters, and "bad actor" disqualification. The final rules modernize the Regulation A filing process for all offerings, align practice in certain areas with prevailing practice for registered offerings, create additional flexibility for issuers in the offering process, and establish an ongoing reporting regime for certain Regulation A issuers.

Under the final rules, Tier 2 issuers are required to include audited financial statements in their offering documents and to file annual, semiannual, and current reports with the Commission on an ongoing basis. With the exception of securities that will be listed on a national securities exchange upon qualification, purchasers in Tier 2 offerings must either be accredited investors, as that term is defined in Rule 501(a) of Regulation D, or be subject to certain limitations on their investment. The requirements for Tier 1 and Tier 2 offerings are described more fully below.

2. Scope of Exemption

Understanding the scope of the exemption is important because not all issuers are eligible to conduct offerings pursuant to Regulation A. Additionally, there are limitations on the types of securities that may be sold and on the amount of securities that may be sold by the issuer and selling securityholders, as well as other issues that may affect the issuer's offering process pursuant to the exemption.

a. Eligible Issuers and Securities

Regulation A is available only to companies organized in and with their principal place of business in the United States or Canada. It is not available to:

- companies subject to the ongoing reporting requirements of Section 13 or 15(d) of the Exchange Act;

- companies registered or required to be registered under the Investment Company Act of 1940 and BDCs;

- development stage companies that have no specific business plan or purpose or have indicated that their business plan is to engage in a merger or acquisition with an unidentified company or companies (often referred to as, "blank check companies");

- issuers of fractional undivided interests in oil or gas rights, or similar interests in other mineral rights;

- issuers that are required to, but that have not, filed with the Commission the ongoing reports required by the rules under Regulation A during the two years immediately preceding the filing of a new offering statement (or for such shorter period that the issuer was required to file such reports);

- issuers that are or have been subject to an order by the Commission denying, suspending, or revoking the registration of a class of securities pursuant to Section 12(j) of the Exchange Act that was entered within five years before the filing of the offering statement; and

- issuers subject to "bad actor" disqualification under Rule 262.

The final rules limit the types of securities eligible for sale under Regulation A to the specifically enumerated list in Section 3(b)(3) of the Securities Act, which includes warrants and convertible equity and debt securities, among other equity and debt securities. The final rules exclude asset-backed securities from the list of eligible securities.

b. Offering Limitations and Secondary Sales

Issuers may elect to conduct a Regulation A offering pursuant to the requirements of either Tier 1 or Tier 2. Tier 1 is available for offerings of up to $20 million in a 12-month period, including no more than $6 million on behalf of selling securityholders that are affiliates of the issuer. Tier 2 is available for offerings of up to $50 million in a 12-month period, including no more than $15 million on behalf of selling securityholders that are affiliates of the issuer. Additionally, sales by all selling securityholders in a Regulation A offering are limited to no more than 30% of the aggregate offering price in an issuer's first Regulation A offering and any subsequent Regulation A offerings in the following 12-month period.

c. Investment Limitations in Tier 2 Offerings

Issuers that conduct a Tier 2 offering should note that Regulation A limits the amount of securities that an investor who is not an accredited investor under Rule 501(a) of Regulation D can purchase in a Tier 2 offering to no more than: (a) 10% of the greater of annual income or net worth (for natural persons); or (b) 10% of the greater of annual revenue or net assets at fiscal year end (for non-natural persons). This limit does not, however, apply to purchases of securities that will be listed on a national securities exchange upon qualification.

d. Integration

The integration doctrine provides an analytical framework for determining whether multiple securities transactions should be considered part of the same offering. This analysis helps to determine whether registration under Section 5 of the Securities Act is required or an exemption is available for the entire offering. Generally, the determination as to whether particular securities offerings should be integrated calls for an analysis of the specific facts and circumstances. Regulation A, however, provides issuers with a safe harbor that offerings conducted pursuant to Regulation A will not be integrated with:

- prior offers or sales of securities; or

- subsequent offers or sales of securities that are:

- registered under the Securities Act, except as provided in Rule 255(c);

- made pursuant to Rule 701 under the Securities Act;

- made pursuant to an employee benefit plan;

- made pursuant to Regulation S;

- made pursuant to Section 4(a)(6) of the Securities Act; or

- made more than six months after completion of the Regulation A offering.

e. Treatment under Section 12(g)

Section 12(g) of the Securities Exchange Act of 1934 requires, among other things, that an issuer with total assets exceeding $10,000,000 and a class of equity securities held of record by either 2,000 persons, or 500 persons who are not accredited investors, register such class of securities with the Commission. Regulation A, however, conditionally exempts securities issued in a Tier 2 offering from the mandatory registration provisions of Section 12(g) for so long as the issuer remains subject to, and is current in (as of its fiscal year end), its Regulation A periodic reporting obligations. Additionally, in order for the conditional exemption to apply, issuers in Tier 2 offerings are required to engage the services of a transfer agent registered with the Commission pursuant to Section 17A of the Exchange Act. The final rules also provide that the conditional exemption from Section 12(g) is only available to companies that meet size-based requirements similar to those contained in the "smaller reporting company" definition under Securities Act and Exchange Act rules.[1] An issuer that exceeds the size-based requirements is granted a two-year transition period before it would be required to register its class of securities pursuant to Section 12(g), provided it timely files all ongoing reports due during such period.

3. Offering Statement

All issuers that conduct offerings pursuant to Regulation A are required to electronically file an offering statement on Form 1-A on the Commission's Electronic Data Gathering, Analysis and Retrieval system (EDGAR). Form 1-A consists of three parts:

- Part I: an eXtensible Markup Language (XML) based fillable form;

- Part II: a text file attachment containing the body of the disclosure document and financial statements; and

- Part III: text file attachments, containing the signatures, exhibits index, and the exhibits to the offering statement.

a. Part I

Part I of Form 1-A serves as a notice of certain basic information about the issuer and its proposed offering, which also helps to confirm the availability of the exemption. The notification in Part I of Form 1-A requires disclosure in response to the following items:

- Item 1. (Issuer Information) requires information about the issuer's identity, industry, number of employees, financial statements and capital structure, as well as contact information.

- Item 2. (Issuer Eligibility) requires the issuer to certify that it meets various issuer eligibility criteria.

- Item 3. (Application of Rule 262 ("bad actor" disqualification and disclosure)) requires the issuer to certify that no disqualifying events have occurred and to indicate whether related disclosure will be included in the offering circular.

- Item 4. (Summary Information Regarding the Offering and other Current or Proposed Offerings) includes indicator boxes or buttons and text boxes eliciting information about the offering.

- Item 5. (Jurisdictions in Which Securities are to be Offered) requires information about the jurisdiction(s) in which the securities will be offered.

- Item 6. (Unregistered Securities Issued or Sold Within One Year) requires disclosure about unregistered issuances or sales of securities within the last year.

b. Part II

Part II of Form 1-A contains the primary disclosure document that an issuer will prepare in connection with a Regulation A offering, called an "offering circular." Issuers are required to provide financial disclosure in Part II that follows the requirements of Part F/S of Form 1-A, while they have the option to prepare narrative disclosure that follows one of two different formats.[2]

i. Offering Circular Format

The Offering Circular format is a simplified and scaled version of the narrative disclosure requirements otherwise required to be provided by issuers in registered offerings on Form S-1. In addition to the availability of certain scaled disclosure items, the Offering Circular format is meant to simplify the process by which an issuer prepares its narrative disclosure by limiting the need for issuers to look outside the form for disclosure guidance.

ii. Part I of Form S-1 or Part I of Form S-11 Formats

Part I of Form S-1 and Part I of Form S-11 contain the narrative disclosure requirements for registration statements filed by issuers in registered offerings. In addition to the Offering Circular format, issuers may provide narrative disclosure in Part II of Form 1-A that follows the requirements of Part I of Form S-1 or, in certain circumstances, Part I of Form S-11. While Form S-1 is generally available for all types of issuers and transactions, Form S-11 is only available for offerings of securities issued by (i) real estate investment trusts, or (ii) issuers whose business is primarily that of acquiring and holding for investment real estate or interests in real estate or interests in other issuers whose business is primarily that of acquiring and holding real estate or interest in real estate for investment. Part I of both Form S-1 and Form S-11 generally describes narrative disclosure requirements by cross-reference to the item requirements of Regulation S-K.

iii. Part F/S (Financial Statements)

Part II of Form 1-A requires issuers to provide financial statements that comply with the requirements of Part F/S. Part F/S requires issuers in both Tier 1 and Tier 2 offerings to file balance sheets and related financial statements for the two previous fiscal year ends (or for such shorter time that they have been in existence). For Tier 1 offerings, issuers are not required to provide audited financial statements unless the issuer has already prepared them for other purposes. Issuers in Tier 2 offerings are required to include financial statements in their offering circulars that are audited in accordance with either the auditing standards of the American Institute of Certified Public Accountants (AICPA) (referred to as U.S. Generally Accepted Auditing Standards or GAAS) or the standards of the Public Company Accounting Oversight Board (PCAOB). Part F/S requires issuers in both Tier 1 and Tier 2 offerings to include financial statements in Form 1-A that are dated not more than nine months before the date of non-public submission, filing, or qualification, with the most recent annual or interim balance sheet not older than nine months. If interim financial statements are required, they must cover a period of at least six months.

c. Part III

Part III of Form 1-A requires issuers to file certain documents as exhibits to the offering statement. Issuers are required to file the following exhibits with the offering statement: underwriting agreement; charter and by-laws; instrument defining the rights of securityholders; subscription agreement; voting trust agreement; material contracts; plan of acquisition, reorganization, arrangement, liquidation, or succession; escrow agreements; consents; opinion regarding legality; "testing the waters" materials; appointment of agent for service of process; materials related to non-public submissions; and any additional exhibits the issuer may wish to file.

d. Non-Public Submission of Draft Offering Statements

Issuers whose securities have not been previously sold pursuant to a qualified offering statement under Regulation A or an effective registration statement under the Securities Act are allowed to submit to the Commission a draft offering statement for non-public review by the staff. Consistent with the treatment of draft registration statements in registered offerings, a non-publicly submitted offering statement must be substantially complete upon submission in order for staff of the Division of Corporation Finance to begin its review. All non-public submissions of draft offering statements must be submitted electronically via EDGAR, and the initial non-public submission, all non-public amendments thereto, and correspondence submitted by or on behalf of the issuer to the Commission staff regarding such submissions must be publicly filed and available on EDGAR not less than 21 calendar days before qualification of the offering statement.

e. Qualification

Issuers are only permitted to begin selling securities pursuant to Regulation A once the offering statement has been qualified by the Commission. The Division of Corporation Finance has delegated authority to declare offering statements qualified by a "notice of qualification," which is analogous to a notice of effectiveness in registered offerings.

4. Solicitation of Interest Materials

Issuers are permitted to "test the waters" with, or solicit interest in a potential offering from, the general public either before or after the filing of the offering statement, provided that all solicitation materials include the legends required by the final rules and, after publicly filing the offering statement, are preceded or accompanied by a preliminary offering circular or contain a notice informing potential investors where and how the most current preliminary offering circular can be obtained.

5. Ongoing Reporting

Issuers in Tier 1 offerings are required to provide information about sales in such offerings and to update certain issuer information by electronically filing a Form 1-Z exit report with the Commission not later than 30 calendar days after termination or completion of an offering. Issuers in Tier 2 offerings are required to electronically file annual and semiannual reports, as well as current reports and, in certain circumstances, an exit report on Form 1-Z, with the Commission on EDGAR.

a. Annual Report on Form 1-K (Tier 2 Issuers Only)

Issuers in Tier 2 offerings are required to electronically file annual reports with the Commission on EDGAR on Form 1-K within 120 calendar days of the issuer's fiscal year end. Form 1-K requires issuers to update certain information previously filed with the Commission pursuant to Part 1 of Form 1-A, as well as to provide disclosure relating to the issuer's business operations for the preceding three fiscal years (or, if in existence for less than three years, since inception), related party transactions, beneficial ownership of the issuer's securities, executive officers and directors, including certain executive compensation information, management's discussion and analysis (MD&A) of the issuer's liquidity, capital resources, and results of operations, and two years of audited financial statements.

b. Semiannual Report on Form 1-SA (Tier 2 Issuers Only)

Issuers in Tier 2 offerings are required to electronically file semiannual reports with the Commission on EDGAR on Form 1-SA within 90 calendar days after the end of the first six months of the issuer's fiscal year. Form 1-SA requires issuers to provide disclosure primarily relating to the issuer's interim financial statements and MD&A.

c. Current Report on Form 1-U (Tier 2 Issuers Only)

Issuers in Tier 2 offerings are required to electronically file current reports with the Commission on EDGAR on Form 1-U within four business days of the occurrence of one (or more) of the following events:

- Fundamental changes;
- Bankruptcy or receivership;
- Material modification to the rights of securityholders;
- Changes in the issuer's certifying accountant;
- Non-reliance on previous financial statements or a related audit report or completed interim review;
- Changes in control of the issuer;

- Departure of the principal executive officer, principal financial officer, or principal accounting officer; and

- Unregistered sales of 10% or more of outstanding equity securities.

d. Exit Report on Form 1-Z (Tier 1 and Tier 2 Issuers)

Issuers in Tier 1 offerings are required to electronically file with the Commission on EDGAR certain summary information on terminated or completed Regulation A offerings in an exit report on Part I of Form 1-Z not later than 30 calendar days after termination or completion of an offering. Issuers conducting Tier 2 offerings are required to provide this information in Part I of Form 1-Z, if such information was not previously provided on Form 1-K as part of their annual report, at the time of filing information in response to Part II of Form 1-Z.

Issuers in Tier 2 offerings that have filed all ongoing reports required by Regulation A for the shorter of (1) the period since the issuer became subject to such reporting obligation or (2) its most recent three fiscal years and the portion of the current year preceding the date of filing Form 1-Z may immediately suspend their ongoing reporting obligations under Regulation A at any time after completing reporting for the fiscal year in which the offering statement was qualified, if the securities of each class to which the offering statement relates are held of record by fewer than 300 persons and offers or sales made in reliance on a qualified Tier 2 offering statement are not ongoing. In such circumstances, an issuer's obligation to continue to file ongoing reports in a Tier 2 offering under Regulation A would be suspended immediately upon the electronic filing of a notice with the Commission on Part II of Form 1-Z.

6. Bad Actor Disqualification

The "bad actor" disqualification provisions contained in Rule 262 of Regulation A disqualify securities offerings from reliance on Regulation A if the issuer or other relevant persons (such as underwriters, placement agents, and the directors, officers and significant shareholders of the issuer) (collectively, "covered persons") have experienced a disqualifying event, such as being convicted of, or subject to court or administrative sanctions for, securities fraud or other violations of specified laws.

a. Covered Persons

Understanding the categories of persons that are covered by Rule 262 is important because issuers are required to conduct a factual inquiry to determine whether any covered person has had a disqualifying event, and the existence of such an event will generally disqualify the offering from reliance on Regulation A.

"Covered persons" include:

- the issuer, including its predecessors and affiliated issuers
- directors, general partners, and managing members of the issuer
- executive officers of the issuer, and other officers of the issuers that participate in the offering
- 20 percent beneficial owners of the issuer, calculated on the basis of voting power
- promoters connected with the issuer in any capacity
- persons compensated for soliciting investors, including their directors, executive officers or other officers participating in the offerings, general partners and managing members

b. Disqualifying Events

Under the final rule, disqualifying events include:

- Certain criminal convictions
- Certain court injunctions and restraining orders
- Certain final orders of certain state and federal regulators
- Certain SEC disciplinary orders
- Certain SEC cease-and-desist orders
- Suspension or expulsion from membership in a self-regulatory organization (SRO), such as FINRA, or from association with an SRO member
- SEC stop orders and orders suspending the Regulation A exemption
- U.S. Postal Service false representation orders

Many disqualifying events include a look-back period (for example, a court injunction that was issued within the last five years or a regulatory order that was issued within the last ten years). The look-back period is measured from the date of the disqualifying event—for example, the issuance of the injunction or regulatory order and not the date of the underlying conduct that led to the disqualifying event—to the date of the filing of an offering statement.

c. Reasonable Care Exception

The final rule provides an exception from disqualification when the issuer is able to demonstrate that it did not know and, in the exercise of reasonable care, could not have known that a covered person with a disqualifying event participated in the offering.

The steps an issuer should take to exercise reasonable care will vary according to particular facts and circumstances. A note to the rule states that an issuer will not be able to establish that it has exercised reasonable care unless it has made, in light of the circumstances, factual inquiry into whether any disqualification exists.

d. Other Exceptions

i. Determination of issuing authority

Disqualification will not arise if, before the filing of the offering statement, the court or regulatory authority that entered the relevant order, judgment or decree advises in writing—whether in the relevant judgment, order or decree or separately to the Commission or its staff—that disqualification under Regulation A should not arise as a consequence of such order, judgment or decree.

ii. Disclosure of pre-existing events

Disqualification will not arise as a result of disqualifying events relating to final orders of certain state and federal regulators or certain SEC cease-and-desist orders that occurred before June 19, 2015, the effective date of the rule amendments. Matters that existed before the effective date of the rule and would otherwise be disqualifying are, however, required to be disclosed in writing to investors in Part II of Form 1-A.

e. Waivers

i. Waiver for good cause shown

The final rule provides for the ability to seek waivers from disqualification by the Commission upon a showing of good cause that it is not necessary under the circumstances that the exemption be denied. Staff has identified a number of circumstances that could, depending upon the specific facts, be relevant to the evaluation of a waiver request for good cause shown: http://www.sec.gov/divisions/corpfin/guidance/disqualification-waivers.shtml. Issuers may view past applications and waivers granted under Regulation A by referring to the following page: http://www.sec.gov/divisions/corpfin/cf-noaction.shtml#3b. Staff in the Office of Small Business Policy is also available to discuss potential waiver concerns over the phone at (202) 551-3460.

7. Relationship with State Securities Laws

a. Tier 1 Offerings

In addition to qualifying a Regulation A offering with the Commission, issuers in Tier 1 offerings must register or qualify their offering in any state in which they seek to offer or sell securities pursuant to Regulation A. Issuers wishing to obtain information on state-specific registration requirements should contact state securities regulators in the states in which they intend to offer or sell securities for further guidance on compliance with state law requirements. Issuers may also obtain useful information on state securities law registration and qualification requirements, including the option to have Tier 1 offerings that will be conducted in multiple states reviewed pursuant to a coordinated state review program, by visiting the website of the North American Securities Administrators Association (NASAA) at www.nasaa.org.

b. Tier 2 Offerings

While issuers in Tier 2 offerings are required to qualify offerings with the Commission before sales can be made pursuant to Regulation A, they are not required to register or qualify their offerings with state securities regulators. Tier 2 offerings by such issuers, however, remain subject to state law enforcement and antifraud authority. Additionally, issuers in Tier 2 offerings may be subject to filing fees in the states in which they intend to offer or sell securities and be required to file with such states any materials that the issuer has filed with the Commission as part of the offering. The failure to file, or pay filing fees regarding, any such materials may cause state securities regulators to suspend the offer or sale of securities within their jurisdiction. Issuers should contact state securities regulators in the states in which they intend to offer or sell securities for further guidance on compliance with state law requirements.

8. Transition Issues

Issuers conducting sales of securities pursuant to a Regulation A offering statement that was qualified by the Commission before June 19, 2015 may continue to do so. Such offerings are considered Tier 1 offerings after the effectiveness of the final rules on June 19, 2015. Qualified offering statements under the preexisting rules for Regulation A are, however, incompatible with the final requirements for Tier 2 offerings, and issuers that wish to transition to a Tier 2 offering need to file a post-qualification amendment to their previously qualified offering statement that satisfies the requirements for Tier 2 in order to do so.

On and after June 19, 2015, issuers conducting Regulation A offerings under the preexisting rules must begin to comply with the final rules for Tier 1 offerings, including, for example, the requirement of electronic filing and the rules for post-qualification amendments, at the time of their next filing under

Regulation A. Additionally, after effectiveness of the final rules, issuers that previously provided offering statements that were qualified using the Model A disclosure format of Part II of the Form 1-A must, at the time of their next filing due under Regulation A, file or amend such offering statement using a disclosure format that is permissible under the final rules for Tier 1 offerings. Model A is no longer permitted for post-qualification amendments of qualified offerings that pre-date effectiveness of the final rules. Lastly, an issuer that is offering securities pursuant to a qualified offering statement under the preexisting rules will, upon effectiveness of the final rules, no longer be required to file a Form 2-A, but instead be required to file a Form 1-Z with the Commission electronically upon completion or termination of the offering.

On or after June 19, 2015, issuers that are in the review process for the qualification of a Regulation A offering statement based on materials filed with the Commission before June 19, 2015 will be required to comply with the final rules, including the requirements for electronic filing and, where applicable, transitioning to a disclosure format that is approved for Regulation A offerings. The issuer may elect to proceed at that time with its offering under the final requirements for either Tier 1 or Tier 2 offerings, provided it follows the requirements for the respective tiers.

9. Other Resources

The adopting release for the amendments to Regulation A can be found on the SEC's website at http://www.sec.gov/rules/final/2015/33-9741.pdf.

Regulation A can be accessed through the "Corporation Finance" section of the SEC's website at http://www.sec.gov/divisions/corpfin/ecfr-links.shtml.

Additional materials regarding the application of Regulation A are available at http://www.sec.gov/divisions/corpfin/cfguidance.shtml.

You can also submit complaints or tips about possible securities laws violations on the SEC's questions and complaints page at http://www.sec.gov/complaint.shtml.

10. Contacting the SEC

The SEC's Division of Corporation Finance is happy to assist small companies with questions regarding Regulation A. You may contact the Division's Office of Small Business Policy by telephone at (202) 551-3460.

* This guide was prepared by the staff of the U.S. Securities and Exchange Commission as a "small entity compliance guide" under Section 212 of the Small Business Regulatory Enforcement Fairness Act of 1996, as amended. The guide summarizes and explains rules adopted by the SEC, but is not a substitute for any rule itself. Only the rule itself can provide complete and definitive information regarding its requirements.

[1] *See* 17 CFR 240.12g5-1(a)(7). Under Securities Act and Exchange Act rules, a smaller reporting company is generally an issuer that has a public float of less than $75 million, determined as of the last business day of its most recently completed second fiscal quarter, or, in the absence of a public float, annual revenues of less than $50 million, as of the most recently completed fiscal year. *See* Securities Act Rule 405, 17 CFR 230.405, Exchange Act Rule 12b-2, 17 CFR 240.12b-2, and Item 10(f)(1) of Regulation S-K, 17 CFR 229.10(f)(1).

[2] The final rules eliminate the Model A (Question-and-Answer) disclosure format under Part II of Form 1-A that was permitted for use in Regulation A offerings before June 19, 2015.

Public Statements of Commissioners at Open Meeting to Adopt Regulation A+

Appendix C contains the comments of the Commissioner of the SEC, presented and made a part of the public record at the hearing adopting the new rules for Regulation A. These give valuable insights into the history of Regulation A, the issues the SEC sought to address and how the SEC views balancing the priorities of facilitating the marketplace with investor protection.

The following are the transcribed public statements of the Commissioners of the SEC at the Open Meeting held March 25, 2015 to adopt the Amendments to Regulation A.

Statement at Open Meeting on Rule 15b9-1 and Reg A+

Chair Mary Jo White

March 25, 2015

Good morning. This is an open meeting of the U.S. Securities and Exchange Commission on March 25, 2015 under the Government in Sunshine Act. The Commission today will consider two recommendations, one from the Division of Trading and Markets and the other from the Division of Corporation Finance—a proposed amendment to Rule 15b9-1 of the Exchange Act and the adoption of Regulation A+ under the JOBS Act.

Rule 15b9-1

[Deleted]

Regulation A+

The second item on our agenda is a recommendation from the Division of Corporation Finance to adopt final rules implementing Title IV of the JOBS Act. The JOBS Act requires the Commission to adopt rules to create a new exemption from registration under the Securities Act for offerings of up to $50 million dollars in a twelve month period.

This mandate, often referred to as Regulation A+, is designed to help enhance the ability of small companies to access capital. Small companies are essential to the livelihood of millions of Americans, fueling economic growth and creating jobs. As I have said in the past, it is critically important for the Commission to consider ways that our rules can facilitate capital-raising by smaller companies. Congress recognized the importance of providing new avenues for capital-raising when it adopted the JOBS Act, which provides for crowdfunding as well Regulation A+.

Existing Regulation A is rarely used by issuers. A 2012 GAO Report cited various factors that have contributed to its lack of use, including the overlapping requirements of federal and state law over such offerings. Our goal in this rulemaking is to make Regulation A+ an effective, workable path to raising capital that also provides strong investor protections. The staff will describe their recommendations for this final rule in more detail, but one issue that I will address first is preemption, an issue of particular interest and importance.

The final rules we are considering today seek to address the challenges presented by federal and state securities registration and qualification by striking an appropriate balance for the roles of federal and state law. In light of the significant investor protections included in the rules and the need to develop a workable exemption, the rules would preempt state registration and qualification laws for certain offerings of up to $50 million in what we call Tier 2 offerings. While the establishment of the North American Securities Administrators Association's (NASAA) coordinated review program is a very positive development, it is a new program and at this stage concerns remain about the costs associated with state securities law registration and qualification requirements, even under a coordinated review program, which may deter issuers from using Regulation A. To create an updated exemption that will be a viable path for capital raising, a calibrated preemption of state securities laws in connection with Regulation A offerings is necessary, at least until there is a track record from which to judge whether the functioning of the coordinated review program may obviate need for preemption.

Importantly, under the rule we are considering today, there continues to be, a strong role for states to play in offerings under Regulation A. NASAA has made great progress in implementing its coordinated review program for Regulation A offerings, and issuers can avail themselves of that program for offerings of up to $20 million, in Tier 1 offerings. It will be informative to see how the program works in practice in connection with these offerings, and the Commission is committed to monitoring the operation of Regulation A to see whether efficiencies in the coordinated program merit further evaluation of whether such a program could effectively operate within the broader context of Regulation A+. It is also important to emphasize that the states retain their full anti-fraud powers and may require that issuers using Regulation A+ file their offering documents with the states. Also, in recognition of the important role of state securities regulators and our relationship with them, we are currently exploring ways to further collaborate with our state colleagues, including establishing a program for a representative of NASAA or a state securities regulator to work with the staff in the SEC's Division of Corporation Finance as it implements these rules and considers other issues of mutual interest.

The final rules we are considering today benefitted greatly from public comment we received and the staff's thorough and careful analysis. I look forward to continuing to work with my fellow Commissioners, the staff, state securities regulators, and market participants to help Regulation A+ become a vibrant capital-raising option that also protects investors in these offerings. As we go forward, the staff will be actively monitoring and assessing the implementation and development of the Regulation A+ regime, which will include a review of the $50 million aggregate offering limitation for Tier 2 offerings, as required by the JOBS Act. As reflected in the release, I have also directed the staff, within five years of the adoption of Regulation A+, to review the impact of both Tier 1 and 2 offerings on capital formation and investor protection and report its findings to the Commission so that we can consider possible changes to the Regulation A+ offering regime.

Before I turn the proceedings over to Keith Higgins, the Director of the Division of Corporation Finance, to discuss the recommendations, I would like to thank the staff for all of their efforts to develop these very important rules. Specifically, I would like to thank Keith Higgins, Betsy Murphy, Sebastian Gomez Abero, Zachary Fallon, ShehzadNiazi, Raquel Fox, Mark Kronforst, Craig Olinger, Lindsay McCord, Jim Budge, Heather Mackintosh, and Sylvia Pilkerton in the Division of Corporation Finance; Annie Small, Rich Levine, Bryant Morris, and Dorothy McCuaig in the Office of the General Counsel; Mark Flannery, Scott Bauguess, Vanessa Countryman, SimonaMola Yost, and AnzhelaKnyazeva in the Division of Economic and RiskAnalysis; and Jeff Minton, Blair Petrillo, Brian Croteau, Kevin Stout and Wes Kelly in the Office of the Chief Accountant. I also would again like to thank my fellow Commissioners and their counsels for their hard and productive work on these rules.

Statement at Open Meeting on Reg A+

Commissioner Daniel M. Gallagher

March 25, 2015

Thank you, Chair White. Today I am delighted that the Commission is fulfilling its JOBS Act mandate to revitalize Regulation A, which has, for too long, been an underused way of raising capital, particularly as compared to its better-known cousin, Regulation D. We have an urgent need to ensure that our rules promote capital formation for small businesses, and I hope that public exempt offerings under Regulation A can take their place beside private exempt offerings under Regulation D and registered offerings as viable means of raising capital. Indeed, I've not been shy about my view that Title IV of the JOBS Act set the stage for us to do something revolutionary to encourage small business capital formation.

I'd like to thank the Division of Corporation Finance, particularly Keith Higgins, Sebastian Gomez Abero, Zachary Fallon, and ShehzadNiazi; the Division of Economic and Risk Analysis; and the Office of the General Counsel for the hard work and dedication put into getting this rule done.

The SEC's rules today generally hew closely to the text and spirit of the JOBS Act, and for that they should be applauded. In particular, the rules raise the offering limit under Tier 2 to $50 million, and preempt offers and sales of securities in Tier 2 offerings. According to a GAO report, a low offering limit and the lack of state preemption have been critical reasons for the lack of Regulation A offerings, and today's rule squarely addresses those two issues. I am also pleased to see some other useful features in the rule, such as a streamlined path for Exchange Act registration of Regulation A securities, and real efforts to scale the Tier 2 periodic reporting regime for smaller-sized issuers, including the novel approach of semiannual reporting. I believe these features balance the need to provide investors with up-to-date, decision-useful information while avoiding unnecessary requirements that would over-burden issuers.

That said, there are a few areas where this rule falls short—where we could have safely done more to facilitate capital formation, but lacked the boldness to take the needed action. With the expectation that we will at some point in the future revisit this rule—perhaps as part of a discrete post-implementation review process that we are required to implement under Executive Order 13579—I wanted to run through a few of these areas.

First, I am quite disappointed that the offering limit was not raised in the final rule. Congress in the JOBS Act gave us a baseline number, $50 million, but also told us in no uncertain terms that we have the authority to raise the cap, and that we are mandated to consider doing so every two years. I don't believe $50 million was chosen out of any particular necessity—perhaps it was just 10 times bigger than the old limit, and Congress knew we needed at a minimum an order of magnitude change in our rule. We should not have felt constrained by Congress's statutory floor, but rather should have done the analysis and picked our own number. Unfortunately, the rule today simply implements Congress's limit and takes a wait-and-see approach on raising it. I look forward to the biennial study of the threshold, to be done by April 2016 according to today's release, and hope we can take bold action then.

Second, the rule introduces a needless transactional friction by failing to deem Regulation A's semiannual reporting to be "reasonably current" for purposes of Rules 15c2-11, 144, and 144A. By not deeming balance sheets with dates up to 9 months to be "reasonably current," issuers may need to file updated financial statements on a "voluntary" basis on Form 1-U in order to bring current the issuer's financial information. Without such "voluntary" filing, issuers may spend half the year—two periods of three months each—in blackout periods during which new quotations cannot be initiated, or resales made under Rules 144 and 144A. In the past, the Commission has assumed that quarterly reporting was necessary to meet the "reasonably current" requirement, but in conjunction with adopting semiannual reporting today, it would have been more than appropriate to provide that such reporting meets the reasonably current requirement. Unfortunately, we have not done so, thereby creating a risk that our rules today backdoor a quarterly reporting requirement on issuers, as securityholders or broker-dealers demand that these more frequent filings be made.

Third, we should have allowed reporting issuers to use Regulation A. It's not entirely clear why issuers already complying with the full periodic reporting regime would have wanted to do a Regulation A offering, but on the other hand Private Investments in Public Equity, or PIPEs, are clearly used from time to time. Perhaps a use for a Regulation A offering, or what I will call a half-PIPE, would have developed too—at which time we could have assessed that use and determined whether additional restrictions were necessary. But it never will now, because we couldn't see our way to giving issuers the flexibility. This is too bad.

While we're on the topic of scoping, I do want to note that, while I agreed with the decision not to extend Regulation A to Business Development Companies, I do think we should consider whether improvements to Regulation E for BDCs would be useful.

Fourth, I think we should have provided a clean 12(g) exemption, without the age-out provision included in the final rule. Exchange Act Section 12(g) was intended to ensure that companies with broad enough public share-holder bases would be required to provide periodic information to investors. Critically, our Tier 2 reporting regime already largely accomplishes that goal. And simple economics dictates that at some point, even a robust Regulation A regime is going to be insufficient for a larger company, which will instead need to do a registered offering, and can enter the full periodic reporting regime at that point.[1]

All this being said, however, we shouldn't let the perfect be the enemy of the good, and let me be clear, this is a good rule that we are adopting today.

But, as good as the rule may be, it should not be the end of the Commission's capital formation agenda. The development of venture exchanges for small cap shares, including Regulation A issuances, would greatly enhance liquidity in these shares, thereby facilitating greater demand and higher prices for the initial issuances of these securities. I am very glad to see that today's rule commits to the continued exploration of venture exchanges, including for Regulation A shares. Congress appears to be thinking about this issue as well—which is all the more reason why we should move forward expeditiously. We shouldn't tempt Congress to force us to promote capital formation when we can do it ourselves, organically. With venture exchanges, we may need Congress's help with certain statutory provisions, but we should be proactively conveying that to Congress rather than passively waiting for Congress to ask us.

Finally, I believe that the amendments we are adopting today don't go far enough to help issuers that are trying to raise under $5 million. Issuers that want to raise more can do so, and the greater offering proceeds will help off-set the offering costs, but companies that are only looking to raise the smaller amount aren't helped by our action. The entity doing the most for these companies is NASAA. If they can make the coordinated review program for state blue sky laws a success—that is, if they can get the remaining states to sign on, and then to stick closely together rather going their separate ways—it will be a significant achievement. I encourage continued SEC cooperation with NASAA on Tier 1 offerings, and will be watching closely to see how the coordinated review program operates in practice. Moreover, we at the SEC should be continuing to look for other ways to help companies that are looking to raise very small amounts of capital. If there are other ways to structure our exemptions so as to provide sufficient protections to investors without being cost-prohibitive for companies, we should do so.

But those are topics for another day (although hopefully another day in the very near future). We have to start somewhere, and today's rule is a very good place to start. I am happy to support it, and I have no questions.

[1] Entry into the full Section 13 reporting regime obviously carries with it several significant, new burdens. And the Commission seems to want to add more burdens every day, even on small companies. Even if these burdens seem to be individually minor, their effect in the aggregate is significant. See, e.g., Rel. No. 33-9723, *Disclosure of Hedging by Employees, Officers and Directors* (Feb. 9, 2015); see also Commissioners Daniel M. Gallagher & Michael S. Piwowar, Joint Public Statement, *Joint Statement on the Commission's Proposed Rule on Hedging Disclosures* (Feb. 9, 2015). This proliferation of regulations (see, e.g., Commissioner Daniel M. Gallagher, Public Statement, *Statement on the Aggregate Impact of Financial Services Regulations* (Mar. 2, 2015), available at http://www.sec.gov/news/statement/aggregate-impact-of-financial-services-regulation.html) creates disincentives for companies to raise capital in the public markets and grow.

Helping Small Businesses and Protecting Investors

Commissioner Luis A. Aguilar

March 25, 2015

The Commission has long recognized that small businesses are essential to the growth and success of our national economy.[1] Our nation's 28 million small business owners create almost two out of every three new jobs and employ more than half of the U.S. workforce.[2] The long-term success of our country's small businesses, however, depends on their access to capital.[3] For this reason, Congress has provided the Commission with authority to pass rules to make it easier for small businesses to raise capital.[4] One rule which has historically been used by small businesses is Regulation A—an exemptive rule that has been around nearly as long as the SEC.[5] Regulation A provides companies with a streamlined and less costly way to raise capital, so long as they provide the investing public with certain critical disclosures about the company and the securities being offered.[6]

To be eligible for the Regulation A exemption, an issuer is limited in the amount of securities that it can offer and sell during any 12-month period. When initially adopted in 1936, this offering limit was $100,000.[7] Subsequently, the offering limit was raised three additional times—to $300,000 in 1945, to $500,000 in 1972, and to $1.5 million in 1978.[8] In 1992, as part of a package that facilitated access to the capital markets for start-up and developing companies, the Commission raised the Regulation A offering ceiling once again to its current cap of $5 million.[9]

Although Regulation A has been frequently relied upon since it was introduced, the use of this exemption has declined over the years. In 1960, for example, more than one thousand companies filed Regulation A notifications with the Commission.[10] By 1997, only 116 offerings were filed under Regulation A, which declined even further to only 19 in 2011.[11] In addition, the number of these offerings that were ultimately deemed "qualified"—meaning securities could actually be sold to investors—went from 57 offerings in 1997 *to only one offering* in 2011.[12]Although these numbers rose slightly between 2012 and 2014, when 26 offerings were qualified, the numbers still remain low.[13] If the success of a regulatory exemption is measured by how often it is used, then Regulation A has been failing.

The reduction in Regulation A offerings has been largely attributed to a few factors. First, the 1982 enactment of new registration exemptions under Regulation D became more attractive options to many issuers who could have used Regulation A.[14] Second, a report by the U.S. Government Accountability Office ("GAO") and many commenters point to the relatively low dollar amounts that could be raised, and the costs and burdens of state blue sky laws, as reasons why issuers chose not to use Regulation A.[15] Today's amendments address both of these concerns, among others.

Protecting Investors While Making Regulation A Work for Small Businesses

First, as mandated by Section 401 of the JOBS Act, the Commission is increasing the dollar amount that can be raised from $5 million to $50 million.[16] Most notably, the amendments create two tiers of issuances that provide a higher ceiling for use of the registration exemption: "Tier 1" for securities offerings of up to $20 million in any 12-month period; and "Tier 2" for offerings up to $50 million in the same period.[17]

In addition to raising the ceiling as to the amount that can be raised, the adopting amendments, commonly referred to as "Regulation A-plus," make other changes to facilitate the use of Regulation A and enhance investor protection.

Currently, Regulation A requires issuers to, among other things, file certain information with the Commission and provide investors with an offering circular that discloses certain narrative and financial information about the issuer and the securities being offered.[18] While these disclosures are important, it is also recognized that these disclosures are far less comprehensive than would be required in a registered offering.[19] This is a particular concern as to investments in small businesses. The statistics demonstrate that investments in small enterprises are inherently riskier than investments in larger companies with proven track records.[20] For example, the U.S. Small Business Administration found that over 50% of small businesses fail within the first five years.[21] According to a separate study, eight out of ten entrepreneurs who start businesses fail within the first 18 months.[22]

In recognition of these concerns, today's Regulation A-plus amendments include new provisions designed to enhance investor protections. Specifically, today's rules strengthen the standards for issuer eligibility.[23] In addition, for higher Tier 2 offerings, the rules require certain new critical disclosures, such as audited financial statements and ongoing disclosures after the offering is completed.[24] Moreover, Tier 2 offerings provide for certain investment limits on what investors can put at risk.[25] Ultimately, although still not as robust as required in a full registration, these new provisions increase the disclosures, transparency, and protections of Regulation A.[26]

The Important Role of State Regulators

Today's rule also addresses the role of state securities regulators. As is well known, this has been a very contentious issue. A 2012 study by the GAO found that, among other factors, the cost of addressing both federal review and state blue sky laws has been an impediment to the greater use of Regulation A by small businesses.[27] Subsequently, at the time the Commission proposed the Regulation A amendments, the rules preempted the application of certain state blue sky requirements with respect to all offerees in Regulation A offerings, and all purchasers in Tier 2 offerings.

At the proposing stage, the Commission recognized that preemption of the state review of Regulation A offerings was a step that required deliberate and serious consideration. State regulators have a long and proud history of protecting investors, and their localized knowledge and resources have been instrumental in detecting and preventing fraud. Moreover, the Commission was also aware that NASAA[28] was developing a coordinated review program intended to lessen the burden of multi-state review of Regulation A offerings.

In that regard, the proposing release urged interested parties to comment on the pros and cons of incorporating state review into the Regulation A process. During the comment period, the Commission received a number of letters on the issue of preemption,[29] and it is fair to say that the commenters' letters reflect a wide spectrum of divergent views.[30] These letters have been very informative and have contributed to the Commission's deliberation on this issue. Letters from NASAA, specific state regulators, and an issuer also informed the Commission that NASAA has made great strides in developing a program to lessen the burdens of multi-state reviews.[31] Specifically, nearly all of the state securities regulators have joined a multi-state coordinated review program[32] that is expected to substantially reduce the compliance costs for small businesses seeking to receive state approval for Regulation A offerings.[33]

After considering all the important factors associated with state involvement in Regulation A offerings, and the creation of the new coordinated review program, the Commission has now determined *not* to preempt blue sky review for offerees in Tier 1 offerings, and, additionally, the Commission is also increasing the ceiling on Tier 1 offerings from $5 million to $20 million.[34]

Furthermore, as to Tier 2 offerings, the Regulation A-plus rules address the concern that preempting state blue sky review will deprive state regulators of the benefit of a preview of certain riskier offerings before these offerings are sold to the public in their states. Accordingly, first-time Regulation A-plus issuers must publicly file their offering statements with the Commission *at least* 21 days before qualification. This filing requirement will allow state securities regulators to require issuers to file such material with them for a minimum of 21 calendar days before any potential sales occur to investors in their respective states.[35]

It is also important to note that nothing the Commission does today limits the ability of state securities regulators to investigate and bring anti-fraud enforcement actions involving Regulation A-plus, or limits the state regulators in investigating and bringing actions against broker-dealers for unlawful conduct in Regulation A-plus transactions.[36]

Information Sharing with State Regulators

In addition, the Commission is currently in discussions with NASAA to allow a representative of a state securities regulator to be embedded with the SEC staff and be involved in staff assessment of Regulation A-plus offerings. [37] One of the goals of this new arrangement is for states to have an unfiltered preview into the Regulation A-plus market for preempted offerings. Among other things, one of the benefits of this arrangement would be that the NASAA representative can be involved as the SEC staff reviews Regulation A-plus filings.[38]

Today, I will vote to approve the rules being considered. There are aspects of the rule that I would have liked to have seen stronger, however—such as additional disclosures as to the equity compensation received by insiders in the year prior to an offering.[39] Nevertheless, despite challenges, today's rules go a long way in balancing the promotion of capital formation and investor protection.

In closing, I would like to thank the staff from the Division of Corporation Finance, the Division of Economic Research and Analysis, the Office of the Chief Accountant, and the Office of the General Counsel for their work on this rulemaking. I appreciate your dedication, and the important work you do to protect investors.

Thank you.

[1] In fact, small firms were responsible for 63% of net new jobs created between 1993 and mid-2013, or more than 14 million of the nearly 23 million net new jobs created during this period. *See* U.S. Small Business Administration Office of Advocacy, *Frequently Asked Questions,available* at http://www.sba.gov/sites/default/files/advocacy/FAQ_March_2014_0.pdf. For these purposes, small businesses are defined as those independent businesses with fewer than 500 employees. The Commission has promulgated a number of regulations aimed at allowing these small businesses to sell securities without having to comply with the full registration requirements of the Securities Act. *See*, for example, Rules 504 and 505 of the Securities Act of 1933 (the "Securities Act").

[2] U.S. Small Business Administration, *Strategic Plan: Fiscal Years 2014-2018*, at 4, *available at* https://www.sba.gov/sites/default/files/aboutsbaarticle/SBA_FY2014-2018_Strategic_Plan_final_update.pdf (last visited Mar. 19, 2015).

[3] *Id.* at p. 5.

[4] *See, e.g.,* Louis Loss, Joel Seligman, and Troy Paredes, *Fundamentals of Securities Regulation,*Vol. 1 (2011), at 529 (noting that Congress "has addressed the problem of financing small business" in various ways, including increasing the scope of the Commission's exemptive power under Securities Act Section 3(b), which provides the statutory authority for Regulation A.).

[5] Regulation A was originally adopted as an exemption from registration in 1936 under the authority of Section 3(b) of the Securities Act of 1933 (the "Securities Act"). *See Amendments to Regulation A*, SEC Release No. 33-9741, (Mar. 25, 2015), at fn. 864, *available at* http://www.sec.gov/rules/final/2015/33-9741.pdf (hereinafter "Regulation A-plus Adopting Release"). By its terms, Regulation A is not restricted to small business issuers. Rather, the rule requires that issuers be one of the following: (i) an entity organized under the laws of the United States or Canada, or any State, Province,

Territory, or possession thereof, or the District of Columbia, with its principal place of business in the United States or Canada; (ii) not be subject to section 13 or 15(d) of the Securities Exchange Act of 1934 (the "Exchange Act") immediately before the offering; (iii) not be a development stage company that either has no specific business plan or purpose, or has indicated that its business plan is to merge with an unidentified company or companies; (iv) not be an investment company registered or required to be registered under the Investment Company Act of 1940; (v) not issue fractional undivided interests in oil or gas rights, or a similar interests in other mineral rights; and (vi) not otherwise be disqualified under the issue ineligibility provisions of Rule 262 of the Securities Act. See Rule 251(a) of the Securities Act. However, the SEC has amended Regulation A in the past to specifically address capital raising issues faced by small business issuers. See, e.g., *Small Business Initiatives*, SEC Release No. 33-6949 (Jul. 30, 1992), *available at* https://www.sec.gov/rules/final/6949.txt. (Noting that "[t]oday, with the adoption of major revisions to Securities Act registration exemptions under Rule 504 and Regulation A and the inauguration of an integrated registration and reporting system for small business issuers, the Commission has completed the first of its Small Business Initiatives announced in March of this year. ... The March proposals were enthusiastically received by the small business commenters as a significant step to facilitating access to the public market for start-up and developing companies, and reducing the costs for small businesses to undertake to have their securities traded in the public markets.")

[6] Regulation A exemption allows eligible companies to publicly offer and sell securities without the costs and obligations of a full registration under the Securities Act of 1933, provided that, among other things, they file certain information with the Commission and provide investors with an offering circular that discloses certain narrative and financial information about the issuer and the securities being offered. See Rules 251 to 263 of the Securities Act, and SEC Form 1-A.

[7] See C. Steven Bradford, *Regulation A and the Integration Doctrine: The New Safe Harbor*, 55 Ohio St. L.J. 255 (1994), at 262, *available at* http://digital commons.unl.edu/cgi/viewcontent.cgi?article=1087&context=lawfacpub.

[8] *Id.* at 262-263.

[9] See *Small Business Initiatives*, SEC Release No. 33-6949 (Jul. 30, 1992), *available at* https://www.sec.gov/rules/final/6949.txt (noting that the Commission proposals that ultimately led to the 1992 amendments to Regulation A "were enthusiastically received by the small business commenters as a significant step to facilitating access to the public market for start-up and developing companies, and reducing the costs for small businesses to undertake to have their securities traded in the public markets."); Louis Loss,

Joel Seligman, and Troy Paredes, *Fundamentals of Securities Regulation,* Vol. I (2011), at 531; C. Steven Bradford, *Regulation A and the Integration Doctrine:The New Safe Harbor,* 55 Ohio St. L.J. 255 (1994), at 262-263.

[10] *See* Harvey Frank, *The Processing of Small Issues of Securities Under Regulation A,* 1962 Duke L.J. 507 (1962), *available at* http://scholarship.law.duke.edu/cgi/viewcontent.cgi?article=1824&context=dlj.

[11] *See* U.S. Government Accountability Office Report to Congressional Committees, *Securities Regulation: Factors That May Affect Trends in Regulation A Offerings* GAO-12-839 (July 2012) (hereinafter "GAO Report"), *available at* http://www.gao.gov/assets/600/592113.pdf.

[12] *Id.* In addition, the GAO Report described that "[b]etween 1992 and May 2012, 214 of the 1,006 Regulation A filings made with SEC were abandoned or withdrawn. As discussed earlier, SEC staff stated that they have received anecdotal information that some businesses abandon or withdraw from the Regulation A filing process to raise capital through different means, such as the issuance of registered public offering." *Id.*

[13] *See* Regulation A-plus Adopting Release at Section III.B.1.a.i. *Regulation A Offerings.*

[14] *See* GAO Report at 2 (noting that "Securities attorneys GAO inter- viewed suggested that the decrease in filings after 1997 could be attributed to a number of factors, including the increased attractiveness of Regulation D.")

[15] *See, e.g.,* Comment Letter from the ABA Business Law Section (Apr. 3, 2014) (noting that "[s]maller companies have limited budgets for capital rais- ing and, in our experience, the cost of state securities law registration and review is often prohibitive."), *available at* http://www.sec.gov/comments/s7-11-13/s71113-99.pdf; Comment Letter from Paul Hastings (Mar. 24, 2014) (stating that "the costs of compliance with state securities laws is a factor that in the past may have contributed to limited use of Regulation A."), *available at* http://www.sec.gov/comments/s7-11-13/s71113-73.pdf; *GAO Report* at 24 (stating that the $5 million ceiling on Regulation A offerings may have been a deterrent to certain businesses and underwriters who would not be interested in $5 million offerings).

[16] *See* Regulation A-plus Adopting Release at Section II.A. (Final Rules and Amendments to Regulation A. Overview).

[17] *See id.* at Rule 230.251(a) (Scope of Exemption).

[18] *See* Rules 251 to 263 of the Securities Act, and SEC Form 1-A.

[19] Compare the instructions to Form S-1, *available at* http://www.sec.gov/about/forms/forms-1.pdf, with the instructions to current Form 1-A, *available at* https://www.sec.gov/about/forms/form1-a.pdf. For example, contrast current Form 1-A's Management's Discussion and Analysis of

Certain Relevant Factors required under Regulation A, which consists of four items for discussion, as compared with the lengthy and more extensive Management's Discussion and Analysis of Financial Condition and Results of Operations required of registrants per Item 303 of Regulation S-K. *See also* Regulation A-plus Adopting Release at Section III.C.3 (Offering Limitations and Secondary Sales) (stating that "[a]n increased maximum offering size in Regulation A offerings could increase the overall amount of securities subject to initial and ongoing disclosure requirements that are less extensive than the requirements for registered offerings being offered to the general public, which may result in less informed decisions by investors."). Moreover, small business issuers relying on the current Regulation A exemption do not have to file audited financial statements with the Commission (unless audited financial statements are otherwise available), and do not have to file ongoing periodic financial reports required of registrants under the Exchange Act.

[20] These risks include, among other things, the likelihood of small business failure, the lower liquidity of these securities, and, unfortunately, the higher risk of fraud in the small business security markets. *See, e.g.,* Robert Longley, *Why Small Businesses Fail: SBA* (2014) (noting that over 50% of small businesses fail within the first five years), *available at* http://usgovinfo.about.com/od/smallbusiness/a/whybusfail.htm. *See also* SEC Website, *Microcap Stock: A Guide for Investors, available at* https://www.sec.gov/investor/pubs/microcapstock.htm ("accurate information about 'microcap stocks'—low-priced stocks issued by the smallest of companies—may be difficult to find. … When publicly-available information is scarce, fraudsters can easily spread false information about microcap companies, making profits while creating losses for unsuspecting investors.") (Website last visited Mar. 16, 2015).

[21] *See* Robert Longley, *Why Small Businesses Fail: SBA* (2014), *available at* http://usgovinfo.about.com/od/smallbusiness/a/whybusfail.htm.

[22] *See* Eric T. Wagner, *Five Reasons 8 Out Of 10 Businesses Fail,* Forbes (Sept. 12, 2013),*available at* http://www.forbes.com/sites/ericwagner/2013/09/12/five-reasons-8-out-of-10-businesses-fail/.

[23] Today's amendments would increase the eligibility requirements for all Regulation A-plus issuers, such as prohibiting issuers who have had their registration revoked by the Commission within the past five years or have failed to file ongoing disclosures, if required, within the past two years. *See* Regulation A-plus Adopting Release at Rule 230.251(b) *Issuer.* In addition, today's amendments would conform the Bad Actor disqualification provisions in Regulation A to those currently applied to Rule 506(d) offerings. The Regulation A-plus final rules, thus, include two new disqualification triggers not previously present in Regulation A: (1) final orders and bars of certain state and other federal regulators; and (2) Commission cease-and-desist orders relating to violations of scienter-based anti-fraud provisions of the federal securities laws or

Section 5 of the Securities Act. *See* Regulation A-plus Adopting Release at Rule 230.262(a)(3) and (5) (Disqualification Provisions).

[24] Today's amendments would require Tier 2 issuers to include audited financial statements in offering circulars and to file audited financial statements with the Commission annually, and to provide ongoing disclosures to investors about the financial condition of the company on an annual and semiannual basis, with additional requirements to provide interim current event updates. *See* Regulation A-plus Adopting Release at Section II.A. (Final Rules and Amendments to Regulation A. Overview). In addition, the financial statements required under Regulation A-plus only require compliance with U.S. GAAS per AICPA standards, rather than the more robust standards promulgated by the PCAOB. While today's rules could have required financial statements to be audited in accordance with the PCAOB standards, audits conducted in accordance with U.S. GAAS, as the adopting release notes, provide protection for investors in Regulation A offerings, especially in light of the requirement that auditors for Tier 2 offerings must be independent under Rule 2-01 of Regulation S-X. Moreover, the staff advises that requiring PCAOB standards would have subjected issuers using Regulation A-plus to audit their financial statements *both* per the PCAOB standards and the AICPA standards as a result of statutory interpretation under Section 2(a)(7) of the Sarbanes-Oxley Act of 2002; this is a burden not shared by companies registered under the Securities Act. *See* Regulation A-plus Adopting Release at Section II.C.3.b.(2).(c) (Final Rules for Financial Statements).

[25] Today's amendments would require that Tier 2 investors either be accredited investors or be restricted to investing only up to 10% of their annual income or net worth, whichever is greater, unless the securities are listed on a national securities exchange. The definition of "accredited investor" applicable to Rule 506 is set forth in Rule 501(a) of Regulation D [17 CFR 230.501(a)] and includes any person who comes within one of the definition's enumerated categories of persons, or whom the issuer "reasonably believes" comes within any of the enumerated categories, at the time of the sale of the securities to that person. The categories include: (A) any natural person whose individual net worth, or joint net worth with that person's spouse, exceeds $1,000,000, excluding the person's primary residence and any indebtedness secured thereby (up to the value of such residence); and (B) any natural person who had an individual income in excess of $200,000 in each of the two most recent years or joint income with that person's spouse in excess of $300,000 in each of those years and has a reasonable expectation of reaching the same income level in the current year. I have spoken several times recently about the need to revise the "accredited investor" definition, and urge the Commission to accomplish this task in the near term. *See* Commissioner Luis A. Aguilar, *Revisiting the "Accredited Investor" Definition to Better Protect Investors* (Dec. 17, 2014), *available at* http://www.sec.gov/news/statement/spch121714laa.html,

and Commissioner Luis A. Aguilar, *The Importance of Small Business Capital
Formation* (Nov 20, 2014), *available at* http://www.sec.gov/News/
PublicStmt/Detail/PublicStmt/1370543532516. The 10% investment
limitation applies only to natural persons. In the case of non-natural persons,
the 10% investment limitation is applied to 10% of the greater of annual revenue and net assets at fiscal year-end. *See* Regulation A-plus Adopting Release
at Section II.A. (Final Rules and Amendments to Regulation A. Overview).

At the proposing stage of today's rules, the Commission asked for comment
on whether there should be investment limits imposed on Tier 1 offerings in
order to provide for state preemption of those offerings. In response, several commenters wrote the Commission stating that in the absence of state
blue sky preemption, the Commission should <u>not</u> impose investment limits
on purchasers in Regulation A offerings (whether Tier 1 or Tier 2 offerings). In
particular, NASAA submitted a comment letter indicating that investment limitations are unnecessary if there is appropriate state oversight. *See* Comment
Letter from NASAA (Mar. 24, 2014), *available at* http://www.sec.gov/
comments/s7-11-13/s71113-75.pdf. In addition, a second commenter
noted that imposing investment limitations in offerings in which the states
are not preempted has the potential to impose conflicting investor protection
standards at the state and federal level, specifically in those instances where
the states impose their own investor limitation standards. *See* Comment
Letter from Groundfloor Finance Inc. (Nov. 18, 2014), *available at* http://
www.sec.gov/comments/s7-11-13/s71113-139.pdf.

[26] We should also be mindful that today's rules will be ineffectual if there
is no liquid, transparent, and fair secondary market for trading in Regulation
A-plus shares. As I have spoken about on several other occasions, we will
need to work to promote a workable secondary trading environment for
the many securities that will be available to the public without the typical
disclosures accustomed to registered securities. *See, e.g.,* Commissioner
Luis A. Aguilar, *The Need for Greater Secondary Market Liquidity for Small
Businesses* (Mar. 4, 2015), *available at* http://www.sec.gov/news/state-
ment/need-for-greater-secondary-market-liquidity-for-small-
businesses.html; Commissioner Luis A. Aguilar, *The Importance of Small
Business Capital Formation* (Nov. 20, 2014), *available at* http://www.sec.gov/
News/PublicStmt/Detail/PublicStmt/1370543532516; Commissioner
Luis A. Aguilar, *Promoting Investor Protection in Small Business Capital Formation*
(Dec. 18, 2013), *available at* http://www.sec.gov/News/PublicStmt/
Detail/PublicStmt/1370542557949. Indeed, today's Regulation A-plus
rules would substantially expand the dollar amount of securities that could be
issued to the public without restrictions, and could therefore be immediately
traded by security holders who are not affiliates of the issuer. *See* Securities
Act §3(b)((2)(C), as added by JOBS Act §401(a); Rule 144 under the Securities
Act. If we do not ensure a viable secondary trading environment for these

securities, investors could be left holding illiquid and hard-to-value securities, and the anticipated capital formation benefits of today's rules will be lost.

[27] *See GAO Report* at 15. As part of the JOBS Act, Congress mandated that the GAO conduct a study on the impact of state blue sky laws on Regulation A offerings. *See* JOBS Act, Section 402.

[28] NASAA refers to the North American Securities Administrators Association, whose members include the 50 states, the District of Columbia, Puerto Rico, the U.S. Virgin Islands, Canada, and Mexico. *See* the NASAA Website at http://www.nasaa.org/about-us/.

[29] To see the comment letters sent to the Commission on the proposed Regulation A-plus rules, *see Comments on Proposed Rule: Proposed Rule Amendments for Small and Additional Issues Exemptions Under Section 3(b) of the Securities Act* (File No. S7-11-13), *available at* http://www.sec.gov/comments/s7-11-13/s71113.shtml.

[30] For example, many commenters objected to the proposed preemption of state securities law registration and qualification requirements. These commenters pointed out that, among other things, state regulators provide important investor protection benefits as a result of their localized knowledge and resources that may assist in detecting and preventing fraud. *See, e.g.,* Comment Letters from: Cornell Securities Law Clinic (Mar. 24. 2014) (suggesting that the "proposed rules increase the potential for fraud by depriving states of the ability to review Regulation A-Plus offerings before they are sold to the public."), *available at* http://www.sec.gov/comments/s7-11-13/s71113-69.pdf; CFA Institute (Mar. 24, 2014) (stating that it questioned whether "removing this important level of review by the states and the investor protection it provides is outweighed by the costs of compliance with state securities registrations."), *available at* http://www.sec.gov/comments/s7-11-13/s71113-61.pdf; and Groundfloor Finance Inc. (Nov. 18, 2014) (stating that Groundfloor "strongly disagree[s] with the proposal to preempt state registration."), *available at* http://www.sec.gov/comments/s7-11-13/s71113-139.pdf. Conversely, many other commenters expressed their support for preemption as proposed. These commenters asserted, among other things, that the added costs and uncertainty of state blue sky compliance was a primary reason that Regulation A was not being utilized as much as other potential offering exemptions. *See, e.g.,* Comment Letters from: OTC Markets (Mar. 24, 2014) (expressing strong support for the preemption proposal, among other things), *available at* http://www.sec.gov/comments/s7-11-13/s71113-77.pdf;

ABA Business Law Section (Apr. 3, 2014) (stating that "[s]maller companies have limited budgets for capital raising and, in our experience, the cost of state securities law registration and review is often prohibitive."), *available at* http://www.sec.gov/comments/s7-11-13/s71113-99.pdf; and Leading

BioSciences (Mar. 24, 2014) (stating that "[b]ecause the Reg A+ Proposal includes robust investor protections, federal preemption should be retained in the final release as a critical piece to making the Tier 2 proposal successful for growing companies like Leading Biosciences."), *available at* http://www.sec.gov/comments/s7-11-13/s71113-58.pdf.

[31] *See, e.g.*, Comment Letters from: NASAA (Feb. 11, 2015) (stating that the coordinated review program "effectively streamlines the state review process and promotes efficiency by providing centralized filing, unified comments, and a definitive timeline for review"), *available at* http://www.sec.gov/comments/s7-11-13/s71113-144.pdf; The Commonwealth of Massachusetts, Secretary of the Commonwealth (Mar. 24, 2014) (stating that "the states, through NASAA, have developed a simple and streamlined coordinated review system for Regulation A and Sec. 3(b)(2) offerings"), *available at* http://www.sec.gov/comments/s7-11-13/s71113-65.pdf; Texas State Securities Board (Mar. 21, 2014) (stating that "[a]s you may know, a new Coordinated Review Program for offerings exempt from registration under Section 3(b)(2), or Regulation A+ offerings, has indeed been developed by the states that will entail a more uniform and streamlined registration process"), *available at* http://www.sec.gov/comments/s7-11-13/s71113-67.pdf; Letter from Groundfloor Finance Inc. (Nov. 18, 2014) (stating that "[w]ith the Coordinated Review program in place, there is no basis for preempting state registration given the practical effects of registering through the program"), *available at* http://www.sec.gov/comments/s7-11-13/s71113-139.pdf.

[32] *See* NASAA Website, *NASAA Members Approve Streamlined Multi-State Coordinated Review Program* (Mar. 11, 2014), *available at* http://www.nasaa.org/29699/nasaa-members-approve-streamlined-multi-state-coordinated-review-program/. *See also* Regulation A-plus Adopting Release at Section H.3.c. (State Coordinated Review Program for Section 3(b)(2) Securities) (noting in a footnote that "[a]t this time, it is our understanding that 49 of NASAA's 53 constituent members have agreed to participate in the coordinated review program.")

[33] Regulation A-plus Adopting Release at Section III.I. (Economic Analysis. Relationship with State Securities Law). *See also*, Comment Letter from CFA Institute (Mar. 24, 2014) (stating that it encouraged reconsideration of state blue sky preemption "in light of the coordinated review process being developed by state securities regulators."), *available at* http://www.sec.gov/comments/s7-11-13/s71113-61.pdf. As of the date of this adopting release, the Commission is also aware of three issuers that have elected to seek qualification at the state level pursuant to this coordinated review program. *See* Regulation A-plus Adopting Release at 234. In fact, one comment letter strongly supporting state involvement came from a company that recently went through the new coordinated review program. *See* Letter from Groundfloor Finance Inc. (Nov. 18, 2014) (stating that "[w]ith the Coordinated

Review program in place, there is no basis for preempting state registration given the practical effects of registering through the program"), *available at* http://www.sec.gov/comments/s7-11-13/s71113-139.pdf.

[34] The Commission is required by Section 3(b)(5) of the Securities Act to review the Tier 2 offering limitation every two years. As stated in the adopting release, in addition to revisiting the Tier 2 offering limitation, the Commission staff is also undertaking to review the Tier 1 offering limitation at the same time. The staff also will undertake to study and submit a report to the Commission no later than five years following the adoption of today's amendments to Regulation A, on the impact of both the Tier 1 and Tier 2 offerings on capital formation and investor protection. The report will include, but not be limited to, a review of: (1) the amount of capital raised under the amendments; (2) the number of issuances and amount raised by both Tier 1 and Tier 2 offerings; (3) the number of placement agents and brokers facilitating the Regulation A offerings; (4) the number of Federal, State, or any other actions taken against issuers, placement agents, or brokers with respect to both Tier 1 and Tier 2 offerings; and (5) whether any additional investor protections are necessary for either Tier 1 or Tier 2. Based on the information contained in the report, the Commission may propose to either decrease or increase the offering limit for Tier 1, as appropriate. *See* Regulation A-plus Adopting Release at Section II.A. (Final Rules and Amendments to Regulation A. Overview).

[35] It is possible, however, that a state's notice filing requirements may reduce the time period in which an offering statement and related materials are on file with the state before Commission qualification. *See* Regulation A Adopting Release at Section II.C.2.c. (Non-public submission of Draft Offering Statements).

[36] *See* Securities Act Section 18(c)(1), as amended by the JOBS Act (stating that "[c]onsistent with this section, the securities commission (or any agency or office performing like functions) of any State shall retain jurisdiction under the laws of such State to investigate and bring enforcement actions, in connection with securities or securities transactions (A) with respect to—(i) fraud or deceit; or (ii) unlawful conduct by a broker or dealer; and (B) in connection to a transaction described under section 4(6), with respect to—(i) fraud or deceit; or (ii) unlawful conduct by a broker, dealer, funding portal, or issuer.")

[37] *See* Regulation A-plus Adopting Release at Section II.H.3.d. (Application of State Securities Law in Tier 1 and Tier 2 Offerings), fn. 832.

[38] *See* Comment Letter from NASAA (Feb. 19, 2014) (stating that "[s]tate regulators have particular strengths that uniquely qualify them to effectively oversee Regulation A+ offerings. Because we are geographically close and accessible to both investors and local businesses, we are often in a better position than the Commission to communicate with them about the offering

to prevent abuse and improve the overall quality of the deal for investor and business alike. Our proximity to investors also puts us in the best position to deal aggressively with securities law violations when they do occur."), *available at* http://www.sec.gov/comments/s7-11-13/s71113-12.pdf.

[39] I would have also liked to see the increased use of tagged data, particularly using XBRL, to allow the SEC and the public to better analyze an issuer's information. Today's amendments require tagged data in XML fillable format in only certain documents, including Part I of Form I-A and Part I of Form I-K. However, unlike registered companies, companies using Regulation A-plus will not be required to submit financial statements using XBRL format. See Regulation A Adopting Release at Section II.C.I. (Electronic Filing; Delivery Requirements) and Section II.E.I. (Continuing Disclosure Obligations).

Statement at Open Meeting on Adoption of Regulation A Amendments

Commissioner Michael S. Piwowar

March 25, 2015

Thank you, Chair White. I am pleased that we are adopting amendments to Regulation A to implement Title IV of the Jumpstart Our Business Startups Act, or JOBS Act. Title IV was enacted to facilitate capital formation by small and emerging businesses. Today's amendments were rooted in a bipartisan bill, championed by Senator Pat Toomey of Pennsylvania and Senator Jon Tester of Montana. So it is quite appropriate—nearly three years after the President signed the JOBS Act into law on April 5, 2012—for the bipartisan Commission to finally adopt the implementing regulations.

Keeping in mind the criticisms of current Regulation A, as thoroughly documented in a report by the Government Accountability Office,[1] the amendments we are adopting today will provide small businesses with additional options for raising capital. Although today's release is not exactly my preferred approach, it is nonetheless a consensus approach that all of the Commissioners can agree fulfills the statutory mandate in a manner consistent with our core mission. In my opening remarks at the proposal stage, I raised the issue as to whether we might consider a new regulatory model in which an issuer could seek qualification of a Regulation A offering from either the Commission or a state securities regulator.[2] I thank Commissioner Stein for working closely with me on the development of this alternative.

With respect to our action today in particular, the new rules will allow an issuer a choice to conduct either a Tier 1 or Tier 2 offering for amounts up to $20 million. This approach will afford the Commission an opportunity to observe choices among issuers as to which approach is more likely to be taken. Moreover, the increased Tier 1 offering level will afford the potential opportunity for state securities regulators to be involved in more offerings under new Regulation A through their new coordinated review program. I thank Commissioner Aguilar for starting the conversation about increasing the maximum Tier 1 offering level, without sacrificing any investor protection, and Commissioner Stein for suggesting the components of a retrospective review that will help the Commission determine whether to adjust the offering limit for Tier 1 in the future.

Our capital formation efforts for small business, however, should not, and will not, stop here. I hope that we will soon consider further expansion of Rule 504 under Regulation D as well as potential exemptive relief under the intrastate exemption to allow for regional crowdfunding conducted pursuant to state securities laws.

Finally, I would like to thank the staff from the Division of Corporation Finance, the Division of Economic and Risk Analysis, the Office of the General Counsel, and others for their efforts in finalizing today's release. I also greatly appreciate the efforts of my fellow commissioners to finalize these amendments. I have no questions and I support the staff's recommendation.

[1] U.S. Government Accountability Office, *Securities Regulation: Factors That May Affect Trends in Regulation A Offerings* (July 2012).

[2] http://www.sec.gov/News/PublicStmt/Detail/PublicStmt/1370542558042.

Statement at Open Meeting on Reg A+

Commissioner Kara M. Stein

March 25, 2015

Today's amendments to Regulation A are the next step in the Commission's effort to respond to changes in our securities offering regulations required by the JOBS Act. While I would have preferred today's amendments take a different approach to preemption, I support the rule today and I truly hope it will successfully provide new options for small and mid-sized offerings.

The Federal securities laws have long recognized that one-size does not fit all. The Commission adopted Regulation A in 1936 as one of the earliest alternatives to full registration of an issuer's securities with the Commission.[1] It was designed to provide smaller companies with a more streamlined approach to obtaining Commission approval to offer securities to the general public. The required disclosures and review by the Commission and the state securities regulators provided the basic investor protections for the offering.

However, over the years Regulation A has been lightly used. Whether it was the ease of making a private offering under Regulation D or other reasons,[2] last year barely any money was raised through the Regulation A offering process. Regulation D private placements, on the other hand, raised over $1 trillion.[3]

So why wasn't Regulation A being used for private offerings? If improvements were made, would it be used more often to raise smaller amounts of capital for smaller companies? Congress believed that it could be improved so that its usage would increase, and directed the Commission to expand Regulation A.

Until today, Regulation A offerings were limited to an aggregate amount of $5 million in a twelve-month period. The amendments we are adopting today create two tiers of offerings and expand the aggregate amount. Tier I can be used to raise up to $20 million in capital in a twelve-month period, while Tier 2, also known as Regulation A+, can be used for offerings of up to $50 million in a twelve-month period.

Tier I offerings are subject to both SEC and state review initially. Upon qualification, however, Tier I offerings have significantly fewer ongoing reporting requirements. I am concerned that this structure too closely mirrors the original Regulation A, and still might not be utilized. However, I hope that the increased offering size will encourage use of this new option. I look forward to seeing how the states work with the issuers to support these offerings, while still thoughtfully protecting investors.

Tier 2 has the potential, I believe, to work effectively for capital raises between $20 million and $50 million. It appropriately includes additional regulatory requirements, such as filing an offering circular which Commission staff will review before qualifying the offering, audited financial statements, and annual reports. Additionally, the amount of securities a non-accredited investor can purchase is capped when buying securities not listed on a national exchange. I am also pleased that any exemption from registration under section 12(g) of the Exchange Act is conditioned upon, among other things, a $75 million or less public float or, in the absence of a public float, revenues of less than $50 million. Today's approach, I hope, allows companies to grow and develop, but ultimately graduate on to full registration status.

Overall, I have ongoing concerns about how well today's changes will work in practice. I do not know if the structure in place will prove as useful as I would like, or as Congress envisioned. I am pleased, though, that the language of the release requires the staff to undertake to study and submit a report to the Commission no later than 5 years following the adoption of today's amendments. Among other things, this report requires the staff to assess the amount of capital raised by the amendments, the number of issuances, and the incidences of fraud and other violations. At that time, the Commission can reevaluate this structure and make appropriate adjustments.

To that end, I look forward to working with investors, small businesses, the states, and others to help us improve the capital formation process so that we can have a palette of options available to companies at different stages in their development.

In closing, I would like to thank Sebastian Gomez, Zachary Fallon, Shehzad Niazi, Raquel Fox, Lindsey McCord and everyone else from the Division of Corporation Finance who worked so hard on the rule. I would also like to thank Blair Petrillo from our Office of the Chief Accountant, Simona Mola Yost and Anzhela Knyazeva from our Division of Economic and Risk Analysis, as well as Dorothy McCuaig and Daniel Morris from our General Counsel's office.

Thank you for your hard work.

[1] Proposed Rule Amendments for Small and Additional Issues Exemptions Under Section 3(b) of the Securities Act, Release No. 33-9497 (Dec. 18, 2013) at 7.

[2] U.S. Government Accountability Office, *Securities Regulation: Factors That May Affect Trends in Regulation A Offerings* (GAO-12-839), July 3, 2012, available at http://www.gao.gov/products/GAO-12-839.

[3] Analysis performed by staff in the Division of Economic and Risk Analysis, cited in Amendments to Regulation A, Release No. 33-XXXX, March 25, 2015, at 255.

D

OTCQX/OTCQB Listing Requirements and On-Ramp Guides

The secondary market for Regulation A securities has a way to go in maturation and sophistication, but important players to stimulating that growth have already entered the fray. Here you find information on one such venue for trading these securities—OTC Markets.

Regulation A+ On Ramp Guide to OTCQB

The SEC recently adopted new rules under Regulation A, known as Regulation A+, that allow companies to raise capital more efficiently and create liquidity for their investors. OTC Markets Group's OTCQB Venture Marketplace enables development stage companies not yet ready to qualify for the higher financial standards of OTCQX to provide a transparent public trading market for their investors. Companies that would like to join OTCQB utilizing Regulation A+ must understand the various steps in the approval process and the role of the SEC, FINRA, broker-dealers/underwriters, and OTC Markets Group. The below guide outlines these steps for companies that choose an offering under Tier 2 of Regulation A+.

STEP 1 (Optional)

Test the Waters: Prior to commencing a Regulation A+ offering by filing a Form 1-A, the company may gauge investor interest by publicizing potential offerings through certain public channels. This period lasts until the offering has been "qualified" by the SEC.

STEP 2

Obtain SEC Approval of Offering	Establish a Security	Apply for OTCQB
Company: Submits Materials to the SEC • Offering Circular: • Files Form 1-A: Initial Disclosure Statement through the SEC's online system, EDGAR • Financial Statements for the past 2 years (audited for Tier 2) • Any materials used during the Test the Water stage **SEC:** Begins the review process. *There must be at least 21 days between filing the Form 1-A with the SEC and qualification*	**Broker-Dealer or Underwriter:** Form 211 is filed with FINRA http://www.otcmarkets.com/content/doc/form-211.pdf Company: • Works with underwriter or other DTC participant to sponsor for eligibility www.dtcc.com/assetservices/underwriting/new-issueeligibility.aspx • Appoints a transfer agent • Applies for a CUSIP number https://www.cusip.	**Company**: • Submits an OTCQB application www.otcmarkets.com/apply-forotcqb

STEP 3

Obtain SEC Approval of Offering	Establish a Security	Apply for OTCQB
Company: Responds to comments on Form 1-A filing	**Company:** May market offering as appropriate under Regulation A+ **Broker-Dealer or Underwriter:** Informs OTC Markets Group of expected pricing date and status of Form 211 clearance (ongoing)	**Company:** Responds to OTCQB application comments

STEP 4

Obtain SEC Approval of Offering	Establish a Security	Apply for OTCQB
Company: Responds to comments on Form 1-A filing	**Broker-Dealer or Underwriter:** Updates OTC Markets Group on expected pricing date and status of Form 211 clearance	**OTC Markets Group:** Responds to OTCQB application comments

STEP 5

Obtain SEC Approval of Offering	Establish a Security	Apply for OTCQB
Company: Completes SEC review and receives qualification on Form 1-A filing *At this point, the company can no longer "Test the Waters"*	**Broker-Dealer or Underwriter:** Updates OTC Markets Group on expected pricing date and status of Form 211 clearance **Company:** Confirms DTC eligibility	**OTC Markets Group:** Provides conditional OTCQB approval letter contingent upon pricing of offering

STEP 6

Obtain SEC Approval of Offering	Establish a Security	Apply for OTCQB
Offering is qualified	**Broker-Dealer or Underwriter:** Informs FINRA of pricing details **FINRA:** • Clears Form 211 and issues a ticker symbol to the company. *If Form 211 is filed 'unpriced', then the broker-dealer or underwriter is required to file an amendment with FINRA noting a priced quotation.* • Notifies OTC Markets Group that Form 211 has been cleared	**Company & Underwriter:** Prices offering and confirms details of offering with OTC Markets Group

STEP 7

Company issues security, non-affiliate investors deposit shares with brokers, and the company commences trading on OTCQB

Regulation A+ On Ramp Guide to OTCQX

The SEC recently adopted new rules under Regulation A, known as Regulation A+, that allow companies to raise capital more efficiently and create liquidity for their investors. OTC Markets Group's OTCQX Best Marketplace provides a platform for established companies to trade their shares on a well-regulated public marketplace through a streamlined qualification process. Companies that would like to join OTCQX utilizing Regulation A+ must understand the various steps in the approval process and the role of the SEC, FINRA, broker-dealers/underwriters, and OTC Markets Group. The below guide outlines these steps for companies that choose an offering under Tier 2 of Regulation A+.

STEP 1 (Optional)

Test the Waters: Prior to commencing a Regulation A+ offering by filing a Form 1-A, the company may gauge investor interest by publicizing potential offerings through certain public channels. This period lasts until the offering has been "qualified" by the SEC.

STEP 2

Obtain SEC Approval of Offering	Establish a Security	Apply for OTCQX
Company:	**Broker-Dealer or Underwriter:**	**Company:**
Submits Materials to the SEC	Form 211 is filed with FINRA www.otcmarkets.com/content/doc/form-211.pdf	• Submits an OTCQX application www.otcmar-kets.com/apply-forotcqx-us
• Offering Circular:	**Company:**	• Appoints a Designated Advisor for Disclosure (DAD) to act as a sponsor on OTCQX. A DAD can be either an approved investment bank or attorney.
• Files Form 1-A: Initial Disclosure Statement through the SEC's online system, EDGAR	• Works with underwriter or other DTC participant to sponsor for eligibility www.dtcc.com/assetservices/underwriting/new-issueeligibility.aspx	
• Financial Statements for the past 2 years (audited for Tier 2)	• Appoints a transfer agent	• A company's current advisor may apply to be a DAD
• Any materials used during the Test the Water stage	• Applies for a CUSIP number https://www.cusip.com/cusip/about-cgs.htm	How to Choose a DAD www.otcmarkets.com/content/doc/how-to-choose-a-DAD.pdf
SEC:		• Subscribes to S&P/Mergent Manual
Begins the review process.		**Mergent:**
There must be at least 21 days between filing the Form 1-A with the SEC and qualification		Joan Felder; Tel: +1 (212) 413-7747
		Email: joan.felder@mergent.com
		Standard & Poor's:
		Frank Spano; Tel: +1 (212) 438-1782
		Email: frank.spano@spcapitaliq.com

STEP 3

Obtain SEC Approval of Offering	Establish a Security	Apply for QTCQX
Company:	**Company:**	**Company:**
Responds to comments on Form 1-A filing	May market offering as appropriate under Regulation A+	Responds to OTCQX application comments
	Broker-Dealer or Underwriter:	
	Informs OTC Markets Group of expected pricing date and status of Form 211 clearance (ongoing)	

STEP 4

Obtain SEC Approval of Offering	Establish a Security	Apply for QTCQX
Company:	**Broker-Dealer or Underwriter:**	**OTC Markets Group:**
Responds to comments on Form 1-A filing	Updates OTC Markets Group on expected pricing date and status of Form 211 clearance	Works with company and its DAD to ensure that the company has met disclosure requirements for OTCQX (requires PCAOB audit)

STEP 5

Obtain SEC Approval of Offering	Establish a Security	Apply for QTCQX
Company:	**Broker-Dealer or Underwriter:**	**OTC Markets Group:**
Completes SEC review and receives qualification on Form 1-A filing	Updates OTC Markets Group on expected pricing date and status of Form 211 clearance	Provides conditional OTCQX approval letter contingent upon the company meeting OTCQX financial standards
At this point, the company can no longer "Test the Waters"	**Company:**	
	Confirms DTC eligibility	

STEP 6

Obtain SEC Approval of Offering	Establish a Security	Apply for QTCQX
Offering is qualified	**Broker-Dealer or Underwriter:**	**Company & Underwriter:**
	Informs FINRA of pricing details	Prices offering and confirms details of offering with OTC Markets Group
	FINRA:	
	• Clears Form 211 and issues a ticker symbol to the company. *If Form 211 is filed 'unpriced', then the broker-dealer or underwriter is required to file an amendment with FINRA noting a priced quotation*	
	• Notifies OTC Markets Group that Form 211 has been cleared	

STEP 7

Company issues security, non-affiliate investors deposit shares with brokers, and the company commences trading on OTCQX

OTCQX RULES RELEASE NO. 9 (PROPOSED AMENDMENTS) June 9, 2015

OTC Markets Group has published proposed amendments to the OTCQX Rules for U.S. Companies, OTCQX Rules for International Companies, and OTCQX Rules for U.S. Banks. The Securities and Exchange Commission's recent amendments to Regulation A become effective on June 19, 2015, and OTC Markets Group has aligned our rules to allow issuers to qualify for the OTCQX Best Marketplace.

Most significantly, a company may use its required disclosure under Regulation A to help meet the initial and ongoing OTCQX disclosure requirements. To qualify for OTCQX, a company using the new Regulation A Reporting Standard must file all reports required to be filed on EDGAR under Regulation A as well as quarterly disclosure and certain other information as outlined below. We have also made clarifying changes to the OTCQX Rules that are applicable to all current and prospective OTCQX companies.

Highlights of Proposed Changes

OTCQX Rules for U.S. Companies:

1. Definitions for "Regulation A" and "Regulation A Reporting Company" were added to the Definitions section.

2. Initial Disclosure Obligations - A Regulation A Reporting Company must have filed all reports required to be filed on EDGAR. The most recent financial statements required to be audited under Regulation A must be audited by an independent public accountant registered with the PCAOB.

3. Ongoing Disclosure Obligations - A Regulation A Reporting Company must file, on an ongoing basis, all annual, semi-annual and other interim reports required to be filed on EDGAR under Regulation A, and within 45 days of the end of each fiscal quarter must publish on EDGAR through Form 1-U quarterly disclosure including all information required in the Company's semiannual report. Each annual report must include financial statements audited by an independent public accountant registered with the PCAOB.

4. For U.S. Premier Companies Only - A Regulation A Reporting Company must publish, on EDGAR through SEC Form 1-U, copies of all proxies, proxy statements and all other material mailed by the Company to its shareholders with respect thereto, within 15 days of the mailing of such material.

5. The initial bid price requirement was updated to indicate that the bid price test will also need to be met at the time of application approval in addition to the time of application submission.

Solicitation of Comments on Proposed Rules:

OTC Markets Group requests your direct feedback relating to the proposed OTCQX Rules for U.S. Companies regarding the disclosure of proxy material by Regulation A Reporting Companies. Specifically, the proposed Rules require that copies of all proxies, proxy statements and all other material be published through EDGAR, and we would like feedback as to whether we should also allow disclosure these materials directly to our OTC Disclosure & News Service through www.otciq.com.

OTCQX Rules for U.S. Banks:

The initial bid price requirement was updated to indicate that the bid price test needs to be met at the time of application approval in addition to the time of application submission.

OTCQX Rules for International Companies:

1. An initial eligibility criterion was added that does not allow a Shell Company or Blank-Check Company to qualify for OTCQX.

2. SEC Reporting Companies may be exempt from the Qualified Foreign Exchange requirement.

3. All OTCQX International Companies are now required to maintain an Updated Profile similar to the OTCQX U.S. and OTCQX U.S. Banks Companies. At least once every six months, the company must submit a Company Update Form via www.otciq.com with the information needed to ensure the Company Profile is current and complete or verify the current Company Profile publicly displayed on www.otcmarkets.com to maintain the "Company Updated Profile" designation on the Company Profile page on www.otcmarkets.com.

Comment Period of 30 days:

OTC Markets Group welcomes your feedback about the proposed changes. Send comments and questions to Mike Vasilios, Vice President of Issuer Compliance at mike@otcmarkets.com by July 9, 2015.

Effective Date of Proposed Changes:

The proposed rules became effective July 10, 2015.

Offering Statement Exemplars

Understanding the scope or requirements of the task undertaken in deciding to file for qualification of Regulation A securities is hard to understand without seeing examples. At http://www.apress.com/9781430257318 you'll find two such examples. They are from the same issuer who has conducted both a Tier I and Tier II offering. By providing for the same issuer, we hope that you can focus on the procedural differences, without having to distinguish differences inherent to different issuers.

Go to the above URL and choose Source Code/Downloads to read the exemplars.

Blue Sky

This appendix provides information from the North American Securities Administrators Association on their Coordinated Review Program for Regulation A securities.

■ **Note**   We have made reference throughout the book to the interplay of state securities law. Detailed examination of this aspect of the regulatory landscape is beyond the scope of this book. We have, however, provided a basic survey of the state registration requirements for Reg A securities (see the Source Code/Downloads section at http://www.apress.com/9781430257318).

NASAA Coordinated Review of Regulation A Offerings Review Protocol

Adopted March 7, 2014

1. Applicants desiring coordinated multi-jurisdictional review of an offering to be conducted under Section 3(b) of the Securities Act of 1933 and Regulation A shall file a request for coordinated review, along with required exhibits and filing fees, through the Electronic Filing Depository. The State of Washington is the program coordinator. Applicants shall indicate in what jurisdictions the offering is to be registered through coordinated review. A listing of all jurisdictions that participate in coordinated review shall be maintained on NASAA's website.

If at the time of application, electronic filing is not available through the Electronic Filing Depository, then the applicant shall remit via e-mail an electronic copy of the application, along with required exhibits, to the program coordinator who shall redistribute the application materials to the jurisdictions indicated on the application. Filing fees must be submitted to the individual states in accordance with their filing procedures. A table of filing fees and remittance addresses for Regulation A offerings by jurisdiction shall be maintained on NASAA's website.

2. Washington will contact all participating jurisdictions to identify both a lead merit examiner and a lead disclosure examiner. If the issuer has not applied in a jurisdiction that applies merit standards, only a lead disclosure examiner will be identified. The lead examiner(s) will be identified within three (3) business days after receipt of the application for coordinated review.

3. The lead examiner(s) will draft and circulate a comment letter to the participating jurisdictions within ten (10) business days after their identification as lead examiner(s) by the program administrator. If the issuer has applied in a jurisdiction that applies merit standards, the lead merit examiner will include comments consistent with applicable NASAA Statements of Policy. The lead merit examiner shall apply and draft comments based on the applicable statements of policy, with the following exceptions:

   a. The Statement of Policy Regarding Promoters' Equity Investment shall not apply;

   b. The Statement of Policy Regarding Promotional Shares shall apply except that one-half (1/2) of any promotional shares required to be locked-in or escrowed shall be released on the first and second anniversary of the date of completion of the offering such that all shares shall have been released from lock-in or escrow by the second anniversary of the date of completion of the offering; and

   c. The Statement of Policy Regarding Loans and Other Material Affiliated Transactions shall apply except that the disclosure document shall not be required to include representations by counsel to the issuer as contemplated in Section VII.C.3. of the policy.

4. The participating jurisdictions shall have five (5) business days from the circulation of the draft comment letter by the lead examiners to submit additional comments or corrections to the lead examiners. If a jurisdiction does not submit comments to the lead examiners within five (5) business days, the lead examiners can assume the jurisdiction has no comments. After the expiration of the five (5) business days for review of the draft letter by the participating jurisdictions, the lead examiner(s) shall have three (3) business days to make any necessary revisions and send the initial comment letter to the issuer.

5. If the initial application is amended by adding more participating jurisdictions, the initial ten (10) business day review period will be extended to five (5) business days from the date the final amendment is received. Amendments to the application for purposes of adding jurisdictions must be made prior to the expiration of the initial ten (10) business day review period. If an issuer seeks to add a jurisdiction after this time, the issuer may be required to pursue registration independently and be subject to non-coordinated review standards in each of the additional jurisdictions.

6. The lead examiners will communicate with the applicant and participating jurisdictions, as necessary, to resolve any outstanding comments. The lead jurisdictions will reply to each issuer's response to each coordinated review letter no later than five (5) business days after receipt of the issuer's response.

7. Participating jurisdictions will receive same-day notice from the lead disclosure examiner and the lead merit examiner when that lead examiner clears the application.

8. Once the lead disclosure examiner has cleared the application, all participating disclosure jurisdictions agree to clear the application.

9. Once the lead merit examiner has cleared the application, all participating merit jurisdictions agree to clear the application.

APPLICATION FOR COORDINATED REVIEW OF REGULATION A OFFERING

Form CR-3(b)

The Applicant hereby requests coordinated multi-jurisdictional review of an application for registration of an offering being made in reliance on the exemption from federal registration under Section 3(b) of the Securities Act of 1933 and Regulation A adopted thereunder.

Please note this coordinated review program is not available to offerings registered under Section 5 of the Securities Act of 1933. Blank check offerings do not qualify for this coordinated review program. This program may not be available to an offering even if the offering fits within the initial screening criteria.

The state of Washington is acting as the Administrator of the coordinated review program. There is no additional fee for coordinated review.

The coordinated review process will take a minimum of 30 days. The Applicant should consider this time frame and file the application as soon as possible after filing with the Securities and Exchange Commission.

The Applicant agrees to resolve comments through the Lead Disclosure and the Lead Merit examiners until such time as the Lead examiners agree that the comment(s) should be resolved through direct contact between the Applicant and the jurisdiction with the unresolved comment(s).

Jurisdictions of Application

Set forth below are the jurisdictions participating in this coordinated review program. [NOTE: The list will be modified to reflect only jurisdictions who agree to participate.] This coordinated review program is available only if the issuer intends to register in two or more of the participating jurisdictions. Please indicate the jurisdictions in which you intend to file an application to register the offering through coordinated review. **Issuers are cautioned to identify all jurisdictions in which they intend to utilize the coordinated review process. In accordance with the review protocol, it may not be possible to include additional jurisdictions at a later date.**

❑ Alabama	❑ Iowa (M)	❑ Nevada (D)	❑ South Dakota
❑ Alaska (D)	❑ Kansas (M)	❑ New	❑ Tennessee (M)
❑ Arkansas	❑ Kentucky (M)	❑ New Jersey	❑ Texas (M)
❑ California	❑ Louisiana (D)	❑ New Mexico	❑ US Virgin
❑ Colorado	❑ Maine (M)	❑ North	❑ Utah (D)
❑ Connecticut	❑ Maryland (D)	❑ North Dakota	❑ Vermont (M)
❑ Delaware	❑ Massachusetts	❑ Ohio (M)	❑ Virginia (M)
❑ District of	❑ Michigan (M)	❑ Oklahoma (M)	❑ Washington
Columbia	❑ Minnesota (M)	❑ Oregon (M)	❑ West Virginia
❑ Hawaii (D)	❑ Mississippi (M)	❑ Puerto Rico	❑ Wisconsin (D)
❑ Idaho (M)	❑ Missouri (M)	❑ Pennsylvania	❑ Wyoming (D)
❑ Illinois (D)	❑ Montana (M)	❑ Rhode Island	
❑ Indiana (M)	❑ Nebraska (M)	❑ South Carolina(D)	

M = Merit Review Jurisdiction   D = Disclosure Review Jurisdiction

Note   While DC, NJ, and WV are disclosure review jurisdictions, they reserve the right to make substantive comments consistent with the coordinated review protocol.

The Applicant understands that any application filed in a jurisdiction subsequent to the initial filing may be reviewed separately and may involve application of non-coordinated review standards. The Applicant should understand that the merit jurisdictions participating in this program will be using certain NASAA Guidelines and/or Statements of Policy as the uniform standard. For information on the standards to be applied, please review the coordinated review program information website at http://www.nasaa.org/regulatory-activity/statements-of-policy/.

Consent to Service of Process

The Applicant irrevocably appoints the Securities Administrator or other legally designated officer of the jurisdiction in which the issuer maintains its principal place of business and any jurisdiction in which this application is filed, as its agents for service of process, and agrees that these persons may accept service on its behalf, of any notice, process or pleading, and further agrees that such service may be made by registered or certified mail, in any federal or state action, administrative proceeding, or arbitration brought against it arising out of, or in connection with, the sale of securities or out of violation of the laws of the jurisdictions so designated. The Applicant further hereby consents that any such action or proceeding against it may be commenced in any court of competent jurisdiction and proper venue within the jurisdictions of application so designated hereunder by service of process upon the Securities Administrators or other legally designated officers so designated with the same effect as if the Applicant was organized or created under the laws of that jurisdiction and have been served lawfully with process in that jurisdiction. It is requested that a copy of any notice, process, or pleading served hereunder be mailed to:

Name _____

Address_____

Dated this ____day of _____, 20____.

Authorized Representative:

Signature _____

Print Name _____

Title _____

Glossary

1933 Act	See Securities Act of 1933.
1934 Act	See Securities Exchange Act of 1934.
After-Market Performance	The price appreciation (or depreciation) in publicly traded offerings is measured from the offering price going forward.
Aftermarket	Trading in a security subsequent to its offering is called the aftermarket.
All-Or-None	A specific type of a best efforts underwriting. If the underwriter can't sell all of the shares being offered, none of the shares will be offered, and the offering will be cancelled.
Alternative Trading System (ATS)	A trading system, platform, or venue, not registered as a National Exchange and regulated by the SEC under Regulation ATS.
Amendment	A subsequent filing or disclosure in a prospectus or offering statement after its initial filing. This is filed by the issuer with the SEC and has additional information regarding the proposed offering for that company.
Analyst	An individual, usually employed by an investment banking firm, who studies and analyzes an industry and the publicly held companies operating in the industry for the purpose of providing investment advice.

Bad Actor	A person or entity who, under rules related to Regulation A and D offerings, has a criminal conviction, a court or regulatory order related to conduct of a disciplinary nature for conduct enumerated under those rules. If the issuer, an affiliate, management member, or significant shareholder of an issuer, or if compensated to assist in placing securities of an issuer, a Bad Actor will disqualify the issuer from offering securities pursuant to Regulation A or D.
Best Efforts	Arrangement whereby investment bankers or underwriters acting as agents agree to do their best to sell an issue to the public, instead of buying the securities outright.
Book	List of all indications of interest for a new issue offering put together by the lead underwriter.
Blue Sky Laws	A term that refers to state securities laws. The origin of the term is somewhat disputed, but versions agree that it comes from characterizations that these laws were intended to stop fraudsters who were selling nothing more than "blue sky."
Book Running Lead Manager (BRLM)	An underwriter who leads the management of a syndicate in a firmly underwritten offering. This underwriter is typically in charge of due diligence, marketing strategy, enlisting other syndicate members, and developing market strategy post-issuance for the firmly underwritten offering.
Bought Out Deal	An underwriter has a commitment to buy all the shares from a company and becomes financially responsible for selling them. Also called a firm allotment.
Broker-Dealer	A person or entity in the businesses of brokering or dealing in securities. Broker-dealers must register, typically with the SEC under Section 15 of the Securities Exchange Act of 1934, must also register under state laws in those states where they want to sell securities, and must become a regulated member of FINRA.

Capitalization	The total amount of a company's outstanding securities. For purposes of display in a registration statement, capitalization includes short-term debt, long-term debt, and equity securities.
Capitalization Table	A table presenting the capital structure of the company prior to the offering, assuming that all securities offered are sold.
Closely Held Company	A company in which the equity interests are held by a few individuals or groups of individuals.
Convertible Securities	Corporate securities (usually preferred stock or bonds) that are exchangeable into a fixed number of shares of common stock at a stipulated price.
Cover Page	The cover page of the offer document covers full contact details of the issuer company, lead underwriter or managing placement agent, and the nature, number, price, and amount of instruments offered, as well as the issue size and the particulars regarding listing.
Disclosure	Material information (e.g., management practices, financial statements, and legal involvements) made public by an issuer as required by the SEC; the purpose is to put investors on notice of information pertinent to their making initial and continued investment decisions about the issuer.
Due Diligence	Reasonable investigation conducted by the parties involved in preparing a disclosure document to form a basis for believing that the statements contained therein are true and that no material facts are omitted.
Earnings Per Share (EPS)	A company's net income, generally divided by the number of its common shares outstanding and adjusted for certain dilutive securities such as stock options, warrants, and convertible debt.
EDGAR (Electronic Data Gathering Analysis and Retrieval)	SEC computer database system that allows issuers to file reports with the SEC by computer instead of having to file physical documents; this data is available to the general public via the Internet.

Effective Date The day a newly registered security can be offered for sale.

Eligible Issuers Issuers can offer securities pursuant to the exemption from registration under Regulation A. See Chapter 5 for discussion of eligibility.

Eligible Securities Securities that can be offered pursuant to the exemption under Regulation A. Eligible securities include any equity or debt security or any convertible security other than fractional interests in gas or mineral drilling/excavation rights and asset backed securities.

Equity Method Method of accounting in which the investor records an investment in the stock of an investee at cost and adjusts the carrying amount of the investment to recognize the investor's share of the earnings or losses of the investee after the date of acquisition. (This generally applies to investments in which stock ownership is between 20% and 50% of the outstanding securities of the investee.)

Exempt Offering A securities offering that does not require a registration statement to be filed with the SEC. Exempt offerings include Regulations A and D and intrastate offerings.

Financial Accounting Standards Board (FASB) A private body that establishes financial accounting and reporting standards in the United States.

Financial Printer A printer that specializes in the printing of financial documents, including registration statements, offering statements, and proxy statements. These printers are also capable of converting documents to an EDGAR format and electronically submitting the document to the SEC.

Firm Underwriting Arrangement whereby investment bankers make outright purchases from the issuer of securities to be offered to the public.

FINRA	The Financial Industries Regulatory Authority. FINRA is the self-regulatory association responsible for oversight of member securities broker-dealer firms and their registered representatives. Broker-dealers registering under the Exchange Act are required to join a self-regulatory organization, typically FINRA.
First Day Close	The closing price at the end of the first day of trading in a registered public offering or traded Regulation A offering. It reflects not only how well the lead manager priced and placed the deal, but what the near-term trading is likely to be. For example, IPOs that shoot up 100% or 200% on their first day of trading are likely to fall back in price on subsequent days due to profit taking. Conversely, IPOs that break offer price immediately are likely to drop further as institutions bail out. Breaking IPO price right out of the box is a poor reflection on the lead manager's pricing and placement.
Float	The number of a company's shares that are available for trading.
Follow on Public Offering (FPO)	When an already listed company makes either a fresh issue of securities to the public or an offer for sale to the public, through an offer document.
Form 1-A	Form through which an issuer makes its initial filing of its offering statement with the SEC to have its securities qualified as exempt from registration under Regulation A.
Form 1-A/A	An amended offering statement filed with the SEC during the qualification process to supplement disclosure or make changes to disclosure requested by the SEC from previous filings.
Form 1-K	Mandated form on which a Tier 2 issuer files the annual report required under Tier 2 of Regulation A.
Form 1-SA	Mandated form on which a Tier 2 issuer files the semi-annual report required under Tier 2 of Regulation A.

Form I-U	Form used to make any current reporting required under Tier 2 of Regulation A.
Go Public	Process by which a privately held company first offers shares of stock to the public; this is done via a registered initial public offering (IPO). Some people also refer to this as when it's Regulation A, particularly Tier 2, as a "going public" event.
Insiders	Persons such as management, directors, and significant stockholders who are privy to information about the operations of a company that is not known to the general public. Insiders are subject to various restrictions and/or limitations regarding equity stock offerings and trading.
Investment Banker	A person or (usually) a firm that, among other things, underwrites securities, functions as a broker-dealer, and performs corporate finance and merger and acquisition advisory services. Investment bankers are usually full-service firms that perform a range of services, as opposed to an underwriter or broker-dealer, which provides only one specific service.
IPO	An initial public offering (IPO) is when a privately held company offers its shares to the public.
Lead Underwriter	Underwriter who, among other things, is in charge of organizing the syndicate, distributing member participation shares, and making stabilizing transactions. The lead underwriter's name appears on the left side of a prospectus cover.
Lock-Up Period	Time period after an IPO when insiders at the newly public company are restricted by the lead underwriter from selling their shares in the secondary market.
Management's Discussion and Analysis (MD&A)	A textual discussion and analysis of a registrant's liquidity, capital resources, and results of operations that must be prepared by management and included in registration statements and most 1934 Act reports.

Market Capitalization	The total market value of a firm. It is defined as the product of the company's stock price per share and the total number of shares outstanding. The market cap should not be confused with the float, which is the amount of shares in circulation. A company's market cap can greatly exceed the float, especially in the case of a new publicly traded company.
Market Value	The market value of a company is determined by multiplying the number of shares outstanding by the current price of the stock.
Managing Broker-Dealer	Interchangeable term for the lead underwriter, managing placement agent, or placement agent in a best efforts offering.
Managing Placement Agent	See Managing Broker-Dealer.
National Association of Securities Dealers Automated Quotation System (NASDAQ)	The NASDAQ is a large electronic stock exchange in the United States.
National Exchange	A securities exchange registered under Section 6 of the Exchange Act and a member of the National Market System. Securities listed on a national exchange are exempt from state registration requirements.
New York Stock Exchange (NYSE)	The NYSE is a large New York-based stock exchange.
Offer Date	The first day the issue is traded publicly.
Offer Document	A prospectus in the case of a public issue registered under Section 5 of the 1933 Act or exempt under Regulation A. An offer document covers all the relevant disclosure to help an investor make his/her investment decision.
Offering Circular	Part II of Form 1-A; the narrative disclosure document for a Regulation A offering.
Offering Date	The first day a security is offered for sale.
Offering Price	Price for which a new security issue will be sold to the public; also known as "issue price."

Offering Statement	The entire filing submission for a Reg A offering. Comprises Parts I and II of Form I-A, as well as Exhibits. Analogous to the registration statement in a registered offering.
Options	A security giving its owner the right to purchase or sell a company's securities at a fixed date and agreed-upon price.
Pipeline	Supply of new issues that are tentatively scheduled to come to market; pipeline is also referred to as "visible supply."
Placement Agent	See Managing Placement Agent.
Preliminary Offering Circular	Refers to the latest iteration of the Offering Circular prior to qualification of securities in a Regulation A offering.
Price Earnings Ratio	A measurement of common stock value calculated as the price per share divided by earnings per share.
Price Range	A proposed price-per-share range is often printed on the cover page of a preliminary prospectus. Example: "It is estimated that the offering price will be $8 to $10 per share."
Private Placement	An offering or sale of securities not required to be registered because it is not made available generally to the public, pursuant to Section 4(2) of the 1933 Act and/or Regulation D.
Proceeds	Money raised in an offering is referred to as proceeds. In every prospectus or offering circular, there is a section entitled "Use of Proceeds." Investors should read this section to find out why the company plans to raise money from the public.
Pro Forma	Financial statements or financial tables prepared as though certain transactions had already occurred. For example, an offering statement might include a pro forma balance sheet that reflects the anticipated results of the offering.

Public Company Accounting Oversight Board (PCAOB)	An organization established by the Sarbanes-Oxley Act to oversee the audit of public companies that are subject to U.S. securities laws. The duties of the PCAOB, as established by the Act, include establishing audit and independence standards; registering public accounting firms; inspecting public accounting firms; and conducting investigations and disciplinary proceedings. The PCAOB, subject to the oversight of the SEC, replaced the accounting profession's self-regulating framework.
Registration	Procedure by which a company registers securities with the SEC pursuant to the 1933 Act. Once registered, the company must also register as a reporting company under the 1934 Act. Registration allows the securities to be listed on a national exchange and sold to anyone without limitations such as those under Regulation A. Registration, however, is expensive and subjects the issuing company to significant ongoing regulatory burdens. If listed on a national exchange, registered securities are exempt from Blue Sky laws. The process requires the issuing company to make filings with the SEC that contain a description of the company, its management, and its financials. The material is reviewed by the SEC for its completeness, amount of disclosure, and its presentation of accounting information before the SEC declares the registration effective, which allows it to be traded to the public.
Restricted Security	Securities that have been sold to investors pursuant to a private exemption, and other transactional exemptions, are "restricted" in their ability to be traded post investment. Typically must comply with requirements of Rule 144 of the SEC's regulations. Most restricted securities have no market in any event because of these requirements and are, thus, very difficult to sell.

Risk Factors The disclosure of the issuer's management to give its view on the internal and external risks faced by the company. Here, the company also makes a note on the forward-looking statements. It is generally advised that the investors go through all the risk factors of the company before making an investment decision.

Road Show Also called the "dog and pony show." A tour taken by a company preparing for a public offering in order to attract interest in its securities; attended by broker-dealers and select potential buyers, including institutional investors, analysts, and money managers by invitation only—members of the media are forbidden to attend.

Rule 12 That portion of the Securities Exchange Act of 1934 that deals with requirements for registration of securities.

SEC The Securities and Exchange Commission, a federal government agency that regulates and supervises the securities industry. The commission administers federal laws, formulates and enforces rules to protect against malpractice, and seeks to ensure that companies provide full disclosure to investors.

Secondary Market Commonly refers to after-issuance trading activity in a security.

Secondary Offering An offering by the company's shareholders to sell some or all of their stock to the public. The proceeds of a secondary offering are received by the selling shareholders, not by the company.

Secondary Transaction A sale or purchase of a security not part of, but after an issuance of the securities by the issuing company.

Securities Act of 1933	The fundamental federal statute for the regulation of securities in the United States. The Securities Act of 1933 sets forth the requirements for when securities sold in interstate commerce must be registered and what exemptions apply. It also prohibits and creates penalties for the issuance of securities without disclosure of material information or on basis of false/misleading information and establishes the authority of the SEC to regulate these securities.
Securities Exchange Act of 1934	The Securities Exchange Act of 1934 was the second piece of seminal federal securities law passed by Congress to regulate exchanges, broker-dealers, and secondary activity. Aspects of the 1934 Act impact initial issuances as well, such as Section 10(b)5.
Selling Group	Group of broker-dealers that helps an underwriting syndicate distribute securities of a public offering.
Selling Group Member	A broker-dealer who is a member of a selling group.
Smaller Reporting Issuer	A U.S. or Canadian entity with revenues of less than $50M and whose public float is less than $75M.
Syndicate Manager	Also referred to as the lead underwriter or managing underwriter who, among other things, is in charge of organizing the syndicate.
Syndicate Member	A broker-dealer participating in a syndicate, depending on context (i.e., best efforts underwritings). Can be used synonymously with selling group member.
Test the Waters	Term used in Regulation A to refer to a process of providing information about a potential offering pre-filing to gauge investment interest. Can commonly refer to marketing in general under Regulation A.

Underwriter

In the strictest use of the term, underwriters are financial intermediaries who buy stock or bonds from an issuer and then sell these securities to the public. Can commonly refer to a brokerage firm that simply raises money for companies using public equity and debt markets.

Unit

A combination of two securities sold for one price. For example, a unit can consists of common stock and warrants of common stock and debt.

Use of Proceeds

How the company plans to use the monies it generated from an offering.

Valuation Multiple

An approach to valuing companies that relies on comparing a company's stock price to its income from operations, cash flow from operations, or earnings per share. The higher the multiple, the more richly valued the company is. Underwriters use valuation multiples of an issuer's peers, or comparables, to determine the appropriate level at which an offering should be priced.

Venture Capital

Source of money for start-up companies, typically raised by venture capital firms who invest in private companies that need capital to develop and market their products. In return for this investment, the venture capitalists generally receive significant ownership of the company and seats on the board.

Volatility

Characteristic of a security that rises or falls sharply in price within a short time.

Warrant

A security entitling its owner to purchase shares in a company under specified terms.

Index

Get the eBook for only $5!

Why limit yourself?

Now you can take the weightless companion with you wherever you go and access your content on your PC, phone, tablet, or reader.

Since you've purchased this print book, we're happy to offer you the eBook in all 3 formats for just $5.

Convenient and fully searchable, the PDF version enables you to easily find and copy code—or perform examples by quickly toggling between instructions and applications. The MOBI format is ideal for your Kindle, while the ePUB can be utilized on a variety of mobile devices.

To learn more, go to www.apress.com/companion or contact support@apress.com.

Apress®
THE EXPERT'S VOICE™

Other Apress Business Titles You Will Find Useful

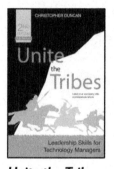

CPSIA information can be obtained
at www.ICGtesting.com
Printed in the USA
FSOW04n1945130416
19188FS